# SOCIAL
# RESPONSIBILITIES
# IN ENGINEERING
# AND SCIENCE

# SOCIAL RESPONSIBILITIES IN ENGINEERING AND SCIENCE

## A Guide for Selecting General Education Courses

*Edited by*
RICHARD H. McCUEN
JAMES M. WALLACE

PRENTICE-HALL, INC., *Englewood Cliffs, New Jersey 07632*

**Library of Congress Cataloging-in-Publication Data**

Social responsibilities in engineering
and science.

Bibliography: p.
1. Technical education—Curricula.
2. Education, Humanistic.   I. McCuen,
Richard H., 1941–    .  II. Wallace, James M.
T65.3.S63 1987      607′.1      86-22527
ISBN 0-13-818253-1

Editorial/production supervision and
  interior design: David Ershun/Nancy Menges
Cover design: 20/20 Services, Inc.
Manufacturing buyer: Rhett Conklin

Printed in the United States of America

10  9  8  7  6  5  4  3  2  1

ISBN  0-13-818253-1   025

PRENTICE-HALL INTERNATIONAL (UK) LIMITED, *London*
PRENTICE-HALL OF AUSTRALIA PTY. LIMITED, *Sydney*
PRENTICE-HALL CANADA INC., *Toronto*
PRENTICE-HALL HISPANOAMERICANA, S.A., *Mexico*
PRENTICE-HALL OF INDIA PRIVATE LIMITED, *New Delhi*
PRENTICE-HALL OF JAPAN, INC., *Tokyo*
PRENTICE-HALL OF SOUTHEAST ASIA PTE. LTD., *Singapore*
EDITORA PRENTICE-HALL DO BRASIL, LTDA., *Rio de Janeiro*

*Dedicated to the memory of*
*PAUL G. MAYER,*
*a professor of engineering*
*who taught both of us*
*the importance of a broad liberal learning*
*and a humanistic attitude.*

*RHM*
*JMW*

# CONTENTS

# PREFACE

The title of this book, *Social Responsibilities in Engineering and Science,* may suggest that the book represents a comprehensive and definitive statement on the social responsibility of engineers and scientists; this is not our intent. The subtitle, *A Guide for Selecting General Education Courses,* reflects a very important limitation on the scope and intention of the book. We have prepared this book for college freshmen in engineering or science programs to develop in them an awareness that they will not practice their professions in a social vacuum. Because engineers and scientists have important social responsibilities, engineering and science curricula include a significant number of required credit hours in the arts, the humanities, and the social sciences. These general education courses have at least three purposes. At the very least, they should help make students aware of the social context in which they will practice their future professions and expose them to some of the breadth of human knowledge and experience. But more important, the general education courses should develop in these students an awareness of their personal values. Such an awareness will help them solve personal problems and will develop in them a sensitivity to social problems affected by their professions.

Why do we believe such a text is necessary? In discussions with students in our specialty areas, civil and mechanical engineering, we found that students are usually not aware of either the social responsibilities of engineers or the reason for including general education courses in their programs. Most students view their education as a utilitarian accumulation of technical knowledge and skills that will serve them in their future careers. It is a rare student who shows any concern about the social role of science and technology in the profession that he or she will practice. Hence, this book. We believe that if it is used during the first semester of the freshman year, students in engineering and science programs will be confronted at the earliest stage of their education with their social responsibilities as professionals and the value of general education courses to both their careers and their personal lives. Thus, the book is not a comprehensive discussion of the social obligations of engineers and scientists; instead, it is intended to spark an interest in freshmen engineering or science majors toward becoming complete professionals who are both technically competent and socially responsible.

## TO THE INSTRUCTOR

Many faculty members in engineering and science recognize the failures of general education courses in meeting the goal of developing a social awareness in their students. A common complaint is that the resources to turn the situation around do not exist. We hope that this book partially fills this resource vacuum, but it cannot stand alone. The development of a social awareness in our students requires additional measures of reinforcement. First, a faculty member from an engineering or science discipline must have a firm belief that general education is important and must be able to convey this belief to the students. Students are willing to believe that thermodynamics, fluid mechanics, and circuit analysis are important only because their instructors identify important applications of the material in these technical courses. Students are not convinced of the importance of the Second Law of Thermodynamics just from reading a thermodynamics text. Similarly, students will not be convinced of the importance of general education just from reading this book. The commitment and enthusiasm of an engineering or science faculty member is necessary to convince students of the importance of general education. If we show little interest in anything but our narrow technical specialties, we should hardly be surprised to find our students following suit.

Second, there is a need for a place in the curriculum for discussions of general education. This might involve the use of guest lecturers from the arts, humanities, and social sciences. The program will be most effective, however, if an engineering or science faculty member leads the discussion and makes liberal use of examples that illustrate the need for general education in the practice of engineering and science.

Third, we certainly would not expect freshmen to identify all of their technical electives for a four-year program; we should not expect any more from them in selecting general education courses. Therefore, the emphasis in the discussion on developing a personal general education program should be on goals and procedures rather than on finalizing a specific, rigid program. Just as many students change interests in the technical discipline of their choice (may even change majors), we should expect that a student who has an interest in general education courses in psychology as a freshman may have an interest in the performing arts when he or she becomes a junior. Classroom discussions carried out in conjunction with this book should help the students set objectives and should clarify how their selections from the catalog courses can help meet these personal and professional development objectives.

Finally, we all recognize the importance of grades to students. If students are told that their grades will not be affected by their efforts on a particular topic discussed in class, they will be less likely to take the material seriously. Therefore, it is suggested that the students be graded on their development of a personal general education program. This should include material on tests as well as assignments related to classwork.

In summary, evaluations of technical courses have shown the following factors to be important: teacher's in-class performance, course organization, text, grading, and student effort. The key factors are no different in teaching the importance of general education.


## ACKNOWLEDGMENTS

We wish to express our appreciation and thanks to Margaret B. Martin, R. Howard McCuen, and Barbara Pequet for the many helpful comments that they made on an earlier draft of the manuscript. We are especially indebted to Lynn Thomas, Carolyn Lee, and Maria Stransky for their successful struggle in typing some very rough first drafts and their patience in making the necessary revisions. This final product would not have been possible without their assistance.

*Richard H. McCuen*
*James M. Wallace*

College Park, Maryland

# CONTRIBUTORS

**David C. Bardach,** Product Development Engineer, Proctor and Gamble, Cincinnati, Ohio

**Michael E. Bohse,** Graduate Research Assistant, Department of Mechanical Engineering, University of Maryland, College Park, MD

**George E. Dieter,** Dean, College of Engineering, University of Maryland, College Park, MD

**Patricia Gaynor,** Civil Engineer

**Michael Gould,** Mechanical Engineer

**Margaret B. Martin,** Storm Water Management Engineer, Public Works Department, Annapolis, MD

**Richard H. McCuen,** Professor, Department of Civil Engineering, University of Maryland, College Park, MD

**Kenyon R. Miller,** Graduate Teaching Assistant, Department of Information and Computer Science, Georgia Institute of Technology, Atlanta, GA

**Barbara Pequet,** a legislative lobbyist for consumer and animal protection issues, Washington, D.C.

**Julie Ann B. Tarr,** Naval Research Laboratory Fellow, Department of Electrical Engineering, University of Maryland, College Park, MD

**Rosemarie Napolitano Thomas,** Electronic Engineer, Telecommunications Engineering Office, U.S. Department of Defense, Bowie, MD

**James M. Wallace,** Professor, Department of Mechanical Engineering, University of Maryland, College Park, MD

# SOCIAL RESPONSIBILITIES IN ENGINEERING AND SCIENCE

**1**

# General Education and Professionalism

*Richard H. McCuen*

## INTRODUCTION

Engineering is not just designing electrical circuits and computers, bridges and roads, robots, space shuttles, military weapons, and nuclear power plants. Science is not just the development of new laws of physics, mathematical theories, and chemical relationships. Engineers and scientists are major players in society, with serious responsibilities to it, both as professionals and as citizens. We cannot stick out heads in the sand; we have an obligation to use our specialized knowledge and skills for human betterment. This philosophy that advances in engineering and science must be made with the public welfare in mind—is not new. The English philosopher and essayist, Francis Bacon (1561-1626), preached the doctrine that the true and lawful end of the sciences is that human life be enriched by new discoveries. In recognition of this responsibility to society, engineering and science curricula are designed to ensure that the student who receives a baccalaureate degree in engineering or science has acquired the fundamentals necessary to meet both the technical and social responsibilities of a professional. Certainly, the technical courses in the educational programs provide baccalaureate recipients with the requisite knowledge and skills to meet their technical responsibilities. But the degree recipient has social responsibilities as well. Engineering and science curricula include a nontechnical component that has the objectives of developing both a social awareness and the ability to evaluate one's own value system. Both technical and societal knowledge and skills must be acquired for the baccalaureate recipient to develop into a socially responsible citizen and professional.

The dual role of engineering and science curricula is illustrated on the cover of the book and is elaborated in Figure 1.1. Half of the caricatures suggest some of the different disciplines in engineering and science, such as electrical engineering and mathematics. The other half of the caricatures are suggestive of some of the disciplines that can help a student develop an awareness of the societal responsibilities of the engineer and scientist. Students of engineering and science are required to take a number of credit hours in the arts, humanities, and social sciences that are illustrated on the cover. A more thorough discussion of these requirements will be presented later. Let it suffice here to say that it is these courses, which will be referred to herein as the general educational requirements (GERs), that are intended to meet the objectives of developing an awareness of both one's own values and one's responsibilities to society. In the figure, each engineering or science discipline is paired with a discipline from the arts and humanities or social sciences; for example, sociology is paired with mechanical engineering. These pairings are not intended to suggest that those in a particular engineering or science discipline must be concerned only with a specific discipline in the arts and humanities. Rather, the pairings were selected to give examples of how an understanding of nontechnical disciplines can affect one's professional life. It is hoped that the following brief points will impress upon the reader the importance of the GERs to the professional engineer and scientist:

- Electrical engineers are responsible for a large proportion of the labor-saving and pleasure-providing technologies that have come about in just the last generation. Their work has also had a profound influence on disciplines in the performing arts, such as music. Electronic synthesizers have revolutionized a large segment of the commercial music industry. Thus, knowledge of music can offer professional opportunities as well as personal pleasure.

- Mechanical engineers are involved in the advancement of the robotics industry. Many people in the labor movement fear that robotics will cause widespread unemployment. Thus, it is important that mechanical engineers know enough about economics and politics to be able to engage in this debate intelligently and conscientiously. At the very least, they have a responsibility to inform the public about what work the robots can now and will be able to take over from human workers.

- Over the last generation, nuclear power has gone through a cycle of rapid growth and decline. The chemical and nuclear engineers who developed this technology have been on center stage in the public debate over the value issue of public safety. Concerns about the risks involved must be weighed as one of the value issues associated with nuclear power. As Francis Bacon stated, technologists have a moral responsibility to ensure that new technologies are in the best interests of society. Thus, an understanding of ethics and values, derived from the study of philosophy, is important for engineers and scientists who are involved in new technologies.

**Figure 1.1** Example relationships between general education and engineering/science disciplines.

- Mathematics and the performing arts are forms of communication. Engineers and scientists communicate among themselves using technical jargon, but they also have a responsibility to communicate with the public. Effective communication, whether in the scientific language of mathematics or the written, oral, musical, or movement languages of literature and the performing arts, is essential in one's profession.

- Civil engineers are involved in much of the land development that takes place. In certain cases, historic sites are located near a property to be developed. Preservation of these historic landmarks provides a continued reminder of past cultures of a society. The civil engineer has a responsibility to preserve these examples of past cultures so that the values they symbolize can be passed on to future generations. An understanding of the importance of history and the culture of past generations can be developed by taking courses in history and culture. Such an awareness may lead the civil engineer to acknowledge the importance of historic sites to a community.

- Throughout history, many new technological developments have been the result of advances in the basic sciences, such as physics. Economic growth depends, in large part, on new technologies. An understanding of the relationship between science and business-based technologies will enable scientists and engineers to be better aware of the economic impact that their work is likely to have.

- Those in the field of chemistry play an important role in world health as well as in personal health. From providing chemicals to control pests on agricultural crops to studying the effect of chemical imbalances on health, chemists are central in the areas of health, fitness, and nutrition.

- A number of participants in the U.S. space program have been psychologists interested in the behavioral issues involved in space travel. If advances in space are to take place during the next generation, those involved will have to provide answers to questions about human behavioral problems associated with extended stays in space, not just answers to the technical issues. The aerospace engineer should not view rocket and propulsion design as the only topics of interest. Solutions to behavioral problems associated with space travel may result from the aerospace engineer's recognition of the relationship between design and behavior. Thus, courses in psychology and human behavior may serve the aerospace engineer well.

- When visiting foreign countries where a different language is spoken, presidents and other dignitaries often include greetings spoken in the native language of the audience as part of their opening addresses. This act conveys to those in the audience that the speaker respects the language and culture of the country. Communication based upon respect is very important in developing cooperation between nations. Engineers and scientists who work in foreign countries act as professional emissaries as well as representatives of their firms. An engineer or scientist who understands the rudiments of a foreign language may be more effective both in generating business and in serving as a representative of our own society.

- Agricultural engineers could play a major role in solving the world's food shortage problem. Major roadblocks to success, however, have been the politics and governmental institutions here at home and in underdeveloped countries. Understanding the politics of food production and distribution will better equip the agricultural engineer to ensure that his or her skills are used with maximum effectiveness. Thus, there are good reasons for students of agricultural engineering to select courses in government and politics.

These examples are intended only to illustrate the importance of nontechnical subjects to the student of engineering and science. However, the importance of these subjects goes much deeper than just augmenting one's technical skills. These subjects have much more to offer. As we will discuss, material within the arts, humanities, and social sciences liberates students so that they can learn from others' experiences; such vicarious experiences provide the basis for developing leadership skills, self-confidence, and a creative attitude—attributes that will serve the students, both personally and professionally, in whatever they pursue.

## ENGINEERING AND SCIENCE CURRICULA

By now, you have examined the program of study required for a baccalaureate degree in the engineering or science discipline of your choice. To facilitate our discussion here, we will separate the program into two parts: general education and technical education. *Technical education* refers to that part of the program in which you acquire the knowledge and specialized skills required for your chosen occupation. *General education* refers to that part of the program in which you acquire the knowledge and skills needed to be a valued member of society. The distinction may be more evident from the following:

> The concept of liberal education first appeared in a slave-owning society, like that of Athens, in which the community was divided into freemen and slaves, rulers and subjects. While the slaves carried on the specialized occupations of menial work, the freemen were primarily concerned with the rights and duties of citizenship. The training of the former was purely vocational; but as the freemen were not only a ruling but also a leisure class, their education was exclusively in the liberal arts, without any utilitarian tinge. The freemen were trained in the reflective pursuit of the good life; their education was unspecialized as well as unvocational; its aim was to produce a rounded person with a full understanding of himself and of his place in society and in the cosmos. (The Harvard Committee, 1948)

One might summarize this by saying that general education courses deal with living, not just with making a living.

## Redfield's Fable

The following fable by Robert Redfield (1941) will illustrate a problem in engineering and science curricula:

> A hen was making an effort to instruct her chicks about their future sources of food supply while she and they were balanced precariously on a chicken coop which was being carried down a river by a flood. It was a long time since she had studied the forest on the bank, and the account she was giving her chicks of forest resources was none too good. So she called to the wise owl on the bank for help. "You know the woods, oh owl, for you stay in this forest and study it," said the hen; "will you not tell me what to teach my chicks about life in the forest?" But the owl had overheard what the hen was telling the chicks about the forest as she came along, and he thought it was scientifically inaccurate and superficial. Besides, he was just then busy completing a monograph on the incidence of beetle larvae in acorns. So he pretended he had not heard the hen. The hen, turned back upon herself, proceeded as well as she could to prepare and put into effect an instruction unit on food resources of forests, meanwhile struggling to keep her chicks from falling off the chicken coop. The chicks took the instruction very well, and later the coop stopped at a point far downstream and the chicks went ashore—to begin their adult life in a treeless meadow.

For our purposes here, we will let the chicks, the hen, and the owl correspond to students of engineering and science, engineering and science faculty, and faculty in the arts and humanities, respectively. The chicken coop in the middle of the flood is analogous to the years a student spends in college; just as the chicks have to worry about not falling into the flood-swollen river, students must cope with the personal problems that they face during the college years. The hen (i.e., the engineering and science faculty) is trying to teach the chicks (i.e., the students) about food resources of forests (i.e., technical courses in engineering and science). Unfortunately for the chicks, the hen was able to give them instruction on only one aspect of knowledge that would be needed (i.e., the technical courses are inadequate by themselves). The conditions at the point far downstream where the coop stopped (i.e., life for students beyond their college years) was quite different from the life portrayed by the hen; finding food in a treeless meadow is not like finding food in a forest (i.e., life as a practicing engineer or scientist is much broader than just the technical dimension of engineering and science that is emphasized in most engineering and science curricula). The hen recognized her deficiencies in meeting all the needs of her chicks, so she asked the owl for help. The wise old owl was too interested in his monograph on beetle larvae in acorns (i.e., arts and humanities faculty do not always recognize the needs of students from other disciplines, and they have their own research careers to develop). Thus, the chicks did not receive a complete education, one that would serve all of their needs under a variety of environments from the forest to the treeless meadow.

The point is that there is more to an education in engineering and science than just the technical courses; preparation for life through a college education involves the development of attitudes that will serve the student for a variety of life experiences. It is hoped that this book will help the chicks overcome the inability of the hen to prepare them for a variety of environments and the understandable disinterest of the owl.

### ABET Guidelines

To ensure that practicing engineers and scientists are qualified to practice their professions, engineering and science programs are structured according to guidelines established by the professions and the accrediting organizations that represent them. For example, the Accreditation Board for Engineering and Technology (ABET) reviews the curriculum for every engineering program that seeks accreditation. To receive ABET approval, a program must meet certain guidelines. With respect to the humanities and social sciences, ABET (1981) provides the following guidelines:

> The curricular content in the area of the *humanities and social sciences* should be planned to reflect a rationale or fulfill an objective appropriate to the engineering profession and the institution's educational objectives. While the objective of a broad liberal education is served through independent humanities and social science courses, the objectives of the profession and of the individual make preferable the selection of some courses in this subject area at an advanced level rather than a selection of totally unrelated beginning courses. It cannot be overemphasized that efforts to present coursework in the humanities and social sciences as an integral part of the engineering educational program are encouraged in the interests of making young engineers fully aware of their social responsibilities and better able to consider related factors in the decision-making process.
>
> (1) Such coursework should meet the generally accepted definitions that humanities are the branches of knowledge concerned with man and his culture, while social sciences are the studies of individual relationships in and to society. Traditional subjects in these areas are philosophy, religion, history, literature, fine arts, sociology, psychology, anthropology, economics, and modern languages beyond the introductory skills courses, while modern nontraditional subjects are exemplified by courses such as technology and human affairs, history of technology, and professional ethics and social responsibility.
>
> (2) Subjects such as accounting, industrial management, finance, personnel administration, and ROTC studies may be appropriately included either as required or elective courses in engineering curricula in satisfaction of desired program objectives of the institution. However, such courses normally do not fulfill the objectives desired of the humanities and social science content. It is the subject matter that is important rather than the department offering the course. Skills courses are acceptable only if a substantial amount of material relating to cultural values is involved as contrasted to routine exercises to enhance the student's performance.

To suggest that courses in the liberal arts, humanities, and social sciences should be taken only because they can enhance an individual's career opportunities would be narrow-minded. In fact, professional advancement of the individual is probably the least important reason for the requirement of general education courses. The examples provided earlier relate to the technical interactions between society and the professional engineer and scientist. The statement of ABET adds a societal dimension to the technical dimension. A third reason for including the GERs in engineering and science curricula is that such courses are important to the social and value development of the student, development that is independent of one's professional life. After receiving a baccalaureate degree, an individual takes on personal, family, and community responsibilities. The GERs are also intended to prepare the individual to meet these personal challenges.


## PROFESSIONALISM AND GENERAL EDUCATION REQUIREMENTS


As noted earlier, we separate engineering and science curricula into two parts: courses that introduce technical topics for the purpose of increasing the students' technical knowledge and skills and courses that provide for the general development of the individual. The latter courses are what we broadly class as the general education requirements (GERs). This does not imply that engineering and science courses cannot be structured to enhance students' understanding of their social responsibilities, only that, in practice, discussions of these responsibilities most often occur in the general education courses. In a society in which economics is a primary source of our values, the effectiveness of a degree program is often narrowly judged by students on its ability to develop the skills necessary to gain long-term, high-paying employment. Students naturally place their primary effort and intellectual interest in those courses that help develop job-related skills. Therefore, the GERs are often viewed as an obstacle to fulfilling the degree requirements, rather than as an integral part of the degree program.

In fact, however, the general education requirements are an essential part of programs in engineering and science. All too often, students fail to see the value of the GERs only because the faculty, including those in the arts, humanities, and social sciences, fail to demonstrate their importance. Students would also probably not recognize the value of many technical courses if the faculty failed to emphasize the importance of the material. The GERs are a necessary part of a professional education in engineering and science because professionals in these specialties must have a wide range of well-developed characteristics, not just technical competency. To delineate the value of the GERs, we will first define what is meant by the term *professional*.

## THE DIMENSIONS OF PROFESSIONALISM

When we hear the word *professional,* we may think of a professional athlete or perhaps even a hired killer. After all, the most general definition of the word *professional,* provided by the *American Heritage Dictionary,* is: "One who is engaged in a specific activity as a source of livelihood." According to this definition, almost all people who work could be classed as professionals. Plumbers, grave diggers, used car salespersons, and chimney sweeps are engaged in specific activities as a source of livelihood. It is not that grave diggers and football players are *not* professionals; they certainly are needed citizens who have skills that are used in a service to society. But certain activities are accorded the status of professions; for example, doctors, members of the clergy, and teachers belong to professions. These professions are usually thought to require a higher level of knowledge than others that might satisfy the dictionary definition of a professional because they serve society in special ways. It is in this sense that we want to classify engineers and scientists as professionals; while engineers and scientists engage in specific activities as a source of livelihood, their work carries special responsibilities to society that accords it the status of a profession. It is these responsibilities that will be outlined here in an attempt to show why the GERs are important to the student of engineering and science in becoming a true professional.

In his discussion of professional development, Dougherty (1961) defines a professional as

> . . . one who uses specialized knowledge and skill in the solution of problems that cannot be standardized. He is actuated by a service motive; he works in a relation of confidence, and observes an acceptable code of ethical conduct.

It must be emphasized that the term *professional* does not apply only to someone who has specialized knowledge and skill. There are other important dimensions of professionalism. In his definition, Dougherty recognized the multifaceted nature of professionalism, and he concluded:

> Professionalism is a way of thinking and living rather than an accumulation of knowledge and power. Knowledge and power are essential and when actuated by the professional spirit they produce the leaders and torch-bearers.

What are the fundamental dimensions of professionalism that are necessary for an individual to be considered a professional? The National Society of Professional Engineers (NSPE, 1976) identified five characteristics of a professional engineer, which also apply to those in the sciences:

1. One who possesses a body of distinctive technical knowledge and art gained by education, research, and experience;

2. One who recognizes a service motive to society in vital and honorable activities;

3. One who believes in standards of conduct, such as represented by ethical rules;

4. One who supports legal status of admission to the profession. The most common forms are registration to practice engineering and graduation from an accredited engineering curriculum; and

5. One who has pride in the profession and a desire to promote technical knowledge and professional ideals.

To these five characteristics, Dougherty's definition suggests a sixth factor that we could add as a fundamental characteristic, even though it may be inherent in the foregoing five characteristics:

6. One who works in a relation of confidence to his employer, the public, and all who use his works.

Considerable time, education, and professional practice are required to obtain the specialized knowledge and skill that characterizes a professional. The professional, in contrast to the artisan or technician, is capable of synthesizing past experience and fundamental principles in solving new problems. Such problem solving requires independent thought and a motivation that is not self-serving. The motivation must stem from a dedication to the service of both society and the profession; otherwise, the knowledge and skill do not maximize human welfare. Because of the interaction of a professional with society and the advantage that the professional has through his or her specialized knowledge and skill, it is important for a professional to have sound moral judgment and to be able and willing to translate this moral judgment into principled professional conduct. Although the six dimensions of professionalism are independent in that any individual may possess one or a few of the characteristics, a true professional must possess all six of the fundamental dimensions.

Although technical design courses could be modified to incorporate material that would foster development of the six dimensions, or a course in ethics and professionalism could be included in engineering and science curricula, it is doubtful that such approaches would be as successful as proper structuring of general education courses. The GERs could enhance development of these six dimensions in the following ways.

1. *Distinctive technical knowledge and art:* This dimension is clearly the intent of the technical component of engineering and science curricula, so it differs from the other five dimensions, which carry a broader perspective. However, this does not imply that growth in the other five dimensions does not enhance one's ability to place technical knowledge in the proper professional and social perspective.

2. *Recognition of a service motive to society:* In professional life, service means more than just completing a job for a client or an employer. Although the job must certainly meet the needs of the client or employer, the completed project must also be consistent with the values of society. General education courses can emphasize the service motive to society. For example, education courses dealing with aid to the handicapped would certainly meet this intent. A health course on the problems of the aging would develop an awareness of the problems of an ever-growing segment of society—problems that engineers and scientists should consider in their work. A sociology course dealing with criminology and the role of police officers would suggest a similarity between engineers and scientists and those in other professions.

3. *Belief in standards of conduct:* Standards of conduct emphasize the ethical requirements of a profession; this is a distinctive characteristic of a profession, all too often honored in the breech. Such standards would certainly be discussed in a number of philosophy courses, as well as in courses on business law or business ethics. Psychology or management courses dealing with issues in human behavior discuss criteria used in evaluating personal behavior, and such knowledge could be transferred to a professional setting. Health courses may discuss the Hippocratic Oath or the legal and moral status of health professionals.

4. *Legal status of admission to the profession:* All professions have specific requirements for admission. Therefore, a prelaw or premed course might be available that would discuss the requirements for those professions and, more important, the need for maintaining the ideals of the profession. A sociology course on unions may discuss the effect of union requirements. A government and politics course on naturalization and the problems of illegal alien issues may provide an understanding of the need for standards. A business law course may discuss the legal requirements of those practicing within a profession, which would demonstrate the need for strict requirements for admission to the profession.

5. *Pride in the profession:* A profession is like a community or a culture. Failures of a few in a community reflect on the entire community, and unacceptable conduct by a few within a profession reflects badly on all members of the profession. Off-the-field misconduct by a few professional athletes reflects badly on their teammates. The same applies to engineers and scientists. Thus, pride and professional ideals among members of the profession are important. Health and fitness courses develop individual pride, and physical education courses that involve team activities can develop pride in joint efforts. The same would apply to courses in the performing arts in which group association may be necessary. A discussion of community activities in a sociology course could provide a set of beliefs that would be transferable to the profession as a community. Similarly, a history course dealing with the problems and privileges of nationalism may identify similarities between nations and thus between professions. A government and politics course that discusses international organizations such as NATO might suggest the importance of unity and pride among countries with similar ideals.

6. *Relation of confidence to the employer and the public:* Loyalty is an im-

portant value in professional practice. A government and politics course dealing with nationalistic loyalty might illustrate this dimension of a professional. A study of past cultures in either a history or a foreign language course might demonstrate the importance of loyalty of the military or public servants to a society. Such an understanding of loyalty should transfer easily to life as a professional, particularly the need for confidence in professional practice.

### Character Enhancement Through the General Education Requirements

Besides being an integral part of a student's professional education, the GERs are also a source of knowledge and skills that are important to personal development. An individual has responsibilities to family, friends, and the community, which increase as he or she moves into adulthood. Some qualities that can be beneficial personally as well as professionally are leadership, creativity, value decision-making ability, and social awareness.

In terms of the family, the community, and the profession, we would probably want to emphasize that the term *leadership* implies success in directing the activities of a group. But real leadership involves more than just directing. A leader must create family, community, or professional purpose; that is, leadership involves initiating and shaping purpose and values, not just executing the activities of the group (Peters and Waterman, 1982). Can courses used to fulfill the GERs develop leadership abilities? They obviously provide diversity in the student's education. This leads to a variety of experiences, even though they are often vicarious experiences. These experiences develop capacities for imaginative sympathy toward others and their experiences. Obviously, a study of history would be one example of vicariously sensed experiences. But even vicarious experiences provide a base from which a leader can initiate action to solve problems at hand. For example, a study of great leaders in history can illustrate desirable characteristics of a leader.

The initiation and shaping of purpose cannot be based solely on experience; it requires the ability to develop creative solutions. Just as new pesticides are necessary because pests develop an immunity to existing pesticides, new problems arise daily in any society, and problem solving goes beyond reshaping past experiences. It requires the confidence and open-minded attitude that are necessary to come up with creative new ideas. Courses in the GERs help develop the self-confidence and free-spirit attitude that are helpful in developing creative solutions to personal, community, and professional problems. For example, a course in radio and television communication may help develop self-confidence. An introductory course in mountaineering can enhance the development of self-confidence while simultaneously developing free-spiritedness. These are the precursors to an attitude of disciplined creativity.

How can creativity be important to an individual? The process of creating something new can be very exhilarating; it can bring much pleasure and happiness. The parents of a newborn baby are thrilled with their "creation." A creative solution to a problem in the community can also be very gratifying. In addition to the feeling of having done something well, creative solutions to problems bring favorable recognition from family and friends, which serves as an ego boost. Achieving personal satisfaction through creative problem solving develops self-confidence and, therefore, self-acceptance; it strengthens self-image and helps one cope with personal shortcomings, whether real or perceived. Creative problem solving provides a feeling of attachment to anyone or anything associated with the solution—a feeling that enhances one's feeling of security. Thus, creative ability touches on many human values, and a planned program for fulfilling the GERs can help form the basis for enhancing creative ability.

Engineering decision making involves more than just selecting the design alternative that has the highest ratio of monetary benefits to project costs; the same is true for decision making in a personal setting. There are value dilemmas that must be resolved in making decisions in both personal and professional settings. How can courses in the GERs enhance one's ability to make value decisions? First, the way value conflicts are resolved depends on an individual's or a company's value system. By discussing moral conflicts in general education courses, the student can come to understand how others weight competing values and what society expects of the individual. The student thereby develops a better understanding of his or her own value system. Second, general education courses broaden the student's value horizon by developing an awareness of a wider array of human values. Third, general education courses provide for a better understanding of the breadth of value responsibility of the individual. Personally, one has value responsibilities to oneself, family, friends, the community, and society. Professionally, one has ethical responsibilities to oneself, the employer, the client, the profession, and society. Although courses that are used to fulfill the GERs may not specifically address the question of ethical responsibilities in one's profession, these courses will certainly affect the individual's value decision-making ability in a professional setting because of their effect on the individual's value system.

For most students, life as a student, whether in high school or in college, does not involve a great deal of interaction with social institutions. Thus, the baccalaureate recipient has a greater value awareness of the individual and of peers than of society as a whole. A greater social sensitivity is needed to function both personally within the community and professionally within the professional community. The GERs are intended to develop such a social sensitivity. *Community service* is more than just a term that describes a form of punishment used by the courts. *Volunteer work* is more than just a term for the free labor that an individual provides for social institutions. Both terms reflect the need for the individual to serve the community in which he or she resides. Community service can take many forms. Boys' and girls' clubs always need coaches for their athletic teams. Handicapped and elderly people often need transportation beyond that provided by public transportation systems. A professional engineer or scientist could volunteer to be a judge at the science fair of the local high school. Many general education courses emphasize society rather than the individual. Discussions of cultures, social institutions, forms of government, historical trends such as the growth of technology, and worldwide problems such as poverty and environmental degradation emphasize society and the need for the individual to function within society.

Some of the diverse benefits of the GERs as part of engineering and science curricula we have seen are:

1. For an individual's personal life, the GERs develop an appreciation of life's rich variety and can help develop an inner peace that will serve the individual in times of personal hardship.

2. A harmonious social life with family and friends requires an array of diverse interests; the diversity of the GERs provides the individual with the confidence that is necessary to function in a variety of social situations.

3. The physical facilities produced by the engineer and scientist provide material comforts and pleasure; many of the GERs provide discussions of societal values, such as beauty, equality, charity, and sympathy.

4. The GERs develop a social awareness that enables the individual to balance nonquantifiable goals and values with the economic benefits associated with engineering projects.

5. The value development of individuals within the profession brought about by the GERs enables individual engineers to enhance collectively the image of the profession so that the reputation of the profession does not limit its ability to serve society.

6. The GERs develop the attitude and honesty that enable the professional to work with the client in a relationship of confidence and trust.

7. The GERs develop an attitude of confidence in providing leadership within the firm and a sense of loyalty to the firm's goals.

8. Within the individual, the GERs develop a creative intellect that maximizes the individual's ability to serve the firm, the client, the profession, and society in terms of the value dimension of a professional.

## SUMMARY

The point of this introductory chapter has been to emphasize the dual responsibilities of a professional. Technical competence alone is insufficient. The professional engineer or scientist also has value responsibilities to society. To meet these dual responsibilities, the educational program must include both a technical component and a component intended to develop social awareness. If the general education requirements are planned properly, are taken seriously, and are fulfilled with an understanding of their importance, the engineer and scientist should be better prepared to meet the demands of professional life.

# EXERCISES

**1.1.** Using the six dimensions of professionalism, evaluate the degree to which a medical doctor and a paid football player are professionals.

**1.2.** Obtain a copy of the Hippocratic Oath and develop a similar oath that would apply to your perception of an engineer or scientist.

**1.3.** Obtain a copy of the Hippocratic Oath and evaluate it in terms of the six dimensions of professionalism.

**1.4.** Discuss why engineers and scientists have a special responsibility to society beyond that of individuals in jobs that do not fulfill the six dimensions of professionalism.

**1.5.** Using human values such as public health and safety, freedom, privacy, and aesthetics, discuss why engineers and scientists must be sensitive to value issues. Provide examples to illustrate your discussion points.

**1.6.** Summarize the benefits of general education courses to (a) professional growth and (b) personal development.

**1.7.** A belief in standards of conduct is one dimension of professionalism. Discuss how failure of members of a profession to follow standards of conduct can lead to a poor public image of the profession.

**1.8.** Provide an example of a situation in which you have shown leadership, and discuss what the consequences might have been had you not provided the leadership.

**1.9.** Each discipline (e.g., physics, electrical engineering, etc.) has a student organization that is affiliated with a professional society. Discuss how participation as an officer of such an organization could enhance one's leadership skills.

**1.10.** Provide an example of a situation in which you provided a creative solution to a problem or were involved in a creative project. How did this affect your self-image?

**1.11.** How has the creativity associated with the U.S. space program enhanced the image of the engineers and scientists associated with the program?

**1.12.** Lawyers have an obligation to do their best in helping their clients, even when the clients admit to committing heinous crimes. With respect to the six dimensions of professionalism, evaluate how law can be referred to as a profession.

**1.13.** Discuss why technical ability alone is not sufficient for someone to be considered a leader.

**1.14.** Sociology is the study of human social behavior, especially with respect to the origins, organization, institutions, and development of human society. Discuss how a course in sociology might help develop leadership skills in an engineering or science student.

**1.15.** Students in engineering and science often view the term *problem solving* as a quantitative process (i.e., a process involving mathematics). Propose types of problems in engineering and science in which mathematical solutions are not possible, and discuss courses in the arts and humanities that might enhance one's ability to make such decisions.

**1.16.** Identify one course of study (such as poetry, history, Renaissance art, or ballet) that you believe has no practical use. Explain your reasons. Does such a course of study have any value at all?

**1.17.** Why has it become necessary for technical education to be increasingly more specialized? Is this detrimental to either the individual or society?

**1.18.** Discuss why both specialized technical education and general education are important in a democratic society.

**2**

# Values and Value Decision Making

*Richard H. McCuen*

## INTRODUCTION

When students of engineering or science think about decision making by an engineer or scientist, they think of decisions associated with the technical aspects of professional life. For example, is the capacity of the computer system adequate for meeting project needs? Will the electrical circuit be adequate to meet power demands? Such technical decisions are obviously part of the responsibilities of a computer scientist or an electrical engineer. But decision making in professional life is not limited to technical aspects. In addition to technical responsibilities, engineers and scientists frequently must make decisions involving human value issues. The news media continually bring to the attention of the public events in which engineers and scientists are involved in value decisions, like it or not. The construction of a dam in Tennessee was halted recently because a little fish called the snail darter was in danger of extinction; in this case, technical progress was stopped not because of a technical issue but because of a value issue—preservation of an endangered species. The press has also widely reported the clash between the public and scientists involved in genetic engineering, which involves a conflict between the freedom to do research and the issue of public health and safety. Some are opposed to genetic engineering because they believe that it represents our attempts to create or alter life. The scientists have also been criticized for their apparent lack of concern about the risks of their work. Their failure to address the endangered species issue or the public health and safety issue in these two cases has prevented the engineers and scientists from completing the technical aspects of their work. The news is filled with other examples of societal issues—such as nuclear power development,

construction of projects by the Corps of Engineers, and military weapon technological development—all of which involve engineers and scientists. Thus, value issues
are an important part of the professional lives of engineers and scientists; we do not
work in a social vacuum. The value responsibilities that we have are as important
as the technical ones. Failure to address these value responsibilities can severely
limit our ability to fulfill our technical responsibilities.

It would be easy to define value decision making as a process of weighting
alternative courses of action according to the importance of values that are in conflict. But the term *weighting* may suggest that we can quantify values and that
value decision making involves merely assigning some numerical weight to each
value involved in the conflict and selecting the decision alternative with the largest
numerical value. Value decision making in a professional context is much more
complicated. A few further examples illustrate some of the various kinds of value
decisions confronting engineers and scientists:

- A chemist employed by a private chemical laboratory is analyzing samples
  taken from a hazardous waste site; the analysis shows that the site does not
  meet state standards. The client is aware that the positive results will require
  large expenditures for cleaning up the polluted site. Therefore, the client offers the chemist $10,000 to provide a report indicating that the site meets
  state standards.

- An engineer in charge of the construction of 200 single-family town houses
  requests county inspection so that the developer can sell the houses. The inspector tells the engineer that he will not inspect the houses for at least a
  month because of a backlog of work; however, the inspector suggests that
  an under-the-table payment of $5000 will ensure speedier attention. The
  engineer recognizes that the unoccupied dwellings represent a loss of $800
  per month per dwelling, and thus the payment appears to be "good business."

- While working on a defense contract for the Navy, an electrical engineer
  recognizes that a weapons system could be vastly improved if an additional
  electronic component existed. Recognizing that the component had not yet
  been developed and that development of the component would not be beyond his technical abilities, the engineer resigns from his company, starts his
  own firm, develops the component, and applies for a patent. When the engineer was hired by his original firm, he had signed a patent agreement in which
  he agreed that any patents originating from knowledge gained while employed by the firm would belong to the firm. The engineer rationalizes that
  his behavior was ethical because he developed the component after leaving
  the firm. Of course, the company claims that the engineer violated the patent
  agreement, both in spirit and by law.

These are just a few examples of what can occur in professional practice. The
practice of engineering and science involves not only technical effort but decision

making that involves value conflicts. But value decision making is not new to a freshman in an engineering or science program. With a little thought, every student could identify value conflicts with which he or she, or a friend, has been involved. For example:

- A high school student conducting a physics laboratory experiment on the linear expansion of a solid finds that his lab measurement does not agree with the expected results. Believing that his grade depends on the accuracy of his results, he decides to report falsely a value close to the expected result, rather than his actual measured value.
- A high school student has not received good grades on the first two quizzes in her trigonometry class. Another student in the class who has done well on the quizzes indicates that he will allow her to copy on the next quiz if she will pay him $10. The student thinks that $10 is a small price to pay for a better grade and improved prestige with her parents and friends.
- A high school student has been going steady with his sister's best friend for 16 months. The sister finds out that her brother has started to see another girl without indicating to his steady girl friend that he wants to date others. Thus, the sister is confronted with the problem of telling her best friend about her brother's conduct, ignoring his behavior, or discussing the matter with her brother.

These are just a few examples of situations in which values are in conflict, and one must make a decision. Whether the value decision is in one's personal life or one's professional life, the alternative consequences of moral (ethical) actions are important. The decision process requires considerable thought as well as an understanding of how to make a decision once the conflicting values have been identified. Very often, incorrect value decisions are made because not all of the values in conflict are identified.

The foregoing examples might suggest that an understanding of values and value decision making are important only in making decisions involving immoral or unethical conduct. This is not the case. Values and value decision making are part of life, both personal life and professional life. A few instances in which values are important to the professional illustrate this:

- It is not uncommon to see a building or a bridge that clashes with its surroundings. All too often, citizens criticize the engineering firm responsible for the design for using function as the sole design criterion while ignoring the need for an aesthetically pleasing design. A sense of beauty can enhance products of engineering and science.
- Safety is an important human value. Improving the safety of the products of engineering and science must be a goal of every engineer and scientist.
- Knowledge is an important value. In itself, it can provide pleasure, and it is

also valuable as a means to other ends. The professional should seek knowledge of his or her profession as a means of personal reward, as a way of supporting an employer, and as a responsibility to serve society.

In one's personal life, values such as the following are also important:

- As the saying goes, variety is the spice of life. Variety is a value that can be
  very important in life. Having a variety of experiences can enhance one's
  self-confidence in social situations. Having a variety of interests can provide
  respite from the stresses of life, both personal and professional.
- Just as knowledge is important professionally, it has many personal rewards.
  Knowledge of other cultures and languages can enhance one's vacation in
  another country. Knowledge of the arts can provide a source of enjoyment
  when one visits a museum, a concert, or a play.
- Self-respect is not a value in itself but, rather, a value through the other values
  that it brings into realization. Someone with self-respect is aware of the values
  that are important and their priorities for himself or herself. A high school
  student who has self-respect does not allow peer pressure to dictate his or
  her attitudes on such issues as smoking, drugs, or the nature and extent of
  sexual activities.

The foregoing examples illustrate the fact that the need to make value decisions is
not a rare occurrence; rather, it is an important common need. Therefore, it may be
worthwhile to provide a broad-brush definition of the concept of human values.

## HUMAN VALUES: A DEFINITION

A value can be defined as follows: "A principle, standard, or quality considered
worthwhile or desirable" (*American Heritage Dictionary,* 1969). As used here, a
human value is a quality that relates directly to the potential for improving the
conditions of humankind. If we accept the premise that only humans are capable
of making value decisions, then the use of two words, *human* and *value,* becomes
redundant. Some might have a problem with the term *human value* since it could
be interpreted to mean that values are concerned only with human betterment,
even at the expense of animals and the environment. This is not the intent here.
It should be assumed that improving the conditions of animals and the quality of
the environment are inherently good, even independent of their effect on humans.

   The ability to make a value decision is one of the characteristics that distinguishes humans from other living things. Along with this ability goes the responsibility to make value decisions in an unbiased and precise way. To make accurate
value decisions, it is necessary that the decision maker understand his or her own
values. This requires a certain commitment to examine critically one's own value
priorities. Unfortunately, too few people take the time to make such an assessment.

Individuals are guided by standards established by their family and friends, and peer pressure is all too often used as an excuse for improper conduct.

Although "life, liberty, and the pursuit of happiness" is probably the most famous value statement, and "I love you" is the most frequently used value statement, there are numerous other values. The following is a partial list of human values:

| | | |
|---|---|---|
| Beauty/aesthetics | Honor | Mercy |
| Cleanliness | Honesty | Pleasure/happiness |
| Courage | Kindness | Public health/safety |
| Diligence | Knowledge | Respect |
| Efficiency | Life | Security |
| Equality | Love | Truth |
| Freedom/liberty | Loyalty | Wisdom |

These values represent feelings or attitudes rather than physical entities. This does not mean that a scale could not be developed in an attempt to reflect variations in a value. For example, industrial engineers are constantly trying to find rules and yardsticks to measure efficiency. Environmental scientists develop standards that define when minimum levels of public health are not being met. Engineering planners attempt to define indices to measure the beauty of an engineering project, and wildlife biologists develop indices to measure changes in the quality of life for animals whose habitat is affected by engineering projects. Although such attempts make it possible to incorporate value issues into the quantitative decision-making framework, engineers and scientists often fail to recognize that not everyone affected by an engineering or science project will agree with the scale used to quantify a human value. Such disagreement is the basis for value conflicts in a professional setting. But at least the engineer/scientist can attempt to incorporate value issues into the decision-making process. The relative effort that an engineer/scientist expends in developing a scale to quantify a value issue may be an indication of the sensitivity of the technical professional to human values.

As noted earlier, human value issues are also important on a personal level. Teenagers expect their parents to respect their privacy. Teenagers also expect a certain level of loyalty among friends. In exchange for their respect for these values, parents expect teenagers to maintain a certain level of cleanliness, honesty with respect to reports on their activities, and respect for rules on such issues as curfews. Value issues are often a source of conflict between parents and teenagers. The conflicts arise from the difference in opinion on the importance of the values. A parent may believe that respect for rules is more important than the teenagers' right to freedom—for example, no curfew. Thus, a conflict between the values of freedom and respect results. The procedure for solving such value conflicts in a personal setting is similar in many respects to the solution of value conflicts in a professional setting.

## VALUE DECISION MAKING

If we accept the premise that values are important to professionals, it should follow that we need an understanding of how values can be incorporated into decision making. Engineers and scientists are often labeled value-insensitive because they do not routinely attempt to incorporate value issues into their decisions; that is, they are accused of placing quantifiable technical goals above nonquantifiable human value goals.

Before trying to outline a procedure for solving value conflicts, we will provide a brief overview of the steps used in technical decision making as a basis for comparison. For our purposes here, technical decision making will be defined by the following steps:

1. Identify goals and objectives.
2. Formulate (a) a performance criterion and (b) a decision model.
3. Specify alternatives.
4. Identify resources and constraints.
5. Evaluate the decision model.
6. Make the decision.

This process can be illustrated by a simplified example of a common engineering problem. We will assume that a particular area of a city is subjected to frequent flooding. In response to complaints and disruption of services, the state hires an engineering firm to evaluate the flooding problem. The following illustrates how the foregoing six steps could be used for solving this well-structured technical problem:

1. Goal: reduce flooding in the city.
2. (a) Criterion: benefit-cost (B/C) ratio; (b) Decision model: select alternative with the highest B/C ratio.
3. Alternatives: one large reservoir or two small reservoirs.
4. Resources: $80,000,000 available.
5. 

| Alternative | Benefits | Costs | B/C |
|---|---|---|---|
| Large reservoir | $75 \times 10^6$ | $68 \times 10^6$ | 1.10 |
| Small reservoirs | $64 \times 10^6$ | $54 \times 10^6$ | 1.19 |

6. Decision: construct the two small reservoirs.

In this case, we assumed that the decision was primarily a technical one. The problem assumed that all sites for the reservoirs were available, and there was no public outcry over the location of the reservoirs. In such a case, the benefits (i.e., reduced flood damage, reduced interruption of public services, recreational use of the reservoirs) and costs (i.e., design and construction costs; costs for relocating roads, utilities, and some homes; and future maintenance costs) are easily quantified, and the benefit-cost ratio is an accepted decision criterion. A number of problems in engineering and science are similarly well structured, and a decision can be based almost solely on the technical and economic merits of the problems.

Many problems in engineering and science are not so well structured, and human value issues or nonquantifiable goals should be considered as important as or more important than the technical aspects of the problem. To show that socio-technical decision making (i.e., decisions involving both value goals and technical goals) is more complex than the technical decision-making process outlined earlier, we can define the following ten-step process:

1. Identify goals.
2. Identify stakeholders.
3. Generate assumptions.
4. Analyze the argumentation.
5. Establish operational objectives.
6. Formulate (a) performance criteria and (b) a decision model.
7. Specify alternatives.
8. Identify resources and constraints.
9. Evaluate the decision model.
10. Make the decision.

It is evident that steps 6 through 10 are identical to steps 2 through 6 of the decision process for well-structured problems given previously. For an ill-structured problem, steps 1 through 5 are necessary, whereas for well-structured problems, step 1 was adequate.

The process of solving ill-structured problems can be illustrated using a variation on the earlier example of controlling flooding in the city. We will now assume that the only technically feasible site for the large reservoir is at the location where two historic landmarks are located and that one of the two feasible sites for the small reservoirs is in a park area considered to be an aesthetic natural treasure. The local historical society rightfully claims that the historic landmarks are used as part of the city's educational programs to teach elementary and junior high school students about early American culture. Therefore, they argue that inundation of the site by the large flood-control reservoir would represent a loss of an irreplaceable community resource. A local environmental group presents an equally valid argument that the park where the engineers have proposed locating one of the small reservoirs would be destroyed and that the inhabitants of the city would lose a site that provides them with much pleasure. It should now be evident that the difference in the benefit-cost ratios identified earlier is probably not very significant, at least when one considers the value issues at stake. Although the engineers in charge of the project could easily place a monetary value on the recreational use of the two alternative sites, it would be much more difficult to place a value on either the cultural benefits of the historic landmarks or the aesthetic pleasure associated with the park site. Thus, a decision model other than the benefit-cost ratio is necessary.

The goal of the engineering project is no longer limited to controlling the flooding. In addition, it is important to preserve the cultural and aesthetic resources of the community. This is no longer a simple technical problem; it is a "people" or value problem as well. Thus, the stakeholders must be identified. Those making the technical decisions cannot fully appreciate the needs and desires of the community without some meaningful community participation. This need leads to a series of community forums, at which those involved in the decision making, including the engineers in charge of the technical details, listen to the stakeholders—those individuals or groups who will be affected by the project. The stakeholders may participate individually or through selected representatives. These forums often involve a considerable outpouring of emotional energy. (One visit to such a meeting by a student of engineering or science would clearly illustrate the importance of values in technical decisions and the importance of general education courses that are intended to emphasize human value issues.)

The next step, argumentation analysis, is beyond our scope here. Let it suffice to say that at this stage, it is necessary for the decision makers to identify the importance and certainty of the stakeholders' assumptions. In our example, those representing the historical society assume that there is no alternative way for the public to learn these specific aspects of past American culture. Similarly, those representing the environmental group assume that the pleasure derived from the aesthetic experience of visiting the park cannot be obtained in other ways. Neither of these assumptions necessarily has a high degree of certainty. It might be possible to move the historic landmarks and recreate their original settings. Similarly, other land might be set aside for a new park that would meet many of the needs provided by the original site. Thus, the assumption-generation step is followed by argumentation analysis in an attempt to evaluate the assumptions of the stakeholders and their reasonableness. This step provides the basis for establishing operational objectives. Whereas the well-structured problem had the goal of reducing flooding, the ill-structured problem has at least two operational objectives: to reduce flooding and to preserve the cultural and aesthetic state of the community.

Although steps 6 through 10 of the problem-solving process for the ill-structured problem are the same as steps 2 through 6 of the process for the well-structured problem, the specific elements are different. The following illustrates the decision process:

6. (a) Criteria: benefit-cost ratio (B/C) and a cultural and aesthetic experience index ($I_{ca}$); (b) Decision model: maximize a function consisting of the sum of B/C and $I_{ca}$.

7. Alternatives: (1) a large flood control reservoir, with the historic landmarks relocated; or (2) two small flood control reservoirs, with a new park constructed elsewhere.

8. Resources: $80,000,000 available.

| 9. *Alternative* | *Benefits* | *Costs* | *B/C* | $I_{ca}$ | *Sum* |
|---|---|---|---|---|---|
| (1) | $\$75 \times 10^6$ | $\$71 \times 10^6$ | 1.06 | 1.04 | 2.10 |
| (2) | $\$64 \times 10^6$ | $\$60 \times 10^6$ | 1.07 | 0.97 | 2.04 |

10. Decision: relocate the historic landmarks and construct the large reservoir.

In this case, we assumed that the value issues could be reduced to a quantitative index; this is often not easy. But the problem suggests (1) that value issues can be just as important as technical issues; (2) that value issues can cause changes in decisions that previously have been based solely on technical criteria; (3) that engineers and scientists must include value issues in their decisions; and (4) that decisions involving value issues are more complex than problems that are based solely on technical details and are easily quantified.

### A Personal Value Conflict

Before trying to put a personal value conflict into the foregoing decision framework, we must agree that there are some value issues that cannot be resolved. For example, abortion is a very emotional topic. Pro-life advocates will not be convinced that a woman should have the freedom to choose; they believe that the life of the fetus should be given priority over the woman's freedom of choice. Pro-choice advocates will also not be convinced that a woman should be required to carry the fetus to term and spend years raising the child. Regardless of the arguments provided and the decision process used, it is unlikely that either side will change its decision. But not all value issues are unresolvable, and decisions often must be made when values are in conflict.

We will use a much-simplified example, previously mentioned, of a common problem to illustrate value decision making in a personal setting. The problem centers on the conflict between a teenager and his parents over the level of freedom and privacy the teen should be allowed concerning his activities with friends. Obviously, the teen believes that he is sufficiently mature to be allowed to go out with his friends without continually reporting his whereabouts to his parents; he believes that he should be given his *freedom* and that he has the right to *privacy*. The parents feel that they have a right to be *knowledgeable* about their son's activities and a responsibility to take the steps necessary to preserve the *happiness* and *security* of the family. They also believe that whatever decision is made, *truthfulness* is an absolute requirement. Thus, this example shows a value conflict between freedom/privacy versus knowledge/happiness/security, with truth as a necessary element in the decision. The ten-step decision process for this problem is summarized in Table 2.1. To maintain simplicity, it should be noted that steps 4 and 8 are of limited use here; details of the application of these steps can be found elsewhere (Mason and Mitroff, 1981; McCuen, 1983a; and Toulmin et al., 1979). It is important to note that human values are used as the performance criteria and then are

**TABLE 2.1   Example of Value Decision Making to Resolve a Conflict in a Personal Setting**

1. Goal: to preserve family happiness and security while allowing the teen as much freedom as possible.
2. Stakeholders: the teen and his family.
3. Assumptions:
   (a)  The teen has a right to some freedom and privacy.
   (b)  The parents have a responsibility to ensure family happiness and security.
   (c)  Truthfulness is valued.
4. Argumentation analysis:

| Assumption | Importance to | | Certainty of Importance | |
|---|---|---|---|---|
| | Parent | Teen | Parent | Teen |
| A | Medium | High | High | Medium |
| B | High | Low | High | Medium |
| C | High | Medium | High | High |

5. Operational objectives:
   (a)  Increase teen's freedom.
   (b)  Provide assurance of family happiness and security to parents.
6. (a)  Performance criteria: ordinal level of freedom, security, and truthfulness.
   (b)  Decision model: select alternative that provides maximal levels of values.
7. Alternatives:
   (a)  Complete freedom for teen.
   (b)  Some freedom with curfew and limited reporting of whereabouts.
   (c)  Limited freedom with strict curfew and continual reporting of whereabouts.
8. Resources/constraints: not applicable.
9. Evaluate decision model:

| Alternative | Freedom | Security | Truthfulness |
|---|---|---|---|
| (a) | High | Low | Not applicable |
| (b) | Moderately high | Moderately high | Promoted |
| (c) | Low | High | Not promoted |

10. Decision: alternative (b).

presented on an ordinal scale of measurement, rather than the interval scale used for the benefit-cost ratio; therefore, the decision model involves a qualitative assessment rather than a quantitative assessment. This is sometimes necessary when dealing with value issues, but it does not prevent us from making a decision. It may make the decision process a little more difficult, but it certainly does not mean that value issues should be avoided when making decisions.

### Value Decision Making and General Education

The intent here has been to bridge the gap between technical and value decision making. The technical courses that form the core of engineering and science programs provide the framework for making technical decisions. However, projects in engineering and science frequently involve human value issues. The ability of engineers or scientists to solve sociotechnical problems depends, to some extent, on their ability to identify, appreciate, and deal with value issues. One goal of the general education requirements that are part of engineering and science curricula is to increase the students' ability to identify and include value issues in the solution of these sociotechnical problems.

## THE ENGINEERING PERSONALITY
## AND VALUE DECISION MAKING

A study by Garfoot and Simon (1963) showed that the average engineer scores high on personality traits associated with quantitative evaluation but low on traits associated with social and political sensitivity. In summarizing studies of the engineering personality that showed that the engineer was indifferent to human relations, Florman (1976) stated that the engineer "would rather deal with things than with human beings." Some hypothesize that people of this personality type are attracted to engineering; others blame it on the stifling nature of engineering education. In either case, the evidence suggests that engineers are relatively insensitive to human value issues.

If we accept this personality typing, there is a clear need for the engineer to develop a sociopolitical sensitivity. If people of this personality type are attracted to engineering, engineering education must be modified so that engineering students become sensitized to human value issues. Likewise, if the problem is the stifling nature of engineering education, appropriate modifications in that education are called for. If the engineering student can learn to design automatic control systems and large steel structures, he or she should certainly be capable of developing a social sensitivity.

## VALUE PREFERENCES WITHIN A PROFESSIONAL CONTEXT

Engineering education emphasizes the technical aspects of engineering. Courses in engineering design and management make up a large part of the undergraduate curriculum. The technical and managerial aspects of each element and relationship of the engineering tetrahedron (Figure 2.1) are probably evident to every reader. The engineer, the firm, the client, the profession, and society have rights and responsibilities from both a technical and a value perspective. For example, society, which demands useful technical products, has the responsibility to provide the engineering community with the resources and the institutional climate in which it can function optimally. When society meets this responsibility, it has the right to be provided well-designed technical products, at an optimum cost, from the engineering community. As another example, the employer of engineers has a responsibility to provide them with acceptable working conditions and the resources to maintain

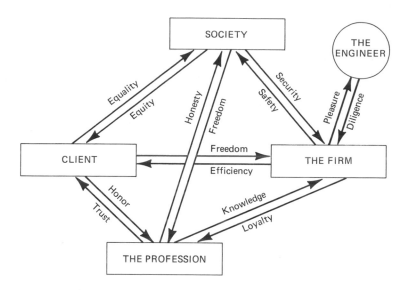

**Figure 2.1**  Professional rights and responsibilities within a value context.

professional competency. For meeting these responsibilities, the employer has the right to receive a profitable level of design or management output. But items like resources, optimum cost, good working conditions, and a respectable level of output are quantifiable goals. These relate to the technical aspects that form the core of engineering education.

In addition to these quantifiable goals, there are value considerations associated with the elements and interrelationships of the engineering tetrahedron. There is no reason to believe that these value preferences are any less important to those involved than the quantifiable goals. Although most students are aware of the importance of the rights and responsibilities associated with these quantifiable goals, it is just as important that they recognize the rights and responsibilities associated with the value preferences.

To illustrate some of the values involved in engineering practice, Figure 2.1 shows one human value for each of the interrelationships between elements of the engineering tetrahedron. Although only a single human value is shown for each path (with the exception of freedom, which appears twice), the figure is meant to illustrate the variety of value issues that arise in engineering. One could identify numerous values associated with each path. The following brief sections discuss the values within a professional context. (Definitions of the terms are given in the last section of this chapter.)

### Society → Profession: Freedom

The economic motivation of a capitalistic system is materialistic accumulation, with pleasure resulting from material goods. A profession can maximize its pleasure only in an unrestrained atmosphere. Therefore, the profession seeks from society the right to self-regulation. Society can provide this through legislation that provides the freedom of self-regulation and the absence of other legislation that would impose restrictions on the practice of the profession.

### Profession → Society: Honesty

Besides being the standard-bearer in interrelationships between the client and the firm, professional societies serve a similar function with respect to society and the profession. Society expects the engineering community to use its specialized knowledge and skills for the betterment of society. Therefore, practicing engineers must not take unfair advantage of members of society, and the profession has the responsibility to ensure that its members act with honesty. Professional codes of ethics (see Chapter 5) are the profession's outward sign to society that it will regulate the ethical conduct of its members.

### Society → Client: Equity

Those in business (i.e., clients) often express concern about the attitudes of society toward them. Specifically, they cite the assumption that "big business" lacks a social conscience, and they believe that various attitudes expressed in the media and in governmental regulations reflect a bias toward the consumer, the worker, the environment, and so forth. This lack of fairness (i.e., equity), they argue, results in a perception of business as socially irresponsible. Furthermore, they argue that regulations and public attitudes toward the business community fail to recognize that the business community also has responsibilities to employees and shareholders.

### Client → Society: Equality

The failure of business to adopt a socially responsible attitude, such as supporting equality, pushes society toward a more regulated and socialistic system, which reduces society's freedom to pursue societal and individual goals. Society responds further with additional legislative action, which, in turn, increases the client's bureaucracy, thereby reducing the efficiency of the client. Thus, it is in the best interests of both the client and society to recognize and follow a policy of equality.

### Society → Firm: Security

An engineering firm has a commitment to the community, and security about its future is necessary for the firm to fulfill this commitment. Society provides this security through legislation, through minimizing institutional constraints, and through actions that enhance the image of the firm and the profession. For example, stability in policies that promote regional growth provides assurance to the firm that it will have continued growth. Thus, physical, institutional, and legislative security are qualities that are important to the firm, and society has a responsibility to provide them to the business community.

### Firm → Society: Safety

Engineers within a firm have specialized knowledge and skills. Society expects the firm to produce designs based on this knowledge in a way that gives public health and safety a high priority. Often, elements of society argue that engineers fail to give adequate consideration to risk assessment in their designs. Even the thought of failure of an engineering design can be disconcerting to people, and studies have shown that the public often perceives the risk to be greater than the actual risk. Even such misperception indicates the importance to society of public health and safety.

### Profession → Client: Trust

The profession, which is represented herein by professional societies, serves as a standard-bearer for the integrity of the firms and individuals that practice in the name of the profession—in this case, engineering. Thus, the profession provides the client with assurance that those practicing within the profession have the technical and moral ability to practice the profession properly. Maintaining the trust of business will ensure proper and efficient functioning of the elements of the profession.

### Client → Profession: Honor

Often, the values of business are considered to be different from the values of the engineering profession. Clients must honor the values and standards of the engineering profession, because failure to respect these nonquantifiable goals reduces the ability of the engineering profession to serve society. The client expresses this respect by giving consideration to the ideals of the profession before seeking to engage an engineering firm in work that fails to adhere to the values of the profession, even when the work meets legal standards. Thus, the client must honor values as well as legal standards.

### Profession → Firm: Knowledge

One of the primary functions of professional societies is the dissemination of knowledge. Besides convening symposia and conferences and forming committees that bring together highly competent and knowledgeable engineers, professional societies distribute journals and conference proceedings that disseminate the most current knowledge on technical, managerial, and professional issues. Through this knowledge, firms are better able to maintain state-of-the-art competency. Continued efforts by the profession to transfer knowledge to those in the business community is a value responsibility of the engineering profession.

### Firm → Profession: Loyalty

For a profession to exist and function, the members and firms involved in the practice of that profession must be loyal to the ideals and standards of the profession. Professional codes of ethics and guidelines for practice may not always appear to be in the best interests of every action by a firm, but without unfailing fulfillment of the firm's obligations to the profession, the responsibilities of the profession to society and to other firms will not be met. Therefore, loyalty of the firm and its employees to the value goals of the profession is necessary.

### Client → Firm: Freedom

Engineering firms seek freedom of practice in the execution of projects for clients. This freedom allows a firm to be creative in solving the client's problem, which makes it possible for the firm to use its specialized knowledge and skills in fulfilling its obligations to the other elements of the engineering tetrahedron.

### Firm → Client: Efficiency

An efficient engineering effort can have both materialistic and nonquantifiable effects on a client. The assurance that the firm will undertake an engineering project in an efficient manner inspires confidence and provides inner contentment to the client. This assurance of efficiency is important, even independent of the materialistic benefits that accompany efficient project management.

### Firm → Employee: Pleasure

A unique characteristic of a capitalistic system is that for a business to show a profit, it must benefit materialistically from inputs by an amount greater than the cost of the inputs, including the labor input. This by itself might suggest that labor is not being treated with equality, which might be true if it were not for the non-materialistic benefits to labor. Employees receive wages for their efforts, and they can trade that income for objects and experiences that provide pleasure. Thus, the value of the labor input is balanced by the sum of the wages used to obtain necessities, the wages used in seeking personal pleasure, and the fulfillment (i.e., professional pleasure) resulting from practice in a profession that serves the needs of society.

### Employee → Firm: Diligence

A firm that must make a profit seeks loyal, diligent employees. In addition to the quantifiable goals achieved by having diligent employees, such employees create a professional atmosphere within the firm. This attitude has benefits to the profession and society as well as to the firm.

### Summary

The examples provided here are much simplified, but they should illustrate the importance of value issues in engineering and science. Value issues arise in all elements of the relationships among employees, employers, clients, professions, and society. Although the value conflicts that usually make the media headlines are those involving society, this does not mean that the other value conflicts are not important. A young engineer or scientist must recognize each of these issues to meet his or her responsibilities and obtain rights that are rightfully theirs.

## COURSE SELECTION

Human values and value decision making are discussed in many disciplines, both in general terms and in terms of applications of the general concepts. A department of philosophy is probably the best source of courses that discuss value issues in general terms, but other departments also offer courses that deal with value issues in a general framework. Course descriptions in the following disciplines should be evaluated: consumer economics, education and human development, industrial technology, microbiology, recreation, sociology, and urban studies. Discussions of values are part of such courses as an introduction to ethics, the philosophy of beauty, the theory of knowledge, consumer product safety, basic microbiology, recreation and leisure, American society, and the city in the development of a national culture. It is important to note that a wide variety of human values would be covered in such courses, including aesthetics, knowledge, public safety, public health, pleasure, and freedom, all of which are important in engineering and science. In taking such courses, however, the student should study the values as they relate to both personal and professional life. Also, some of these courses can show the extent to which values affect our lives.

In addition to courses that deal with values, courses that include discussions of decision making, especially value decision making, should be included to fulfill the general education requirements. The philosophy department would be the most likely program in which to find a basic course in decision making; in such a course, moral aspects of decision making would be a central topic of study. Other programs in which courses on decision making may be found include business management, economics, family and community development, speech, and sociology. Again, the frameworks for the discussions may differ. In a business management course, the emphasis might be on conflict resolution within a business setting. In a course in family and community development, the emphasis might be on solving family and community conflicts. Despite the differences in setting, however, the courses will have the common thread of resolving conflicts that involve values. The student should recognize that value conflicts, as well as value responsibilities, occur between each pair of elements in the responsibility tetrahedron of Figure 2.1. In courses on value decision making, these sources of value conflicts should be considered so that the professional implications are recognized.

In addition to courses on values and on value decision making, general education courses are available that discuss value issues in a practical setting. Such courses can also be found in the programs cited earlier. For example, an economics course might discuss the role of values in the development of economic philosophies and systems. A microbiology course might discuss the importance of microscopic life forms to human welfare. A recreation course might discuss techniques for evaluating environmental, historic, and natural features of recreation sites and the quality of recreation visits to these sites. Instead of discussing values and value decision making in general terms, these courses put the general concepts into specific contexts. It is hoped that students will be able to recognize the importance of the concepts and transfer the knowledge to both personal and professional life.

## CONCLUSIONS

The central theme of this chapter has been the importance of values to the professional engineer and scientist. After providing a definition of the term *human value,* we presented a framework for decision making when value issues are involved and briefly compared it with decision making using a benefit-cost criterion. However, the process of making decisions that involve value goals is more complex than decision making when all goals are quantifiable. A knowledge of values is important, because value conflicts can arise in every aspect of engineering and science. The responsibility tetrahedron was used to emphasize the diversity of values that are important in professional practice. Finally, we discussed types of courses that deal with human value issues and value decision making. It should be emphasized that material in this chapter is not independent of the discussion in Chapter 1; a primary purpose of general education courses is to develop an awareness of values and value issues.

The public is the ultimate beneficiary of engineering works. But the public also pays for the projects. Thus, the use of decision criteria such as the benefit-cost ratio has an obvious basis. These quantifiable criteria are important, but the widespread support for community protest organizations and environmental groups is an indication that the public believes that other criteria are important, many of which are related to nonquantifiable goals. Fundamental human values such as aesthetics, tranquility, environmental quality, and public health are important to the public. Obviously, some sectors of the public believe that these value issues are more important than the benefit-cost ratio; other sectors place different rankings on competing nonquantifiable goals.

Which human values are most important to the public? And at what point does the public believe nonquantifiable value issues are more important than the quantitative criteria? These are not questions for which easy answers are possible. But an attempt at answering should show the importance of value issues to the decision making involved in engineering projects.

If there is any doubt that values are important or that value issues will receive more attention in the future, we need only consider the notoriety that recent technological developments have gained. Topics such as genetic engineering, computers, and robotics are laden with value issues. With the development of genetic engineering, the public is concerned with public health and safety and with life as we know it. The scientists and engineers involved with genetic engineering want the freedom to pursue their research. Thus, there is a value conflict that to many is far more important than the technical details. In computer technology, value issues such as privacy, freedom, and knowledge are central. One conflict centers on the public concern about the storage of vast amounts of personal information and the problem of controlling access to such information. A second conflict centers on the government concern about the transfer of new computer technologies to foreign countries that could use them in weapons systems; the conflict here arises between national security and the desire for (economic) freedom on the part of those who could profit from the sale of the new technologies. As robots enter the work force, many people are concerned about the effect of robot technology on social values. How will such technology affect unemployment and personal self-worth, leisure, and equality? The point here is that value issues are currently very important to engineers and scientists, but it is very likely that such issues will be even more important to the engineers and scientists of the future.

## DEFINITIONS FOR SELECTED HUMAN VALUES

The following are definitions of the human value terms that appear in the responsibility tetrahedron (Figure 2.1):

> *Diligence:* Long, steady application to one's occupation or studies; persistent effort; attentive care.
>
> *Efficiency:* The quality or property of acting or producing effectively with a minimum of waste, expense, and unnecessary effort.
>
> *Equality:* The state or instance of being equal; especially, the state of enjoying equal rights, such as political, economic, and social rights.
>
> *Equity:* The state, ideal, or quality of being just, impartial, and fair.
>
> *Freedom:* The condition of being free of restraints; the power to act, speak, or think without the imposition of restraint.
>
> *Honesty:* The capacity or condition of not lying, cheating, stealing, or taking unfair advantage; characterized by an absence of deception or fraud.
>
> *Honor:* Esteem, respect, reverence, reputation; applicable to both the feeling and the expression of these characteristics.

*Knowledge:* Familiarity, awareness, or understanding gained through experience or study; cognitive or intellectual mental components acquired and retained through study and experience—empirical, material, and that derived by inference and interpretation.

*Loyalty:* Feelings of devoted attachment; the condition of being faithful; the unfailing fulfillment of one's duties and obligations in a close and voluntary relationship.

*Pleasure:* An enjoyable sensation or emotion; satisfaction; sometimes, though not invariably, suggests superficial and transitory emotion resulting from the conscious pursuit of happiness.

*Safety:* Freedom from danger, risk, or injury.

*Security:* Freedom from doubt; reliability and stability concerning knowledge of the future.

*Trust:* Firm reliance on integrity, ability, or character of a person or thing; implies depth and assurance of such feeling, which may not always be supported by proof.

## EXERCISES

**2.1.** What values are most important to you and why? What are the sources of your value system?

**2.2.** To what extent do the friends you have made in college exhibit the values identified as being important professionally specifically, knowledge, honesty, loyalty, diligence, orderliness, and responsibility?

**2.3.** What values should be important to a practicing engineer or scientist? How would they differ from the primary values of other professions, such as law or medicine? How would they differ from the primary values of a plumber, a service station attendant, or some other skilled laborer?

**2.4.** Identify someone in public life (e.g., a politician, national sports figure, actor or actress) whom you respect greatly. Discuss the values that characterize this individual's life and why you believe he or she serves as a good role model.

**2.5.** Evaluate variety as a human value. Discuss its implications in both personal and professional life.

**2.6.** Evaluate equity as a human value. Discuss its implications in both personal and professional life.

**2.7.** Knowledge as a human value has obvious professional implications. Discuss its role in one's personal life.

**2.8.** If both social welfare and profit are considered to be important goals of the engineering profession, how does one reconcile these two conflicting goals in making professional decisions?

**2.9.** Discuss the values transmitted through television, both programs and advertisements. Use examples to illustrate your discussion.

**2.10.** Values such as freedom, pleasure, honesty and truth, diligence, and loyalty are affected by peer relationships during one's teen years. Discuss how peer pressure can affect such values.

2.11. The Golden Rule is "Do unto others as you would have others do unto you." Discuss the merits of using the Golden Rule as a guide in personal value decision making.

2.12. Evaluate the Machiavellian philosophy that the end justifies the means from a human value standpoint. Discuss its use as a basis for professional relationships.

2.13. The study by Garfoot and Simon and Florman's personality summary suggest that engineers are insensitive to human welfare and lack interest in public policy. Do you believe this is detrimental to society? Why?

2.14. In the introduction to this chapter, an example is given in which a high school student finds out that her brother is cheating on his girl friend, who is the sister's friend. What value conflict does the girl face? What action would you recommend that she take, and why?

2.15. In the introduction to this chapter, an example is given in which a chemist is offered money by a client to falsify data. What value conflict does the chemist face? Which value is most important, and why?

2.16. In the responsibility tetrahedron (Figure 2.1), identify and discuss other values that you believe would be important between the individual engineer and the employer (i.e., the firm).

2.17. In the responsibility tetrahedron (Figure 2.1), identify and discuss other values that you believe would be important between society and the other elements of the tetrahedron.

2.18. Engineers and scientists are often blamed for the detrimental effects of new technologies, such as nuclear power. Identify the value issues, as opposed to the technological details, involved with a new technology and evaluate how the engineer or scientist can affect these values. What are the roles of the public and their elected government representatives, the courts, and the business managers in these value issues?

2.19. Identify specific courses in your undergraduate course catalog that might discuss human value issues and value decision making.

2.20. Recognizing that personality affects one's value system, identify specific courses in your undergraduate course catalog that might discuss the relationship between personality and value development.

2.21. Some behaviorists argue that genetic factors determine an individual's value development; others argue that experiences in everyday life are the primary determinant. This is known as the nature–nurture controversy. Identify specific courses in your undergraduate course catalog that might discuss value development.

2.22. How can specialized education in an engineering or science discipline change an individual's values? What values would be emphasized? How can general education shape an individual's value system? What values are emphasized in general education courses? Discuss the similarities and differences in the values emphasized in technical and general education courses.

2.23. You are an engineer working for a company that drills for, ships, and processes natural gas. A rich gas field is located near a historic trail that was used by settlers in their move west. Many local citizens believe that there is historic significance to the trail and that extensive development of the field would damage the ecology of the trail. Discuss the value issues and the factors you would consider in resolving the value conflict.

**3**

# Values in Conflict:
# The Social Impact
# of Changing Technology

*James M. Wallace*

## INTRODUCTION

There are two major themes running through this book: developing and strengthening your system of values and helping you choose courses to satisfy your general education requirements. What do they have to do with each other? Isn't the first your private affair and the second simply a set of courses you must get through in order to graduate? We hope that you will come to see how importantly they are related. Within these pages, we are urging that you choose these courses most carefully, so that they will form a meaningful whole, expanding your experience and grounding your values. They should help you better understand the many sides of human life in society and your role within it. They should help you examine what you value, and why, by comparing your values to what others have considered worth valuing. They should help you develop the ability to determine when social values are in conflict and to sort out the issues that are at stake in the competing needs and wishes of individuals and social groups.

Why is this especially important for aspiring engineers and scientists? As we will try to make clear in this chapter, the changes that technology has wrought in the 400 years since the rise of science in Western Europe and in the 150 years since the beginning of the Industrial Revolution have radically transformed the way we live and relate to one another. You hope to become part of that ongoing saga of change. You can be an active, knowledgeable participant—shaping this change for human good—or you can passively function as a tiny cog in this seemingly inexorable machine. To be an active participant requires that you learn to see how technology is embedded in a political, economic, and cultural matrix that determines its effects. Examining that matrix is the intent of this chapter.

## TECHNOLOGY AND DAILY LIFE

Our lives are so thoroughly pervaded by the products, processes, and even the mind-set of technology that most of us are only vaguely aware of just how much our view of the world around us is shaped by it. Consider for a moment some of the most important aspects of your life: food, shelter, clothing, transportation, education, and entertainment. How is technology involved in each of these? Start by examining some of the technologies used in producing the food you ate today.

Today's food comes to you from an amalgam of different technologies. First, there is farm machinery. Beginning with the steel plow of John Deere in 1857 and followed by the mechanical reaper of Cyrus McCormick in 1883, design improvements led to the modern combine, which was introduced in the 1920s. Second, there have been remarkable breakthroughs in agronomy, with the development of fertilizers, new strains of plants and defoliants, soil conservation, and irrigation systems. There are also the farm workers themselves. The number of Americans in the labor force that produces the food we consume has declined from about 70 percent at the beginning of the nineteenth century to about 3 percent today. In fact, these relatively few farmers produce so efficiently that huge surpluses are available for export. Third, there have been major changes in transportation. Before appearing in your local grocery store, grapefruit grown in Texas, beef raised in Kansas, and asparagus from New Jersey are transported in refrigerated trucks, railway cars, and airplanes over asphalt and concrete roads, on thousands of miles of steel track, or to and from huge metropolitan airports. Fourth, these foodstuffs are packaged in metal cans, cardboard boxes, and plastic wrappings that require lumbering, papermaking, mining, metalworking, and plastic extrusion. Fifth, the advertisements that make you aware of these foods roll off high-speed printing presses or flicker incessantly across your television screen. Sixth, when you go through the checkout counter of the grocery store, your bill is rapidly calculated on a large central computer, utilizing the universal product code. Simultaneously, the inventory of the items you purchased is instantly altered on the computer. Seventh, the food is brought home, refrigerated, and cooked by electrical or chemical energy conversion processes that you take for granted. You serve the food on dishes shaped by automatically controlled ceramic lathes and eat with cast stainless-steel utensils. The chain of technological activities that take place before you sit down to a meal seems almost endless. As you might imagine, similar processes occur in the other areas of your life.

The house or apartment you live in is made of brick, concrete blocks, lumber, nails, sheets of drywall, steel reinforcing rods, plastic and copper and galvanized iron pipes, glass windows, ceramic tiles, and copper conducting wire. Electricity, natural gas, and purified water are available to you at the turn of a valve or the flip of a switch. Your clothes, made of subtle blends of natural and synthetic fibers, are held together by plastic buttons and metal zippers and are shaped and stitched on weaving, cutting, and sewing machines before you see them in your favorite shop or boutique. You move about your town or city in automobiles, buses, or subways that are technical marvels hardly imaginable to people even 100 years ago. These vehicles are powered by gasoline, diesel fuel, and electricity produced by huge industries employing hundreds of thousands of people. The books that you study and the newspapers and magazines that you read are composed and typeset on word processors. You are entertained by television programs and films made up of images and sounds miraculously captured by thousands of miniature electronic circuits. Just think of all the technical steps needed to make available to you the cassette recorded music of your favorite rock band! The list could go on and on.

But technology does not affect only you as an individual. You live in social groups made up of ever-widening concentric circles—your family, your neighborhood, your town or city, your nation, and the world (Figure 3.1). This framework for viewing technology and society is not intended to imply that the individual is the center of attention. Instead, it suggests that our horizons must continually expand as our responsibilities increase.

We need to ask ourselves how technology—as it has evolved and changed over centuries, decades, and even from year to year—changes us and the societies in which we live. These changes have made our lives longer and more mobile, more comfortable, and more efficient. Some of them, though, threaten our environment

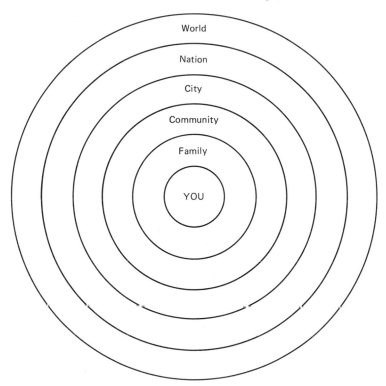

**Figure 3.1** Layers of social relationships.

and safety and bring benefit to some members of society only at the expense of others.

As future engineers and scientists, you are no doubt aware of many of the benefits that technology provides us; perhaps you are less aware of the ill effects technology sometimes carries with it. With such knowledge, you will be better prepared to help shape technology to benefit society. But before examining the impact of changing technology on society, it might be helpful to clarify what we mean by the terms *technology* and *society*.

### What Is Technology?

When we talk about technology, do we mean only technical products, such as gears, rubber tires, nuclear power plants, airplanes, microchips, computers, and washing machines? Is there more to technology than these material products? Is there even more to technology than the technical processes and knowledge incorporated in mathematical formulas, computer algorithms, and assembly lines that are used to design and fabricate these products? A little thought will make clear that technology is much more. In the broadest sense of the word, technology encompasses a considerable part of human activity and life. Goldman and Cutcliffe (1979) define technology as referring

> . . . to the product of a particular *social* process in which abstract economic, social, and cultural values shape, develop and implement the concrete artifacts and techniques generated by the engineer.

Winner (1977) distinguishes three parts of technology:

1) *apparatus,* . . . the class of objects we normally refer to as technological tools, instruments, machines, appliances, weapons, gadgets—which are used in accomplishing a wide variety of tasks,
2) *technique,* . . . the whole body of technical activities—skills, methods, procedures, routines—that people engage in to accomplish tasks, and
3) *organization,* . . . factories, workshops, bureaucracies, armies, R and D teams.

Noble (1977) makes clear that the people who build and use technical objects, using a variety of techniques, are themselves part of the technology:

> [Technology] is not merely man-made, but made of men. Although it may aptly be described as a composite of the accumulated scientific knowledge, technical skills, implements, logical habits, and material products of people, technology is always more than this, more than information, logic, things. It is people themselves undertaking their various activities in particular social and historical contexts, with particular interests and aims.

Technology is made up of things, methods, and people, connected in quite complicated and changing relationships. It has political, economic, and cultural as well as purely technical dimensions. The social effects of technology will depend on how it is used as well as on how it works.

### What Is Society?

This question is a little easier to answer. *Webster's New World Dictionary of the American Language* (1958) defines (human) society as "all people, collectively, regarded as constituting a community of related, interdependent individuals." Community is defined, in turn, as "a society of people having common rights and privileges, or common interests, civil, political, and others, or living under the same laws and regulations." Society and community are clearly somewhat interchangeable ideas. They both imply interdependence of people through language, race, nationality, economics, law, government, and culture. Implied, also, is at least a partially shared system of values.

If you live in a dormitory at your college or university, your immediate society or community is made up of your fellow residents, who live under a common set of dorm rules, observe the same customs, such as shared meals, and hold at least some values, such as education, in common. Students who play their stereo equipment through 40-watt amplifiers can disrupt study in the entire dorm. The use of this technology must be regulated so that the common value of education is fostered while still allowing those who value it the pleasure of listening to their favorite music.

Another broader level of society of which you are a member is the whole university community. The introduction of computers for course registration has made the process much more efficient, has enabled you to make changes with ease, and has freed your professors of much laborious record keeping—all valued benefits. But because of the introduction of this technology, you probably feel the loss of personal interest and help from professors. Those are but two small ways in which changing technology affects the different social layers in which you live and work. In the following section, we will examine how technology, broadly defined, is central to one of the most fundamental human activities—our work.

## TECHNOLOGY AND WORK

One of the most important ways in which technology affects us is in the sphere of work. In fact, it is probably not much of an exaggeration to say that this is the *basis* of all the other effects. Without the fundamental reconstituting of work implements, methods, and organization ushered in over centuries by changing technology, we would not have the products of technology that so permeate every corner of our lives today.

To understand how technology affects work, we need to outline briefly the economic system in which our work is done in the United States. This system is a highly developed form of liberal capitalism, which has evolved over the past 150 years. Heilbroner and Thurow (1982) distinguish five differences between precapitalist and capitalist economic life, which began to emerge in Europe in the sixteenth century. First, in most earlier societies, slaves never owned property and peasants only rarely did. Land was held by a small, powerful group of aristocrats. Second, there was no organized social arrangement for buying and selling land, labor, and their products, which we now call the market system. Of course, there was also no legal right to withhold labor; it was at the disposal of the lord. Some small-scale bartering and trading occurred, but it was a minor part of economic life. Third, making money was not held in high regard, and lending money at interest, called *usury,* was one of the seven deadly sins. Fourth, wealth was primarily controlled not by rich people, as it is today, but rather by powerful military and political leaders—who were often one and the same persons. Fifth, economic life was stable. The way people dressed, ate, were housed, traveled, and fought did not change much in the twenty centuries between the Golden Age of the Greeks and the end of the Renaissance.

Slowly, almost imperceptibly, during the course of the sixteenth century, that most necessary social arrangement of a capitalist economy—an extensive market system—emerged. Economic activities began to be dictated by the impersonal opportunities and discouragements of the marketplace, rather than by personal commands of noblemen. Wealth began to shift from the aristocracy to a new merchant class, who combined land, labor, and capital—the so-called factors of production—to generate products for sale. This occurred first in a trickle, then in a stream, and finally in a flood in which we almost drown daily, as seen through television, newspaper, and radio advertisements.

In all of this change, technology played and continues to play a vital role. Without technology, capitalism would not be possible. Precapitalist technology, though highly developed—as seen from the Egyptian pyramids, the Great Wall of China, Greek temples, and Roman aqueducts—was lavished on the needs of rulers, priests, and warriors for ceremony, religious ritual, and warfare. In the late eighteenth and early nineteenth centuries, however, a new class of entrepreneurs emerged who saw technology as a means of lowering costs by increasing the productivity of workers and of introducing new products on the market. For example, in England between 1701 and 1802, the introduction of spinning and weaving machines to produce clothing increased the use of cotton by 6000 percent! The Industrial Revolution had begun.

Heilbroner and Thurow cite seven major changes that occurred. First, "things" became common; beds, forks, shoes, carriages, and stoves were no longer the possessions of only the privileged few. Second, the size of work places increased enormously as factories replaced small craft shops. Third, the organization of work also increased in complexity to keep pace; managers, supervisors, and manufacturing processes were required. Fourth, the nature of work changed with the introduction of the division of labor, so that a single craft worker could no longer produce an article from beginning to end. Work became fragmented and often monotonous. Fifth, travel became available to masses of people. This created a mobile work force and led to the waves of immigration to the United States in the late nineteenth century of people seeking economic opportunity. Sixth, people often lost their skills as their work was fragmented; as a result, some industries dried up as new ones emerged. Even today, this process proceeds unabated as manufacturing industries in the United States are moved to the Sun Belt or the Third World, leaving displaced workers to either retrain for the available hi-tech jobs or face unemployment. Seventh, democratic parliamentary institutions arose as economic and political power shifted from the aristocracy to the mercantile class and later, to a lesser extent, to the workers themselves.

With the advent of machines and better transport, and with labor division techniques culminating in the assembly line, the productivity of workers (the value of their product compared to their labor costs and the costs of materials and machinery) increased manyfold. This economic system is by far the most productive ever devised. Powered by its technological engine, it has produced unimagined wealth. This wealth has been unequally shared, however, and the technology that has produced it has had many unintended detrimental effects on society and the environment. And equally important, values have come into conflict in the process.


## CHANGING TECHNOLOGY/CONFLICTING VALUES

In Chapter 2, we defined a human value as a principle, standard, or quality that is considered worthwhile. We discussed how value conflicts arise because of differences in opinions about whether or not a value should be considered in decision making and because of differences in the perceived importance of a value by the various individuals and groups affected by the decisions. The process of technological innovation that fuels economic growth almost always brings values into conflict. This is vividly illustrated if you think about the aforementioned seven changes that the Industrial Revolution brought with it.

That a vast array of consumer items have become available to many more people is surely considered of great benefit by almost everyone. The health, safety, and pleasure of all of us have been immeasurably increased. With the increase in the size of work places and the organization of work, efficiency and production have been greatly improved. This is what we mean by "economy of scale." Products can be made more cheaply per unit when they are made in large quantities. The parliamentary democracies that arose in the late eighteenth century extended equality, equity, and freedom to larger numbers of their populations. As excluded citizens (originally everyone but the white, male, property-owning class) fought for their rights to be included, the numbers of people with some control over these parliamentary institutions became larger. These are desirable results. However, with the labor division that came with large-scale and complex organization of work, much of the pleasure of doing creative work and the freedom that comes with having a wide variety of skills were also lost. The mobility that came with high-speed transportation systems in the late nineteenth and early twentieth centuries increased our freedom but surely eroded the stability and security of families and communities and has seriously degraded the environment.

The Industrial Revolution had two faces. It championed some values of some people but diminished or overran other values of other people. In short, this era raised for many people the political question we face daily: Who decides which values will have priority? Are our social and political institutions designed so that everyone has an equal voice?

In the remainder of this chapter, we will look at two examples of technological change—one well established and one brand-new—that have affected or will greatly affect our individual and social lives. These technologies have brought values into conflict. We will ask ourselves how these changes were introduced, how the values inherent in the changes were weighted, and by whom. We will also explore whether the social benefits of the changes outweigh their costs.

### Values in Conflict: The Automobile

The automobile is a *technical* marvel. Think about all the engineering skills that go into designing and producing the car that you or your family own. The combination of pistons, cylinders, ignition, electrical and cooling systems, and drive train, with its high-performance engine linked to axles and tires through gears and joints, is a true wonder of design, fabrication, and construction. Your car can whisk you from place to place in air-conditioned comfort while entertaining you with your favorite music on cassette tapes or providing you with the latest breaking news over the radio. You may even be able to make calls from your car over a modular telephone or watch a miniature television set. The seats can recline and are individually adjustable to the length of your legs and your preferred posture. These luxuries seem standard today, but they were brought with a price. With the advent of the automobile at the end of the nineteenth century, some human values were achieved or reinforced while others were lost or diminished.

Human values are goals and standards that we strive to achieve or maintain for our benefit. What are some of the strived-for goals and benefits that have been achieved by the development and widespread use of automobiles? The most obvious one is convenient mobility or freedom. Never has it been so easy for people to move from place to place at any time of the day or night. The immediate accessibility of cars is a wonderfully convenient and, conditions permitting, rapid means of transportation. Indeed, in the United States we are often so caught up in our own convenience and speed that the government must regulate the top speed at which we are allowed to drive cars. Not only does the privately owned car give us the freedom of timing and controlling our travels, it also lets us go anywhere we want, over any route, for any distance, near or far—from house to school, from the movie to the grocery store, from the parking lot on Main Street to a campsite beside the Grand Canyon—door to door. This flexibility is impossible with all forms of public transportation, which have to provide common routes that are convenient to all their users; it is one of the great appeals of the automobile. Because of its convenience, speed, control, and flexibility, the automobile has become enormously attractive. Almost 10,000 automobiles are produced every day by American manufacturers. At the turn of the century, there were about 8000 cars and trucks in the United States; this number expanded to 118 million by the mid-1970s. Today there is an automobile for every 2.3 persons in our country; 80 percent of American families own one car, and over 20 million families own two or more.

*Detrimental effects.* As a beginning college or university student, you have been licensed to drive for only a few years and are probably still fascinated with your own or your family's car. But have you thought about some of the values that have been lost with the emergence of the automobile as almost our sole means of convenient transportation? Some of them are familiar: congestion, environmental pollution, and human life and property losses through accidents. We will examine these in a little more detail later. A not-so-obvious loss is the automobile's part in changing the character of most modern cities into sprawling, ugly, dirty, crime-ridden places, marginally fit for healthy life and work.

*The city and the automobile.* Schaeffer and Scalar (1975) have traced the evolution of cities in relation to their modes of transportation. They argue that cities were invented to minimize the need for transportation. In their first phase, urban centers were "walking cities." Work was done on a small scale in shops. The material used in this craft manufacturing was brought in from the nearby countryside, and the products for sale were delivered about town on foot or by using dray animals. For thousands of years, human beings lived in such small and medium-sized towns; we know what they looked like from drawings, paintings, and woodcuts. Even today in many places in the world, such towns, without mechanized transportation, still exist. We should not romanticize the quality of life in these preindustrial cities; they were and are dirty, smelly, and crowded places in which to live and work. One need only visit towns in the Third World today to quickly get a taste and smell of this form of urban life.

Given our specific interest in human values, it is important to recognize the social values that dominated life in these "walking cities." Certainly, the family and community and, most important, religion were the dominant institutions that shaped values. They stressed the importance of respect for authority above all. But because neighbors lived and worked so intimately with one another, there almost certainly was also a greater sense of mutual communal responsibility. With respect to work, diligence, which was characterized by more than 60-hour workweeks for employees, was highly valued.

With the advent of the Industrial Revolution came the railroad. Not only did this provide high-speed transportation between urban centers, it also allowed people to move from the commercial and industrial center of towns into more pastoral surroundings and to commute back and forth to work. As discussed by Schaeffer and Scalar (1975), the "tracked city" provided for the rapid movement of people and, to a much lesser extent, for the rapid intracity transportation of raw materials and products. The centers of commerce and industry were still concentrated in towns and cities, but people began to disperse to the outskirts to find more pleasant living space. This mobility between suburb and town became available first with the steam street railway and later with the electric streetcar. Between 1890 and 1902, electric streetcar track mileage in the United States jumped from 1200 to 21,900. Elevated railways and subways were added in many U.S. cities by the latter part of the nineteenth century. The suburbs in the "tracked city" of this period were not nearly so stratified by economic class and position as they later became with the emergence of the automobile. Each suburb required its own butcher, baker, grocer, tailor, firemen, and schoolteachers, all of whom lived as well as worked there. These suburbs spread out radially along the streetcar and railway lines, producing the star-shaped pattern we still recognize today in older American cities.

The growth of rail transportation set the stage for many value changes associated with the automobile. It was the first stage in the decline in importance of the community in shaping values. Individuals and families no longer lived in the same community where their parents grew up. Greater emphasis was placed on freedom and mobility. Values such as mutual responsibility and respect for authority declined in importance as people loosened ties with their community and church or synagogue. An emphasis on efficiency rather than diligence probably emerged during this period. Although it is easy to quantify changes in rates and miles of railroad track, value changes may not be so apparent, but they were certainly occurring.

At the turn of the century, shortly after the emergence of the automobile, American cities were in their heyday. Pictures of major U.S. cities from this period stand in sharp contrast to the potholed, crime-infested, filthy metropolitan centers we know today. For a brief period, when a balanced transportation system—including the streetcar, the trolley, the subway, commuter railroads, buses, automobiles, and bicycles—was available, cities, large and small, were pleasant places in which to live and work. This period was short-lived; with the coming, in the years after World War I, of what Schaeffer and Scalar call the "rubber city," cities radically changed, losing much of what had once made them, at least for a brief time, such attractive places.

First of all, paved roadways and parking began to require ever-larger proportions of urban space. Taebel and Cornehls (1977) show that streets and parking take from 40 to 60 percent of available space in American cities today. Because both goods and people could be moved with unprecedented convenience and flexibility with trucks and automobiles, the familiar phenomenon of urban sprawl began to take place. Land developers gobbled up surrounding farmland, creating pockets of look-alike single-family homes, connected to work places, shopping centers, and each other by miles of paved roads, increasingly lined with unsightly gas stations and fast-food chain shops. These "hamburger boulevards" are indistinguishable from one another in any American city today. The once star-shaped "tracked city" now became the amorphous, ever-expanding "rubber city." Shops and stores moved from downtown to satellite shopping centers on high-speed beltways and access roads, following their more affluent customers. With easy access by automobile to food, clothing, haircuts, and movies, suburban communities could become stratified groupings of similar age, race, and economic class. The rich diversity of the older cities began to disintegrate. The center cores of the cities were left to those without adequate access to automobiles: the poor, the elderly, and the handicapped. For these people, suburbia was not an attractive place to live, because the public transportation available to them was grossly inadequate. Most of the people left in the inner cores of cities were renters, not homeowners, so the property tax base of cities was eroded. Business and industry no longer needed to be located near railheads or harbors because of the flexibility of truck transportation. They slowly began to move out from the centers of cities into industrial and commercial parks on the outskirts, since most of the executives, managers, and many of the workers now lived nearby. As corporate taxes began to dry up, the tax base of cities was further eroded. Public services—from schools and hospitals to street repair, fire, and police protection—as well as recreational and cultural institutions such as parks, art museums, symphony orchestras, and live theater suffered from lack of financial support. Taebel and Cornehls depict the automobile and its effects as a centrifugal force, which pulls apart the inner city, with its ethnic, cultural, racial, and age diversity, and fragments a variety of activities made up of business and commerce, manufacturing, housing, recreation, and entertainment. These once-integrated elements of city life were flung outward into burgeoning suburbs that were accessible only by automobiles over vast ribbons of concrete.

Recent attempts to reverse urban blight and decay have often included efforts to rebuild social values, as well as rebuilding the physical facilities of cities. In some cases, careful urban redevelopment has tried to utilize specific historical facets of the city, such as underground Atlanta and the harbor in Baltimore. These attempts to rebuild community spirit and connectedness result from the recognition that not all changes produced by technology are in the best interests of society. We engineers and scientists, who are often the harbingers of technical "progress," always need to look carefully at what we mean by progress to see what is being swept away in its path.

*Environmental pollution.*   More than half of the nation's air pollution is due to the internal combustion engine; this proportion is closer to 75 to 80 percent in Los Angeles and New York City. Cars alone deposit about 180 billion pounds of contaminants into the air each year. The most immediate adverse health effects of these pollutants are that they aggravate already existing conditions of respiratory and cardiovascular disease and increase death rates, particularly for older people and infants. Water pollution occurs through several sources: the runoff of rainwater containing petroleum products from streets and highways is a major source; the pollution from petroleum refineries and mining and steel industries is an additional large source. We are all familiar with the oil spills from the giant supertankers, which have ruined beaches. Most recently, we have also become aware of the acid rain that is killing forests in the United States, Canada, and Europe. Noise pollution certainly is related to the enormous growth of automobile use in our century. The constant din of traffic noise presents a serious psychological problem, which is ubiquitous but hard to quantify. Our quest for convenience, speed, control, flexibility, and freedom has certainly had its cost in polluted air and water, dying forests, and increased noise.

*Energy consumption.* The transportation sector in the United States consumes 25 percent of all the available domestic energy supplies, including 60 percent of all petroleum, a nonrenewable resource. Trucks and cars together account for three-fourths of the energy consumption in the transportation sector. Although the extent of the world oil reserves is much debated, there is considerable evidence that sometime in the next century we will deplete the supply if we continue consuming at current and projected rates. For a society that has reduced its passenger system and much of its freight system to an almost exclusive use of petroleum-fueled vehicles, this will likely result in a social and economic catastrophe in the not too distant future. Here again, we pay a price for what we value so much from the automobile.

**The politics and economics of automobile technology.**   As noted earlier, the automobile is a *technical* marvel. But as we have seen, technology is not solely the product of technical design and fabrication. It is made up of things, methods, and people in social interdependency. The uses of technology depend on a complex matrix of political, economic, and cultural forces that develop and distribute the products of technical innovation. In this section, we will examine some of the forces that have shaped the effects of the automobile on our society.

Values—the principles, standards, or qualities to which we aspire—are partially allocated in a society by the political process. The government, which is the seat of political authority, sanctions some economic activities over others in order to reinforce certain values with the resulting neglect or loss of others. Thus, we have seen that convenient, flexible, and rapid mobility—the principal value provided for us by cars—has been given precedence over the values of clean air and water, energy conservation, transportation accessibility for everyone, and aesthetically harmonious and ethnically and culturally diverse cities.

*Federal transportation policy.*   Urban transportation policy in the United States has gone through four stages. The first period, which Taebel and Cornehls (1977) call the "Laissez-Faire Stage," was a period in which urban transportation development was completely given over to the cities themselves. The Federal Road Act of 1916 provided for some funding for intercity and rural roads but excluded aid to cities of populations over 2500.

Taebel and Cornehls call the second period the "Depression Era Stage." The Emergency Relief and Construction Act of 1932, at the beginning of Roosevelt's first term, and the Hayden-Cartwright Act four years later provided aid for road construction in cities as well as for farm-to-market roads, but they were principally aimed at providing public jobs for the vast numbers of unemployed. The Hayden-Cartwright Act also set the stage for the later Highway Trust Fund by making it, as the legislation explicitly stated, "unfair and unjust to tax motor vehicle transportation unless the proceeds of such taxation are applied to the construction, improvement, or maintenance of highways." Road and street construction during this period was largely unplanned and served mainly to help get the nation out of the Depression by economic pump-priming.

The third period is called the "Highways-Only Stage." Immediately following World War II, in a time of economic prosperity and after the automobile industry had greatly expanded its capacity, the Federal Aid Highway Act of 1944 reinitiated federal involvement in road construction. With the passage of the Federal Aid Highway Act of 1956, Congress instituted a national interstate and defense highway system of unprecedented scale, marked by the familiar red, white, and blue signs. No other action of the federal government has ever had anything like the effect of this act on American transportation. The large federal share, 90 percent of the funding of this vast system of highways, left only 10 percent to be picked up by states and cities. The act established the Highway Trust Fund to finance the system out of gasoline and certain other highway-related taxes, not out of the general revenue. Because of the availability of these enormous sums for the exclusive use of highway construction and maintenance under this taxing system, other forms of transportation naturally withered.

In the 1960s and 1970s, beginning with the Urban Mass Transportation Assistance Act of 1964, Congress attempted to redress some of the imbalance during the "Balanced System Stage" by providing some funds for other forms of transportation. But in contrast to the 90 percent federal share of interstate highway funding, only 70 percent was provided, leaving cities and states to come up with the remaining 30 percent. Funded by this act, new urban subway systems in San Francisco, Washington, D.C., Cleveland, and Atlanta have been built.

This brief historical sketch of federal policy for road and highway construction illustrates how thoroughly the growth of the automobile industry in the United States was undergirded by political policy decisions to the detriment of other forms of transportation. Political decisions are almost always reflective of economic power. Where does economic power in the American transportation sector reside?

*The economics of transportation.* At the beginning of the century, dozens of small companies, including Oldsmobile, Hudson, Nash, Ford, Cadillac, Packard, Buick, and Chevrolet, were producing cars in the United States. In time, some of these bought up the weaker firms or forced them out of business until we are left today with the big three in the United States: General Motors, Ford, and Chrysler, as well as struggling American Motors. Recently, even Chrysler was close to bankruptcy until the federal government bailed it out with massive low-interest loans. As the largest of these companies, GM serves as the price leader; the others quickly make price adjustments for their new cars so that competition between them is minimal. In addition to the automobile industry itself, the related industries of petroleum, rubber products, iron and steel, and machinery are closely tied to automotives. Of the twenty largest American industrial corporations listed by *Fortune* magazine, automotive and related industries account for about 70 percent of their total sales, assets, and net income and almost 60 percent of their total employees. These automotive and related corporations occupy a commanding position in American economic life. If we look beyond these giants, however, we see that textile industries, the concrete and construction industries, and even the food and entertainment industries are indirectly tied to the production of automobiles, as illustrated in Figure 3.2.

How has the automobile industry used its power to achieve dominance over the American transportation system? Has it simply been that American consumers, acting through their marketplace choices, have shown an overwhelming preference

**Figure 3.2** The automotive and related industries (courtesy of Kennikat Press, from *The Political Economy of Urban Transportation*).

for automobiles over other forms of transportation available to them—such as streetcars, trams, and subways? If this were the whole story, then we should simply live with our choices; unfortunately, however, the truth is a good deal more disturbing. The automobile industry *directly* undertook to eliminate its competition in three phases: (1) the substitution of intercity buses for rail passenger transportation, (2) the acquisition and dismantling of local electric streetcar systems to be replaced by city buses, and (3) the replacement of city buses with passenger cars. The story is fascinating and frightening.

In 1925, GM purchased the nation's largest producer of buses, the Yellow Coach Company, and proceeded to assist in the formation of the Greyhound Corporation. Greyhound agreed to buy all of its buses from GM, which, in turn, agreed not to sell any buses to Greyhound's competitors. With continued financial backing from GM, Greyhound eventually displaced most of the nation's railroad commuter lines and was transporting nearly half of all intercity passengers by 1950. General Motors remained the largest shareholder of Greyhound until 1948. With phase one well under way, GM then formed the United Cities Motor Transit, a holding company that systematically bought up electric streetcar companies around the country, tore down their power lines, and ripped up their rails. In New York City, this was begun in 1936 and was completed within 18 months. By corporate fiat, the world's largest electric streetcar system was completely scrapped and replaced by diesel-powered buses in this brief period.

At the end of the 1940s, GM had participated in converting more than 100 electric transit systems to buses in 45 cities. In 1949, GM was convicted—together with Standard Oil of California, the Firestone Company, and others—of economic conspiracy and monopoly. These giants were fined only the ludicrous sum of $5000, adding social insult to social injury. The way to complete control of passenger transportation was now clear. Having converted almost all of the nation's public transportation systems to city buses and now controlling the production of these buses, the automobile industry proceeded to allow bus technology to fall behind, making buses less economically competitive with the private passenger car. Although most cities today continue to have bus systems, which have been somewhat revived in the past two decades, the automobile still has a near-monopoly on American transportation.

To survey this history is to see that the products of technology never stand in isolation. They are embedded in the political, economic, and cultural processes that shape the use and misuse of these products. In the case of the automobile, an exciting new technology won the American consumers' hearts. The industry that produced it used all the enormous economic and political power at its disposal to ensure that this love affair would become a marriage.

### Values in Conflict: Robotics

We have discussed the impact on society of an old technology, the automobile, and we have seen, perhaps to our surprise, how greatly it has affected the way we live. We now turn to a brand-new technology, robotics, which is attracting a flood of new students into computer science and mechanical and electrical engineering. Robotics is already beginning to be used in aeronautical, chemical, civil, and mechanical engineering practice. Perhaps you are one of the students who wants to be on the forefront of this technical revolution. Before you graduate to go out into industry and design or use robots, however, you need to think about what they are going to mean for the lives of large numbers of people whose jobs will be affected by them in the decades ahead.

*What are robots?*  If you are a science-fiction fan, you may think robots look like C3PO or R2D2 in the movie *Star Wars,* or perhaps like some Ray Bradbury creation. No, these "steel-collar workers" are much more mundane in appearance; they are awkward-looking machines with long mechanical arms and grippers. They are programmed to move through a series of points in space and to perform various operations. The Robot Institute of America defines a robot as

> a reprogrammable, multifunctional manipulator designed to move materials, parts or specialized devices through variable programmed motions for the performance of a variety of tasks.

The key word in the definition is *reprogrammable*. With this capability, the same robot can be directed to perform many different operations in an industrial setting, including spot welding, monitoring and feeding die-casting machines, loading and unloading machine tools and presses, spray painting, and a variety of materials-handling tasks. About one-third of American-made robots are simple pick-and-place devices that are used in materials handling to move objects from one position to another. All programmable robots are servo-controlled; that is, their direction can be altered in midmotion without tripping a mechanical switch. The microprocessor controlling device memorizes a sequence of arm and gripper movements that can be indefinitely repeated until reprogrammed. "Smart" or "intelligent" robots are those that can optimize their instructions and alter their own software to improve their work routine. The most sophisticated machines—sensory robots, which are still rare—have artificial senses of sight and touch that allow them to adapt much more readily to their tasks. Using digital image-processing techniques, a sensory robot is able to distinguish and select a part by its shape, grip it in the proper orientation, and put it into place in an assembly operation—all at high speed.

*Robots in use today.*  The automobile industry is the single largest user of robots, mostly for spot welding. With model changeovers, robots can easily be taught the new welding locations on the new car models. In Japan, it is reported that a single operator of spot-welding robots in an automobile assembly plant can handle a work load that once required ten people. Arc welding, which is dirty and is a health hazard because of the gases, fumes, and heat generated, is also being handled by robots. Spray painting and coating, the third largest application, is rapidly growing in both the automobile and home appliance industries. The quality of the finished coat can be very carefully controlled, and the consumption of paint or coating material is significantly reduced when robots are used. This is also a job that has health risks for human operators. At the General Electric refrigerator plant in Chicago, a robot spray paints refrigerator linings twice as fast as the two-person crew it replaced. Hotpoint dishwashers are being sprayed with porcelain enamel in Milwaukee by robots that saved the company $19,000 through waste reduction in the first year of operation. In this case, one person on each of two shifts was replaced by the robots. Robots are also being used in numerically controlled machining operations, where they are able to respond much more flexibly to changes in production volume.

*What will robots do in the future?*   Although only a few assembly tasks are currently performed by robots, many researchers expect such tasks to be the next big area of application. The difficulty encountered in these assembly tasks is to recognize, pick up, and manipulate into place the part to be assembled when it is mixed with dissimilar or even randomly oriented parts. In Japan, however, a factory robot is currently in service that assembles electronic machinery and appliance parts at a high rate of speed with a positioning accuracy of 8 micrometers. Using magnetic repellants, the parts literally float over the work table, and the high precision is achieved by sixteen visual sensors controlled by a microprocessor.

The ultimate aim of robot designers is to integrate them into an entire operation called a flexible manufacturing system (FMS), popularly known as an unmanned factory. In such factories, computers and robots are expected to perform almost all operations now carried out by people. Inventory control, tool management, machining, assembling, finishing, and inspection will all be done automatically. The product line can vary with consumer demand by simply reprogramming the robots. Such factories will even be able to reproduce themselves by manufacturing the components for new factories.

*The social impact of robots.*   These "steel-collar workers" are designed to replace human workers. So long as the jobs they replace are inherently hazardous or boring tasks that no one wants to do, this is of great benefit. But when robots begin to take over jobs that are the livelihood of human workers, this new technology obviously poses a great threat. If increased productivity through robotics leads to more leisure time and/or higher wages, workers who learn to use them will benefit from their implementation. If workers replaced by the robots have the opportunity to retrain for more rewarding and safer jobs, they will benefit. But what will happen to those workers who are displaced and not retrained? Labor unions in the United States are beginning to stir in the face of a significant rise in the production of robots and the research efforts toward extending their application.

The main argument for the implementation of robots is that they will increase productivity. Unlike human workers, they can operate around the clock, and they do not require breaks except for maintenance and reprogramming. They perform repetitious tasks with nearly unfailing accuracy, which greatly reduces slumps and spurts, thus giving smoother production flow. They can operate in hazardous and hostile working conditions without requiring the ventilation, lighting, and air conditioning needed by human workers. Also, by conforming to exacting specifications, they reduce waste of materials.

*Benefits.* Society should welcome robots that can take over unsafe and unhealthy jobs. Jobs such as forging operations; acid, chemical, or paint spraying; sand blasting; nuclear waste manipulation; and arc welding, which produces hot sparks and smoke, can all be done by robots, thus freeing human workers for jobs in safe environments. On-the-job health and safety are obviously important social values. Boring, tedious jobs such as assembly-line work involving hundreds of daily repetitions of the same operation are dehumanizing and are perfectly suited for machines rather than people. Robots can do physically demanding tasks, providing more opportunities for handicapped people. Resources are conserved through the use of robots because of accurate application of materials and because retooling is replaced by reprogramming, thereby reducing waste. Minimizing waste will also contribute to improvements in plant cleanliness, providing for a safer and more aesthetically pleasing work environment. Moreover, robots can work for virtually unlimited periods of time, thus better using the investment in plant and equipment.

*Cost.* The effect of robotics on national employment is probably the most hotly debated question surrounding this technology. Will robots produce a net reduction of jobs? If so, how many and of what type? Who will be responsible for retraining the displaced workers? None of these questions can be answered with certainty, and predictions vary widely. Proponents of robots argue that the number of new jobs created will more than make up for the jobs lost.

New jobs will be created in programming, maintenance, and operations. Retraining people to operate robots appears to be a minor problem. Maintenance, however, is a different story, in that it requires considerable knowledge of hydraulic systems, basic electronics, and numerical controls. Programming specialists will be required as robots become "smarter" and more adaptable. Manufacturing engineering is a new occupation emerging in this so-called *second industrial revolution.* Some studies predict that the robot manufacturing industry will employ between 60,000 and 100,000 workers by 1990.

Many labor economists are not so sanguine, however, about the net employment picture. Harley Shaiken, a research fellow at MIT and a former consultant to the United Auto Workers, estimates that 100,000 autoworkers could be replaced by 32,000 robots by 1990 (Martin, 1982). A Carnegie-Mellon University study (Martin, 1982) concludes that nearly 500,000 workers in the manufacturing, automotive, electric equipment, machinery, and fabricated metals industries could be replaced by nonsensory robots; this figure doubles if sensory robots are used. The study estimates that over the next twenty years, servo-controlled robots could replace up to three million manufacturing workers, out of a total U.S. work force in this sector of eight million. In 1980, General Electric implemented an automation program that was intended to replace nearly half of its assembly workers with robots. Italy's giant auto company, Fiat, hopes to reduce its work force by 90 percent using sensory robots. The director of the Carnegie-Mellon Robotics Institute, computer science professor Raj Reddy, draws a parallel between the robotics revolution and the mechanization of agriculture in the early part of this century (Martin, 1982). Industrial workers will be displaced, he says, into other jobs as farm workers were then, with society receiving the net benefit. However, just as the displaced farm workers, arriving in cities without skills and jobs, undoubtedly questioned this benefit, today's displaced industrial workers are not so certain what part of society is principally benefitting.

*Retraining for the automated future.* Retraining of workers is likely to become an area in which labor unions will make increasing demands in the years ahead. The chairman of DuPont reported in the *New York Times* ("Few on Layoffs," 1983) that his company's capacity for producing synthetic fibers had doubled in the ten years from 1973 to 1983, but that the operating manpower required had increased by only 4 to 5 percent because of mechanization and robotics. He further stated that 7 percent of the company's total work force of 174,000 had to be laid off during the recession of the early 1980s, and few of them would be rehired because their jobs had been taken over by automation. This was a conclusion that was shared by most of the chief executive officers of major American corporations, such as GM, Ford, AT&T, and GE, who gathered with the leaders of government at a 1983 National Business Council meeting. In a feature article ("Robots in the Labor Force," 1980), *Business Week* expressed concern about job displacement and retraining:

> It would be pure wishful thinking to assume that the conversion can be made painlessly and that the problem of displaced workers will solve itself. As the robots move in, human workers will have to be retrained and shifted to jobs that do not represent demotions. This is fairly easy to arrange when the robots are taking over only the most dangerous and distasteful jobs in industry. It will be far harder when the automation starts replacing workers in light assembly operations.

The article goes on to say:

> US companies should decide what sort of retraining they can offer and how they can break down and restructure jobs to provide work for those who can not be reeducated.

*Comparison of Japanese and American robot use.* The fact that Japan is the leading user of robots in the world and appears to have accomplished the changeover with considerably less social disruption than appears likely in the United States seems to be, at least in part, the result of Japan's labor-management structure. Employees in Japan, who value job security, are guaranteed employment until the age of 55 or 60. Every worker receives two bonuses each year, which are based on the company's profits. Japanese unions are not structured around skills; rather, they are organized to include all the workers in an entire company. Employees thus identify with the company and more easily move from one job to another within it. Japanese companies assume the responsibility for retraining workers who are displaced, because the lifetime employment arrangement gives the companies little opportunity to recruit from outside. In this environment, the advantages of using robots for hazardous and monotonous jobs are self-evident, and increased productivity directly benefits the workers. For these reasons, it seems that Japanese workers welcome robots.

In the United States, however, the prevailing business mentality often uproots companies, moving them to the American South or abroad in search of cheaper labor and higher profits and leaving laid-off workers and their communities to bear the social costs. In such an environment, the prospect of robots being used on a massive scale rightfully strikes fear in the hearts of American workers. It is argued that efficiency and productivity are the keys to the economic issues at stake. Advocates of increased robot use in American industry believe that without such an increase here, foreign competitors will be able to produce their products at lower costs and thus will be able to reduce prices, thereby undercutting American trade.

Seen from a national perspective, increased productivity with robotics is clearly beneficial to the whole economy. But how will that benefit be distributed, and who will decide? The central value issue at stake here is *democracy*. Will the workers, who must use this new technology and can potentially be displaced by it, have significant control over its development and implementation? Or will it simply be forced upon them, traumatically disrupting their lives? Until those whose jobs are at risk have gained more democratic control over the work place, these ingenious technical devices will continue to be seen as threats to what workers value most—their security and livelihood. The values of safety, freedom, and creativity, which robots could enhance, will not sufficiently compensate for these losses. Companies that successfully implement robotics to increase productivity will surely become more profitable, but the question of who will be the principal beneficiary is still not answered.

As with automobiles, the costs and benefits of this new technical innovation depend on how the society organizes its use. This organization is a social, political, and economic question that ultimately determines whether technology serves people or people serve it.

## CONCLUSIONS

We have taken a brief look at some of the ways technology affects our daily lives, and we have seen that almost no area is left untouched, making them profoundly different from those of our great-grandparents. These effects are not limited to us

as individuals. More important, technology changes the way we relate to one another in the various social groupings in which we are intertwined: our families, communities, cities, nation, the world (see Figure 3.1). Changes in human methods of
work, reorganized to fit the needs of the technologically driven Industrial Revolution, were seen to be its most fundamental effect. The natural environment, with
all its resources necessary for our continued healthy, productive existence, has also
been radically altered by the growth of technology in the 300 years since the Renaissance. Our scientific and technological knowledge has gone so far as to bring the
world under constant peril, threatened by the once-unimagined power contained
in unseen atoms.

Technology is much more than merely its technical products. It is a social
process made up of methods devised by engineers and scientists, organized and used
by businesspeople and economists, and sanctioned by politicians. All of these
people, their decision-making processes, and their manufacturing techniques and
products are part and parcel of the human undertaking we call technology.

We have considered in some detail how these actors in the development of a
now well-established technology—the automobile—played out their roles to reduce
a once-diverse American transportation system to one almost solely dependent
upon cars. We have seen how the human value of convenient mobility was served
in this drama, to the detriment of the environment; the conservation of precious,
nonrenewable energy resources; the accessibility of public transportation for all—
rich and poor, young and old, healthy and handicapped; and the preservation of
aesthetically harmonious, ethnically and culturally diverse cities. We have also considered how an emerging technology—robotics—with the potential of taking over
hazardous and monotonous jobs and of making many other manufacturing and
assembly jobs more economically productive, is seen as a looming threat to the
livelihood of workers who may be displaced by these technical inventions. That
these American workers do not embrace this technical innovation, as Japanese
workers appear to be doing, was seen to result from their lack of voice in deciding
how and when robots will be used. This structure of American labor-management
relations is itself part of robot technology as understood in the broad sense we have
been considering here.

As an aspiring engineer or scientist, you will be at the very heart of this multifaceted undertaking. If you take seriously your profession's expressed aim of creating socially beneficial technical products, you will need to know much more than
most engineers and scientists have in the past about the economic, political, and
cultural forces that determine the development and uses of new technologies. Your
educational experience must include considerable exposure to the rich variety of
human endeavor: social studies such as history, economics, government and politics, psychology, sociology, and business; the literary, performing, and fine arts;
and languages, philosophy, and contemporary cultural courses, such as women's
studies and Black studies. Not only will you be personally enriched by these diverse
areas of study, but you will be far better prepared to take your place as a responsible professional and citizen.

## EXERCISES

**3.1.** List ten ways that technology developed during your lifetime affects you today.

**3.2.** What technologies were involved in the food you ate for breakfast this morning before it appeared on your table? Which of these technologies were involved in the breakfast of an average American 250 years ago?

**3.3.** Which technologies were involved in the clothes you wore today before you bought them? Which of these technologies were involved in the clothes of an average American 250 years ago?

**3.4.** What technical inventions were necessary before a cassette tape recorder could be built with which you can listen to your favorite music?

**3.5.** How has use of the universal product code changed grocery shopping? What are some of the economic and cultural dimensions of this change?

**3.6.** List a recent technological development by each of the engineering disciplines (aeronautical, chemical, civil, electrical, industrial, mechanical, and nuclear) that, in addition to benefits it has provided, has also had detrimental social effects.

**3.7.** Name three nineteenth-century entrepreneurs and describe how they used technology to create a new product that became a commonplace consumer article.

**3.8.** List three mass assembly-line-produced consumer articles that were once made by individual craft workers. How do you think the change has affected those who produce the articles?

**3.9.** How do you think the rise of democratic parliamentary institutions and the rise of the Industrial Revolution, at about the same time in history, are related?

**3.10.** Think of a recent political decision involving technology. Which individuals or groups most influenced the decision?

**3.11.** How is work organized and done differently in countries that operate under a socialist economic system compared to the American capitalist system?

**3.12.** Discuss the values that have been brought into conflict by a technology developed during your lifetime. How has the government acted to give some values priority over others in the use of this technology?

**3.13.** List all the ways you can think of that your life would be different if you had no access to a car. How would the city or town you live in have to be reconstructed for you to be able to move about by public transportation? What would be the best forms of public transportation?

**3.14.** Discuss all the individual advantages you have if you own a car. Are there any societal advantages? Discuss the societal advantages.

**3.15.** List some areas not mentioned in this chapter in which robots might be used. Can you think of any social costs besides loss of jobs? How would you suggest overcoming these social costs?

**3.16.** How could the work place be more democratically organized so that workers *and* society would both benefit from the use of robots? What inhibits such changes from taking place?

**4**

# Understanding Professional Ethics

*Richard H. McCuen*

## INTRODUCTION

The topics of the preceding chapters lead into a central topic that is important to professional engineers and scientists: professional ethics. As will be discussed in Chapter 6, leadership is extremely important in engineering and science. One characteristic of a leader is the ability to establish value goals; a leader who has this characteristic is referred to as a *pathfinder*. Through example and inspiration, the pathfinder encourages others in an organization to be sensitive to these values in all phases of their professional work. It is thus important for all professionals to act in accordance with guidelines provided by professional societies in recognition of the social responsibilities of its members. Such guidelines are expressed in a professional society's code of ethics, which presents the human values that are important to members of the professional society and serves as a guide to conduct that reflects these values. An understanding of the profession's goals as well as the ability to apply the guidelines properly will benefit the professional, the profession, and the public.

Although an entire book could be devoted to the issue of professional ethics, we will limit our discussion of the subject in this chapter to three areas. First, we hope to develop an awareness that the engineering and science professions consider human value issues a very important part of professional practice. Second, because they recognize that engineers and scientists have social responsibilities (many of which are discussed in other chapters of this book), professional societies have formulated and adopted professional codes of ethics. We will discuss one such code—the code of ethics of the National Society of Professional Engineers (NSPE)—in some detail. Third, because such codes are based on human values, practicing engineers and scientists must understand how to incorporate the value goals of the professional society into their professional practice in order to meet their social responsibilities. We will discuss the application of a code to three ethical dilemmas that arise in professional practice. The chapter will also discuss courses that could be taken to gain a better understanding of value goals.

## PROFESSIONAL CODES OF ETHICS

Almost all professional societies have codes of ethics. Although they are not meant to be means for disciplining members of the professional society, any violation of the code can result in disciplinary action by the professional society; if a member is found guilty, the penalty may be suspension for a period of time or expulsion.

There are several purposes in having a code of ethics. First, it establishes the goals of the society, one of which is a concern for the public interest. This serves to enhance the profession's public image, but the code is not developed simply for this egoistic reason. Second, a code identifies the values that must be held paramount by members of the professional society. Such values as honesty, public safety, knowledge, and equality are central to all professional codes of ethics. Third, a code of ethics identifies the rights and responsibilities of all parties involved. The parties, which were identified in the responsibility tetrahedron in Chapter 2, include the individual, the client, the profession, and society. Although an individual has specific value responsibilities to each of the other parties, he or she also has rights. Thus, a code of ethics should demonstrate clearly that professional life is not self-sacrificing. Individual members have moral responsibilities to themselves and their families, just as they have moral responsibilities to the other parties in the responsibility tetrahedron. The individual must weigh each of these value responsibilities in making any decision. A fourth goal of a code of ethics is to provide guidance and inspiration for proper professional conduct, as well as serving as a force in deterring improper professional conduct. By establishing the ideals of professional practice, a code of ethics attempts to maximize human welfare. In summary, a professional code of ethics establishes goals, identifies important human value issues, identifies rights and responsibilities, and provides guidance for proper professional conduct.

Unfortunately, a perfect code is not possible; all codes of ethics have limitations. Although some of these limitations are significant, the balance is strongly in favor of a professional society having a code. The limitations are as follows. First, codes of ethics are not legal documents. Therefore, they have limited value in disciplining members. A professional society may expel a member, but this does not prohibit the member from practicing in a professional capacity. Expulsion from the National Society of Professional Engineers may exclude an individual from performing many design functions, but the individual can still serve in a number of engineering management functions. Second, having a code of ethics places the profession under a "value microscope"; therefore, the profession must establish a bureaucracy to police the code. Although there are obvious benefits to establishing the necessary bureaucracy, additional bureaucracy is not usually greeted with enthusiasm, and it is always hoped that public scrutiny is not necessary. Third, it is sometimes difficult to compose a code of ethics that does not include parts that appear to be self-serving. After all, just as members of professional societies have responsibilities, they also have rights. Parts of codes that relate to these rights may be misconstrued as self-serving, even though they are necessary to provide a necessary balance between rights and responsibilities. Fourth, some segments of a professional society may have different rights and responsibilities than other segments. For example, a society that has members in both academia and professional practice must recognize the different needs and responsibilities of these two groups. Fifth, codes of ethics often do not provide members with insights into how and why the code was formulated, the values stressed in the code, and the process by which value conflicts can be resolved. The human values imbedded within the code may not be evident to the average member. Also, as suggested in Chapter 2, value decision making is more complicated than decision making based on quantitative indices. A professional society should not arbitrarily assume that its members know how to make value decisions. This should be an important consideration when a professional society elects to formulate a code of ethics. Sixth, a member who is also a member of another profession with a different code of ethics may find that the different codes stress different responsibilities. This may lead to conflicts in performing his or her duties. For example, the codes of ethics for lawyers and engineers stress different values, and conflicts may arise when an individual whose practice involves both legal and engineering work must make a value decision. The foregoing limitations suggest that a professional society must give serious thought to the formulation of a code and then must provide the necessary education for its members after the code has been formulated and adopted.

## CODE OF THE NATIONAL SOCIETY
## OF PROFESSIONAL ENGINEERS

Although the various professional societies in engineering and science have different codes of ethics, the code of the National Society of Professional Engineers (NSPE) can be used as an example. The NSPE code, reproduced at the end of this chapter, has four primary sections: Preamble, Fundamental Canons, Rules of Practice, and Professional Obligations.

The Preamble serves several functions. In general terms, it establishes the value goals of the profession. The Preamble is very value oriented; specifically, it notes the following values: quality of life, honesty, impartiality, fairness, equity, and public health, safety, and welfare. The Preamble also notes the parties involved: the engineer, the public, clients, employers, and the profession. The Preamble could stand alone as an ethical guide by which members could practice within the engineering profession.

The Fundamental Canons are slightly more specific than the Preamble; however, the canons are still based on human values, especially those identified in the Preamble. The first canon emphasizes the important responsibility the engineer has to society. The second canon is important because violation of it can undermine the values indicated in the first canon; the probability of mistakes is greatly increased when an engineer works outside his or her area of competence. Violation of the third canon would be dishonest, could damage the reputation of the employer or client, and would degrade the image of the profession. Public statements should be made only after an attempt has been made to resolve issues within the firm. An informal chain of command exists, with the issuing of public statements at the end of the chain. It is in the best interests of all parties involved to follow this chain of command, because it promotes such values as loyalty to the firm, maintaining the image of the profession, and enhancing public welfare. The fourth canon suggests truth, loyalty (to the employer and client), reliability, and trust; these values are necessary in order to meet the obligations the employer has to society and to the client. The fifth canon is based on the values of honesty and trust; failure to abide by this canon can lead to disharmony within the profession, which decreases the efficiency by which the profession serves society.

The first Rule of Practice emphasizes the primary values of public safety, health, and welfare. Rule 1a goes one step further in that it suggests that the public welfare is best served when the engineer who is aware of something that does not serve the best interests of the public follows the proper chain of command in rectifying the problem. Loyalty is an inherent value in Rule 1c; this rule suggests that a lack of loyalty is not in the best interests of public welfare. Honesty and truth are inherent in Rule 1d; the rule is important because it emphasizes the importance of honesty and truth in maximizing human welfare. Rule 1e indicates that knowledge of wrongdoing brings with it a responsibility; failure to bring code violations to the attention of the proper authorities is, in itself, a violation of the code. Both fraudulent activity and the failure to report it are actions that are not in the public's best interests. Thus, although it is important for the engineer to execute his or her professional duties so as to ensure public safety, health, and welfare, the components of Rule 1 suggest that violation of other values, such as loyalty and honesty, results in a violation of the values of public safety, health, and welfare; these human values are interdependent.

Rule of Practice 2 and its components are important because violation could be detrimental to public safety, health, and welfare. This rule deals with knowledge, and as indicated in Chapter 1, one element of a professional is specialized knowledge and skills. Recognizing the high degree of specialization in most engineering and science disciplines, Rule 2 has increasingly become more important. When an individual lacks competence in a specific area of a technical field, the individual may jeopardize public safety, health, and welfare by trying to practice in that area.

In addition, individuals are ignoring other values if they perform professional services outside their area of competence. Specifically, it suggests a lack of honesty in their dealings with the client. Furthermore, it reduces the efficiency of the firm. In summary, Rule of Practice 2 deals with human values of knowledge, performance, honesty, and efficiency, as well as public safety, health, and welfare.

It is readily evident that Rule of Practice 3 deals with truth. Again, truthfulness is important because it serves the interests of public welfare. But it is necessary to recognize that truthfulness is also important to the firm, the client, and the profession. Rule 3b is related to Rule 2 in that the importance of professional competence is stressed. Whereas Rule 2 relates more to the importance of professional competency than to the relationship between the individual and the firm in technical matters, however, Rule 3 relates more to the issue of communicating outside the firm—but still with regard to competency. Obviously, the values of truth, knowledge, and honesty are central to Rule 3; they are additionally important because of their relationship to public safety, health, and welfare.

Rule of Practice 4 deals with the values of faithfulness, loyalty, honesty, truthfulness, and respect. Again, within the framework of Rule 4, these values are necessary for serving society. Rule 4 and its components reflect ethical problems that arise in interrelationships of engineering practice. Failure to recognize that conflicts of interest can arise in practice can be detrimental to the individual's career and harmful to public welfare.

Rule 4c is of special interest because it addresses the problem of gratuities. Gratuities are not just a problem for engineers and scientists. Elected public officials have been criticized for accepting gifts and not reporting them according to the procedure specified by law; a recent case that received wide attention in the media involved an appointed advisor to the President who accepted a watch and failed to report the gift. Some engineers come under public scrutiny, and violation of Rule 4c can cast a shadow of doubt on the integrity of the individual. Rule 4c suggests that the concept of "zero gratuity" is the best policy. Zero gratuity means that an individual should accept nothing from anyone other than the direct compensation provided by the employer. Any policy other than zero gratuity would require drawing a line on what is acceptable. If one believes that it would be acceptable to receive a free lunch from a contractor, then is a dinner acceptable? If a dinner is acceptable, then how about an overnight, all-expense-paid trip to a resort? These are some of the "freebies" that citizens criticize elected public officials for accepting. It is no different with engineers. The zero gratuity policy of Rule 4c is the best policy.

Rules of Practice 4d and 4e are also worthy of special attention. Chapter 16 emphasizes the importance of participation by engineers and scientists in public processes. Public participation by engineers and scientists can enhance the public welfare, which is a value central to the NSPE Code of Ethics. But when public participation results in a conflict of interest, it detracts from, rather than enhances, the public welfare. This is a reason for including Rules 4d and 4e in the code. In the long term, such conflicts of interest also can damage the reputation of the

profession. Thus, engineers and scientists should participate actively in public processes, but only when their participation does not lead to a conflict of interest and violate the spirit of professional codes of ethics.

Rule of Practice 5 again deals with the interdependencies between elements of the responsibility tetrahedron in Chapter 2. Values inherent in Rule 5 include honesty, truthfulness, pleasure (i.e., personal gain), and performance. Violation of Rule 5 would not be in the best interests of the public welfare. In addition, some of the relationships embedded in Rule 5 involve the employee and the employer (i.e., the firm), the firm and the client, and the client and society (i.e., public authorities and contributions to elected officials). Besides violating the code of ethics, many of the concepts in Rule 5a are also illegal. However, it is important to recognize that the fact that an action is legal does not necessarily mean that it is ethical.

The fourth part of the NSPE Code of Ethics is the section on Professional Obligations. The values inherent in this part are the same as those in the other parts. Because of its length, we will not undertake a detailed analysis here.

## CODES IN PRACTICE

An initial reading of a professional code of ethics may leave one with the impression that they are too general to be applied. Whereas a code of law may state, "Theft of a car is punishable by five years in prison," a code of ethics is written in value terms and does not suggest a punishment for violation. The difference between a legal statement and a rule of professional practice is evident from a comparison of the foregoing statement of law to a rule of practice such as "Engineers shall hold paramount the safety, health, and welfare of the public in the performance of their professional duties." Although legal codes and codes of ethics both have a base in human values, and although both can be used to discipline violators, codes of ethics are written in general terms and require the ability to recognize the underlying values and to weigh alternative courses of action. Legal codes indicate punishments that will result from violations, while codes suggest the array of responsibilities that professionals have to the firm, the client, society, and the community. In practice, a professional who has been involved in a wrongdoing may find himself involved in both a lawsuit and a hearing with the professional society on a code of ethics violation.

To illustrate codes of ethics in practice, we will discuss three types of questionable practice: bid-rigging, kickbacks, and whistle-blowing. We will not fully describe these practices but will provide a brief outline of each. The goals of this discussion are to identify some of the value issues involved and to illustrate how the practices violate both the spirit of the professional codes and specific elements of the codes. We will leave discussions of the use of codes for punishing violators to sources that provide more detailed discussions of professional ethics; let it suffice here to say that a member of a professional society who violates the society's code of ethics can be disciplined by either expulsion or suspension from the professional society, either of which can be detrimental to the professional's career.

### Bid-Rigging

In simplified terms, the process of bid-rigging is as follows. A client requires a certain task to be completed and is not capable of doing the work. Therefore, the client, which could be either a private company or a public agency (i.e., federal, state, or local government), puts out a public notice that the work is open for bids. When a task is open for bids, companies that have the expertise and facilities to complete the task develop proposals that detail a proposed plan of operation, a schedule for completion, and a statement describing the company's qualifications. A budget may also be submitted. If a contractor believes that he will be one of only a few firms that will bid on the request for a proposal, he might try to rig the bid in one of a number of ways. The contractor might approach other firms that are likely to bid on the proposal and suggest that the other firms submit proposals with very high price tags so that he can submit a bid that is slightly lower than the other bids but higher than it should be. In return for the other firms submitting highly inflated bids, the contractor promises either to give them a piece of the action or to submit an unreasonably high bid on some future request for proposal so that the other firms can rig a bid. Thus, the client gets the work done, but the cost of the work exceeds the amount for which the work could have been completed honestly.

Before identifying the elements of a professional code of ethics that are violated by bid-rigging, it would be useful to evaluate the situation from a value standpoint. The end result of bid-rigging is that the client pays more for the work than is necessary. When the client is a public agency, the public is paying more for a project than is really necessary. This represents, at the least, a misuse of public resources, resources that could have been used to satisfy other public needs are being paid to the contractor for his private use. The misused funds could have been used for a public safety or health improvement project, improved educational facilities, or a piece of sculpture that could be displayed in a public area. These represent the values of health and safety, knowledge, and aesthetics. By rigging the bid, the contractor has placed his personal pleasure above these social values. But the violation of values does not stop with health, knowledge, and aesthetics. The contractor has also violated the trust that society places in the profession. When the contractor's bid-rigging scheme is exposed, the image of the profession will be tarnished. If more than one instance of bid-rigging is exposed, governmental bodies may place restrictions on the bidding process. Such restrictions can increase the costs of projects, which means that the opportunity for other public facilities is forgone. The length of completion of projects might also increase as a result of restrictions imposed because of past bid-rigging activities; this represents inefficient use of public resources. In addition, when the image of the profession is tarnished, the respect that society has for the profession is diminished and the practices of other professionals may be affected adversely. Thus, unprofessional conduct such as bid-rigging has many value implications; it is not just a materialistic (i.e., money) problem.

A professional code of ethics does not specifically state that a professional should not participate in a bid-rigging scheme; a code should not make such state-

ments. This does not imply, however, that the code does not prohibit such conduct. One could reasonably argue that bid-rigging violates a number of rules in the NSPE code, such as Rules of Practice 3, 4, and 5 as well as Professional Obligations 1, 1f, 3, 3a, and 7. Certainly, Professional Obligation 1f—"Engineers shall avoid any act tending to promote their own interest at the expense of the dignity and integrity of the profession"—would be violated by a bid-rigging scheme. The contractor receives a larger sum of money than he would have received if he had submitted the bid legally. The inflated bid promotes the interests of himself and his firm, but it will result in injury to the reputation of the profession when the scheme is exposed. Furthermore, Rule 4 states: "Engineers shall act in professional matters for each employer or client as faithful agents or trustees." In a bid-rigging scheme, the contractor is clearly not acting faithfully to either the employer or the client. Thus, besides being illegal, bid-rigging violates numerous elements of a professional code of ethics and represents a serious violation of human value conduct.

### Kickback Schemes

In some respects a kickback scheme is similar to bid-rigging. A kickback scheme involves a contractor and a client—usually a public employee. In simplified terms, a kickback scheme works as follows. The contractor responds to a request for a proposal and submits a bid of $X$ dollars on a project. The client, who is using public funds, approaches the contractor and states that he will award the contractor the bid only if the contractor revises his bid upward to $X + \Delta X$ dollars. The amount $X$ is retained by the contractor to complete the job, and the amount $\Delta X$ is returned to the client "under the table." In some cases, the kickback of $\Delta X$ is funneled back to the client through a dummy company under the heading "For services rendered."

In a kickback scheme, the public is clearly being defrauded. The public is paying $X + \Delta X$ dollars for work that has a monetary value of $X$ dollars. As in a bid-rigging scheme, the amount $\Delta X$ cannot then be used to meet other social needs. The evaluation of values would be the same for a kickback scheme as for a bid-rigging scheme, and the same sections of the code of ethics would be violated. Both the public and the profession suffer because of the actions of the individual.

### Whistle-blowing

The term *whistle-blowing* refers to an action taken by one party (an individual employee or a group of employees with a common purpose) in which information is released to another party (usually the public) against the wishes of a third party (usually the employer). Whistle-blowing may be better understood through an example. Assume that a chemist who works for a manufacturer is responsible for testing the wastewater released from the manufacturing plant into the local river. The chemist tests the wastewater for various pollutants and reports the findings to the plant manager. The manager should take corrective action or stop the manufacturing process when the quality of the wastewater falls below the standards required by the state water quality standards. If the chemist finds that the quality of the wastewater is below these standards and the plant manager is not taking the necessary action to improve the quality of the wastewater, the chemist faces a value dilemma. Does he allow the company to continue to pollute the local river or does he report the pollution to the state? If he goes to the local press, he is "blowing the whistle." Of course, whistle-blowing is a last resort. The chemist should first try to resolve the value conflict within the company. Most companies have specific procedures for solving such value conflicts. Since details of such procedures are not central to the goals of this book, the following simple procedure will suffice for our purposes here: (1) try to resolve the issue with the immediate supervisor; (2) proceed up through the company chain of command in an attempt to resolve the issue; (3) obtain private legal counsel; (4) approach the appropriate public agency about the matter; and (5) report the concerns to the public media—that is, blow the whistle. Before any of these steps are taken, the individual should first collect, document, and organize all pertinent information; even when the problem may not involve a legal issue, all evidence should be gathered to support a case. Again, it should be emphasized that whistle-blowing is a last step.

Our goal here is not to describe the process of whistle-blowing but to discuss the value issues involved; the process should be left for a more detailed discussion of professional ethics. In the case of the chemist, he recognizes that the discharge of wastewater that does not meet quality standards may represent a public health hazard, may pose a threat to fish and aquatic organisms in the river, may degrade the aesthetic quality of the river environment, and may limit the value of the water to downstream users. Although there is clearly a monetary value associated with the substandard wastewater, the value issues of public health, rights of aquatic life, and aesthetics are at least as important as the monetary value. But the dilemma is difficult to solve because competing values exist. The chemist has value responsibilities to his employer, to the other people who work for the firm, and to his family, who depend on him for support. The firm values loyalty. If the plant is shut down, employees will lose pay and benefits, and the public will lose tax receipts that are used for social services. If the chemist blows the whistle, he may lose his job and thus not be able to meet his responsibilities to his family. The dilemma is to weigh the value and monetary issues on both sides. The point we are making here is that value issues are important to engineers and scientists. When values are in conflict, the engineer or scientist must be able to assess the risks involved and weigh his or her responsibilities to self, family, community, firm, client, and society.

## COURSES ON PROFESSIONAL ETHICS

Unlike such topics as history, the fine arts, and literature, courses that deal with professional ethics are not consigned to one specific academic department or program. The topic could be included in courses in many disciplines. For our purposes here, we will consider courses that deal with the subject as it relates to a specific discipline and courses that deal with it in general terms. Obviously, courses that cover ethics in business, medicine, law, or journalism would provide insights into how other disciplines tackle value issues within their professions. One should not expect the goals to be the same. For example, one should expect loyalty to the client to be given higher priority in legal ethics than in engineering ethics, and the relationship between a doctor and patient would be central to a discussion of medical ethics. Although there are obvious and important differences between ethics in engineering and science and ethics in other professions, courses dealing with ethical issues in these other professions can still be of value to students of engineering and science because there are also important similarities. Some issues that might be discussed include the problem of policing professional conduct, the weighting of professional versus personal value responsibilities, the influence of professional codes of conduct on the professional, the role of the public in decisions involving violations of professional codes, and the degree to which codes of ethics restrain economic freedom in a free-enterprise system. A study of such issues would certainly make discussions of codes for professional societies in engineering and science more meaningful.

In addition to courses that address specific codes of ethics and ethical issues, a number of courses deal with general concepts related to professional ethics. Certainly, some in a philosophy program would discuss such issues as moral obligations, human rights and values, moral conflicts, value decision making, ethical theories (e.g., utilitarianism, deontological theories), moral reasoning, and ethical relativism. Courses in sociology might deal with such subjects as discrimination, civil rights, privacy, occupational safety, and rights of employees and employers. Such issues have a measure of interdependency with professional ethics in engineering and science. Other programs that might discuss concepts that can be transferred to professional practice include courses in women's studies (equality), economics (accounting for risk in decision making), and computer ethics.

## CONCLUSIONS

Professional societies recognize the social responsibilities of engineers and scientists and have adopted codes of ethics to detail the importance of these responsibilities. Codes of ethics are not lists of dos and don'ts. Rather, they outline the human values that are important in professional practice. In discussing the value basis of parts of the NSPE Code of Ethics, we noted that the emphasis in this code is on the safety, health, and welfare of the public. To meet this value goal, engineers must practice in an atmosphere of honesty, truthfulness, loyalty, trust, and respect; they also must be knowledgeable and must practice with efficiency.

Interpreting a code of ethics involves more than just reading the words. An individual must understand the moral basis of a code and must be able to apply the codes, which are usually written in very general terms, to a variety of situations. Such an ability to interpret requires an education in human values and value decision making. Since this is generally not part of the technical component of engineering and science programs, it is important for the student to develop this ability through general education courses. We noted a number of these courses in this chapter, and many other types of courses may also help develop these abilities.

## NSPE CODE OF ETHICS FOR ENGINEERS

### Preamble

Engineering is an important and learned profession. The members of the profession recognize that their work has a direct and vital impact on the quality of life for all people. Accordingly, the services provided by engineers require honesty, impartiality, fairness and equity, and must be dedicated to the protection of the public health, safety and welfare. In the practice of their profession, engineers must perform under a standard of professional behavior which requires adherence to the highest principles of ethical conduct on behalf of the public, clients, employers and the profession.

### I. Fundamental Canons

Engineers, in the fulfillment of their professional duties, shall:

1. Hold paramount the safety, health and welfare of the public in the performance of their professional duties.
2. Perform services only in areas of their competence.
3. Issue public statements only in an objective and truthful manner.
4. Act in professional matters for each employer or client as faithful agents or trustees.
5. Avoid improper solicitation of professional employment.

### II. Rules of Practice

1. Engineers shall hold paramount the safety, health and welfare of the public in the performance of their professional duties.
   a. Engineers shall at all times recognize that their primary obligation is to protect the safety, health, property and welfare of the public. If their professional judgment is overruled under circumstances where the safety, health, property or welfare of the public are endangered, they shall notify their employer or client and such other authority as may be appropriate.
   b. Engineers shall approve only those engineering documents which are safe

for public health, property and welfare in comformity with accepted standards.

c. Engineers shall not reveal facts, data or information obtained in a professional capacity without the prior consent of the client or employer except as authorized or required by law or this Code.

d. Engineers shall not permit the use of their name or firm name nor associate in business ventures with any person or firm which they have reason to believe is engaging in fraudulent or dishonest business or professional practices.

e. Engineers having knowledge of any alleged violation of this Code shall cooperate with the proper authorities in furnishing such information or assistance as may be required.

2. Engineers shall perform services only in the areas of their competence.

a. Engineers shall undertake assignments only when qualified by education or experience in the specific technical fields involved.

b. Engineers shall not affix their signatures to any plans or documents dealing with subject matter in which they lack competence, nor to any plan or document not prepared under their direction and control.

c. Engineers may accept an assignment outside of their fields of competence to the extent that their services are restricted to those phases of the project in which they are qualified, and to the extent that they are satisfied that all other phases of such project will be performed by registered or otherwise qualified associates, consultants, or employees, in which case they may then sign the documents for the total project.

3. Engineers shall issue public statements only in an objective and truthful manner.

a. Engineers shall be objective and truthful in professional reports, statements or testimony. They shall include all relevant or pertinent information in such reports, statements or testimony.

b. Engineers may express publicly a professional opinion on technical subjects only when that opinion is founded upon adequate knowledge of the facts and competence in the subject matter.

c. Engineers shall issue no statements, criticisms or arguments on technical matters which are inspired or paid for by interested parties, unless they have prefaced their comments by explicitly identifying the interested parties on whose behalf they are speaking, and by revealing the existence of any interest the engineers may have in the matters.

4. Engineers shall act in professional matters for each employer or client as faithful agents or trustees.

a. Engineers shall disclose all known or potential conflicts of interest to their employers or clients by promptly informing them of any business association, interest, or other circumstances which could influence or appear to influence their judgment or the quality of their services.

    b. Engineers shall not accept compensation, financial or otherwise, from more than one party for services on the same project, or for services pertaining to the same project, unless the circumstances are fully disclosed to, and agreed to, by all interested parties.

    c. Engineers shall not solicit or accept financial or other valuable consideration, directly or indirectly, from contractors, their agents, or other parties in connection with work for employers or clients for which they are responsible.

    d. Engineers in public service as members, advisors or employees of a governmental body or department shall not participate in decisions with respect to professional services solicited or provided by them or their organizations in private or public engineering practice.

    e. Engineers shall not solicit or accept a professional contract from a governmental body on which a principal or officer of their organization serves as a member.

5. Engineers shall avoid improper solicitation of professional employment.

    a. Engineers shall not falsify or permit misrepresentation of their, or their associates', academic or professional qualifications. They shall not misrepresent or exaggerate their degree of responsibility in or for the subject matter of prior assignments. Brochures or other presentations incident to the solicitation of employment shall not misrepresent pertinent facts concerning employers, employees, associates, joint venturers or past accomplishments with the intent and purpose of enhancing their qualifications and their work.

    b. Engineers shall not offer, give, solicit or receive, either directly or indirectly, any political contribution in an amount intended to influence the award of a contract by public authority, or which may be reasonably construed by the public of having the effect or intent to influence the award of a contract. They shall not offer any gift, or other valuable consideration in order to secure work. They shall not pay a commission, percentage or brokerage fee in order to secure work except to a bona fide employee or bona fide established commercial or marketing agencies retained by them.

## III. Professional Obligations

1. Engineers shall be guided in all their professional relations by the highest standards of integrity.

    a. Engineers shall admit and accept their own errors when proven wrong and refrain from distorting or altering the facts in an attempt to justify their decisions.

    b. Engineers shall advise their clients or employers when they believe a project will not be successful.

    c. Engineers shall not accept outside employment to the detriment of their regular work or interest. Before accepting any outside employment they will notify their employers.

d. Engineers shall not attempt to attract an engineer from another employer by false or misleading pretenses.

e. Engineers shall not actively participate in strikes, picket lines, or other collective coercive action.

f. Engineers shall avoid any act tending to promote their own interest at the expense of the dignity and integrity of the profession.

2. Engineers shall at all times strive to serve the public interest.

a. Engineers shall seek opportunities to be of constructive service in civic affairs and work for the advancement of the safety, health and well-being of their community.

b. Engineers shall not complete, sign, or seal plans and/or specifications that are not of a design safe to the public health and welfare and in conformity with accepted engineering standards. If the client or employer insists on such unprofessional conduct, they shall notify the proper authorities and withdraw from further service on the project.

c. Engineers shall endeavor to extend public knowledge and appreciation of engineering and its achievements and to protect the engineering profession from misrepresentation and misunderstanding.

3. Engineers shall avoid all conduct or practice which is likely to discredit the profession or deceive the public.

a. Engineers shall avoid the use of statements containing a material misrepresentation of fact or omitting a material fact necessary to keep statements from being misleading; statements intended or likely to create an unjustified expectation; statements containing prediction of future success; statements containing an opinion as to the quality of the Engineers' services; or statements intended or likely to attract clients by the use of showmanship, puffery, or self-laudation, including the use of slogans, jingles, or sensational language or format.

b. Consistent with the foregoing, Engineers may advertise for recruitment of personnel.

c. Consistent with the foregoing, Engineers may prepare articles for the lay or technical press, but such articles shall not imply credit to the author for work performed by others.

4. Engineers shall not disclose confidential information concerning the business affairs or technical processes of any present or former client or employer without his consent.

a. Engineers in the employ of others shall not without the consent of all interested parties enter promotional efforts or negotiations for work or make arrangements for other employment as a principal or to practice in connection with a specific project for which the Engineer has gained particular and specialized knowledge.

    b. Engineers shall not, without the consent of all interested parties, participate in or represent an adversary interest in connection with a specific project or proceeding in which the Engineer has gained particular specialized knowledge on behalf of a former client or employer.

5. Engineers shall not be influenced in their professional dutues by conflicting interests.

    a. Engineers shall not accept financial or other considerations, including free engineering designs, from material or equipment suppliers for specifying their product.

    b. Engineers shall not accept commissions or allowances, directly or indirectly, from contractors or other parties dealing with clients or employers of the Engineer in connection with work for which the Engineer is responsible.

6. Engineers shall uphold the principle of appropriate and adequate compensation for those engaged in engineering work.

    a. Engineers shall not accept remuneration from either an employee or employment agency for giving employment.

    b. Engineers, when employing other engineers, shall offer a salary according to professional qualifications and the recognized standards in the particular geographic area.

7. Engineers shall not compete unfairly with other engineers by attempting to obtain employment or advancement or professional engagements by taking advantage of a salaried position, by criticizing other engineers, or by other improper or questionable methods.

    a. Engineers shall not request, propose, or accept a professional commission on a contingent basis under circumstances in which their professional judgment may be compromised.

    b. Engineers in salaried positions shall accept part-time engineering work only at salaries not less than that recognized as standard in the area.

    c. Engineers shall not use equipment, supplies, laboratory, or office facilities of an employer to carry on outside private practice without consent.

8. Engineers shall not attempt to injure, maliciously or falsely, directly or indirectly, the professional reputation, prospects, practice or employment of other engineers, nor indiscriminately criticize other engineers' work. Engineers who believe others are guilty of unethical or illegal practice shall present such information to the proper authority for action.

    a. Engineers in private practice shall not review the work of another engineer for the same client, except with the knowledge of such engineer, or unless the connection of such engineer with the work has been terminated.

    b. Engineers in governmental, industrial or educational employ are entitled to review and evaluate the work of other engineers when so required by their employment duties.

    c. Engineers in sales or industrial employ are entitled to make engineering comparisons of represented products with products of other suppliers.

9. Engineers shall accept personal responsibility for all professional activities.
   a. Engineers shall conform with state registration laws in the practice of engineering.
   b. Engineers shall not use association with a nonengineer, a corporation, or partnership, as a "cloak" for unethical acts, but must accept personal responsibility for all professional acts.
10. Engineers shall give credit for engineering work to those to whom credit is due, and will recognize the proprietary interests of others.
   a. Engineers shall, whenever possible, name the person or persons who may be individually responsible for designs, inventions, writings, or other accomplishments.
   b. Engineers using designs supplied by a client recognize that the designs remain the property of the client and may not be duplicated by the Engineer for others without express permission.
   c. Engineers, before undertaking work for others in connection with which the Engineer may make improvements, plans, designs, inventions, or other records which may justify copyrights or patents, should enter into a positive agreement regarding ownership.
   d. Engineers' designs, data, records, and notes referring exclusively to an employer's work are the employer's property.
11. Engineers shall cooperate in extending the effectiveness of the profession by interchanging information and experience with other engineers and students, and will endeavor to provide opportunity for the professional development and advancement of engineers under their supervision.
   a. Engineers shall encourage engineering employees' efforts to improve their education.
   b. Engineers shall encourage engineering employees to attend and present papers at professional and technical society meetings.
   c. Engineers shall urge engineering employees to become registered at the earliest possible date.
   d. Engineers shall assign a professional engineer duties of a nature to utilize full training and experience, insofar as possible, and delegate lesser functions to subprofessionals or to technicians.
   e. Engineers shall provide a prospective engineering employee with complete information on working conditions and proposed status of employment, and after employment will keep employees informed of any changes.

"By order of the United States District Court for the District of Columbia, former Section 11(c) of the NSPE Code of Ethics prohibiting competitive bidding, and all policy statements, opinions, rulings or other guidelines interpreting its scope, have been rescinded as unlawfully interfering with the legal right of engineers, protected under the antitrust laws, to provide price information to prospective clients; accordingly, nothing contained in the NSPE Code of Ethics, policy statements, opinions, rulings or other guidelines prohibits the submission of price quotations or competitive bids for engineering services at any time or in any amount."

### Statement by the NSPE Executive Committee

In order to correct misunderstandings which have been indicated in some instances since the issuance of the Supreme Court decision and the entry of the Final Judgment, it is noted that in its decision of April 25, 1978, the Supreme Court of the United States declared: "The Sherman Act does not require competitive bidding."

It is further noted that as made clear in the Supreme Court decision:

1. Engineers and firms may individually refuse to bid for engineering services.
2. Clients are not required to seek bids for engineering services.
3. Federal, state, and local laws governing procedures to procure engineering services are not affected, and remain in full force and effect.
4. State societies and local chapters are free to actively and aggressively seek legislation for professional selection and negotiation procedures by public agencies.
5. State registration board rules of professional conduct, including rules prohibiting competitive bidding for engineering services, are not affected and remain in full force and effect. State registration boards with authority to adopt rules of professional conduct may adopt rules governing procedures to obtain engineering services.
6. As noted by the Supreme Court, "nothing in the judgment prevents NSPE and its members from attempting to influence governmental action. . . ."

*Note:* In regard to the question of application of the Code to corporations vis-a-vis real persons, business form or type should not negate nor influence conformance of individuals to the Code. The Code deals with professional services, which services must be performed by real persons. Real persons in turn establish and implement policies within business structures. The Code is clearly written to apply to the Engineer and it is incumbent on a member of NSPE to endeavor to live up to its provisions. This applies to all pertinent sections of the Code.

NSPE Publication No. 1102 as revised, July 1981 [used with permission of N.S.P.E.]

### EXERCISES

4.1. Summarize the goals of professional codes of ethics.
4.2. Summarize the limitations of professional codes of ethics.
4.3. Obtain a copy of the code of ethics for a professional society in your chosen

academic major and evaluate the human value basis that underlies each section of the code.

**4.4.** Formulate a code of ethics for student conduct in an academic community. What human values are emphasized? How would cheating on an exam violate the code? How would falsifying lab data violate the code?

**4.5.** For the NSPE Code of Ethics, identify the parts of the code that suggest that there are ethical obligations to (a) the individual engineer, (b) the firm or employer, (c) the client, (d) society, and (e) the profession.

**4.6.** Discuss how an action can be legal but still unethical. Illustrate with examples.

**4.7.** Consider the following two cases: (1) A high school math teacher who has no background in English literature is assigned to teach a one-semester course in English literature. (2) A teaching assistant who has a B.S. in mathematics but no prior teaching experience is assigned to teach as a recitation instructor for a college freshman calculus class. Discuss the value issues involved. What is the likely outcome of this practice? Discuss the applicability of Rule of Practice 2 of the NSPE Code of Ethics.

**4.8.** An engineering firm finds that a contract it has signed requires that it design a small flood control dam. The firm realizes that it does not have an engineer with the specific design experience, and the budget for the contract does not include sufficient money to hire someone with expertise. The design of the dam is assigned to the engineer whose experience most nearly compares with the experience needed to design a dam. Discuss the values involved. What is the likely outcome of this practice? Discuss the applicability of Rule of Practice 2 of the NSPE Code of Ethics.

**4.9.** A city councilman receives a case of expensive scotch for Christmas from a cable TV firm that is involved in bidding on the rights to run the cable TV franchise in the city. What are his alternative courses of action? If he decides to keep the scotch, would he be violating the spirit of Rule of Practice 4 of the NSPE Code of Ethics? Discuss the case.

**4.10.** An engineer who works for a local government is responsible for evaluating proposals submitted by engineering firms. After evaluating the proposals, she makes recommendations to the city council on who should be awarded a contract. One engineering firm offers box seat tickets to the engineer for ten games of the local major league baseball team. What value issues are involved in this case? What actions could the engineer take? If she accepts the tickets, would she be violating Rule of Practice 4 of the NSPE Code of Ethics? Discuss the case.

**4.11.** Evaluate the value basis of Professional Obligations 1 and 10 of the NSPE Code of Ethics.

**4.12.** To what extent does Professional Obligation 11 of the NSPE Code of Ethics obligate engineering firms to provide engineers employed by the firm with time off to obtain advanced degrees and compensation for tuition, books, and fees?

**4.13.** Discuss how padding a resume that is used for obtaining employment is a violation of a code of ethics. Identify specific elements of the NSPE code that would apply. Padding here means to lengthen the resume with extraneous material. What elements of the code would be violated if inaccurate material were included on the resume?

4.14. A college senior accepts an all-expenses-paid trip to a city in another state to interview a firm for employment upon graduation. The student accepts the travel compensation knowing that he or she will not accept a job even if it is offered. Would this be a violation of the NSPE Code of Ethics? If so, identify specific elements of the code that apply.

4.15. An employer instructs an engineer in the firm to charge his time to one project when, in fact, the engineer is working on another project for which the budget has been expended. What sections of the NSPE Code of Ethics does this violate? What human values are brought into question? What are the engineer's alternative courses of action?

4.16. Rationalization is the act of falsifying the outcome of one's own actions so that one has no regret for the actions. Explain the irrationality of the following rationalization provided by an engineer who has just made a kickback:

> I made a business decision to make the kickback. No one was hurt. The public got the project completed, and the job enabled me to keep from laying off some of my employees.

4.17. Provide an excuse that someone who rigged a bid might use as rationalization. Discuss the compromise of values that takes place when someone rationalizes an unethical action.

4.18. The following excuse is provided by a student who cheated on an examination:

> I know that many other people have cheated on exams, so by cheating, I am only bringing my grade up to what it would be if the other people had not cheated.

Explain the irrationality of this rationalization and discuss the compromise of values that the student has made.

# 5

# History, Technology, and Professional Values

*Richard H. McCuen*

## INTRODUCTION

Chapter 2 provided a general introduction to human values and briefly discussed sources of personal values; Chapter 3 dealt with the impact of technology on society and the role of engineers and scientists in shaping technological change; and Chapter 4 discussed the importance of values in professional practice and the codes of ethics that reflect these professional values. This chapter will bring together these points and will show how technology and past cultures have shaped professional practice as we know it now. To accomplish this objective, we will draw an analogy between the factors that influence the development of personal value systems and the forces that have shaped professional values.

To put this in perspective, we suggest that historical roots are to the profession's value system as genetic factors are to the individual's value system; similarly, society affects the profession's value system in much the same way as environmental factors (i.e., experiences in life) influence an individual's value system. Although the emphasis in this chapter is on the historical aspects of technological growth, some thoughts on the nature-nurture debate may be in order. It is hoped that an understanding of the evolutionary process of professional value systems will provide the basis for sensitizing students of engineering and science to their societal obligations.

## THE NATURE-NURTURE CONTROVERSY

Developmental psychobiologists have given considerable attention to the role of heredity and environmental factors in shaping human value systems. Some suggest that behavior is primarily controlled by genetics; others argue that the experiences of life determine behavior. This debate is referred to as the nature-nurture controversy. Heredity plays an important part in human development, not the least of which is to place a limit on the value capacity of an individual. Primary value sensations, such as pain and hunger, are the primary determinants of the fundamental human values; secondary human values—including the moral, social, and ethical principles of an individual—appear to be the result of both genetic factors and environmental conditioning experiences. An individual's maturation process, and thus his or her value system, is also shaped by various aspects of the environment. Bremer (1971) has identified the primary environmentally related value input sources of past American generations as the agricultural society, family, town and community, religion, and education. Bremer further hypothesizes that the values of the business community of today are becoming society's values. The effect of the various value input sources varies from person to person; whereas a particular educational experience may have a significant impact on the values of one individual, another individual may be more influenced by a religious affiliation. There is also strong evidence that television, which may be viewed as an appendage of business, has a significant impact on the values of an individual and, thus, on our society (Rubinstein, 1978). Although heredity most likely determines the basic patterns of human value development, the genetic determinants only find expression in interaction with various aspects of the environment (Levine, 1960).

Of specific interest here are the value systems of professional engineers and scientists. Engineers and scientists have been accused of being insensitive to the social concerns of society, and studies have suggested that engineers are indifferent to public affairs (Florman, 1976). Garfoot and Simon (1963) measured the relative prominence of six basic interests or values—theoretical, economic, aesthetic, social, political, and religious—and concluded that theoretical and economic values were the most prominent values of professional engineers, while aesthetic and social values were the least prominent. Are these value characteristics the result of hereditary factors, or have they resulted from environmental influences?

Recognizing the dominant role of engineers in a technological society, one would hope that professional engineers would be highly sensitive to the social concerns of society. If the results of the study by Garfoot and Simon (1963) are true, then there is an apparent need to sensitize engineers to their societal obligations; this is the intent of the humanities requirements in engineering education programs. As any educator will attest, the courses that satisfy accreditation requirements often contain very little material that will increase engineering and science students' sensitivity to social concerns. However, we cannot place the blame totally on a technically oriented education. As Florman (1976) has indicated, "Engineering does not create this sort of person. It is this sort of person who is choosing engineering." Engineering and science students are usually given considerable latitude in selecting courses to fulfill the general education requirement, and the courses selected often lack the potential to humanize the student. The results of a study by McCuen (1979) indicate that one-third of engineering graduates are not sufficiently sensitive to human welfare in making engineering decisions. If a technically oriented education is going to have a positive influence on the social sensitivity of students of engineering and science, it is necessary to identify the responsible factors and make appropriate modifications within the curriculum. If environmental factors (i.e., education) can shape professional value sensitivities, then courses that can affect the value systems of future professionals must be included as part of the curriculum.

## GENETIC AND ENVIRONMENTAL VALUE INPUT SOURCES

It must be emphasized at the outset that it is not presently possible to quantify the relative importance of genetic and environmental contributions to the formation of value systems. The nature-nurture controversy, which has its roots in the work of Darwin, has had a significant impact on American culture (Cravens, 1977). However, there is little agreement on the effect of evolution on human value systems. Some have argued that human value systems, if derived solely from evolutionary processes, would be highly immoral because of the emphasis on such qualities as ruthlessness and brute force. Others, such as Julian Huxley, have argued that evolutionary processes are the only way that human values such as knowledge and selfless morality could have survived under the diverse economic and political systems man has created. The Social Darwinists and the new evolutionists, who based their ideas on experimental science, have significantly influenced the shaping of moral development theories.

Piaget (1948) and Kohlberg (1976) have demonstrated that individuals progress through several stages of moral development. Kohlberg (1973) has shown that humans are basically egoistic in their early years. This may be the result of the evolutionary process, of social organization, which has required thousands of years and has pitted man against a hostile environment. The quest for survival may have created a genetically aggressive personality. Recognizing that environmental factors can modify the behavior of humans, it is reasonable that individuals would progress through stages of moral growth such as those defined by Piaget and Kohlberg. The moral growth of any one individual will depend on both genetically defined moral capacity and the environmental factors to which he or she is subjected.

Researchers in the behavioral sciences have proposed a number of conceptualizations for the development of a value system. Thornburg (1973) indicates that value development takes place in five stages: childhood, preadolescence, adolescence, young adulthood, and adulthood. The primary influences of value development in these stages are parents, parents and peers, peers, peers and society, and society, respectively. During childhood, there is a very consistent pattern between behavior and values because the locus of the individual's initial value development is within the family. The association between behavior and values is similarly consistent in adulthood, but society is the primary influence at that stage. Adolescence is the period of greatest inconsistency between values and behavior. According to Thornburg (1973), the following factors influence the trend toward inconsistency: (1) the family as an influential unit is severely challenged; (2) the preadolescent is increasingly concerned about the socialization process in school; (3) peers take on an increasingly important role in behavior; and (4) growth and development patterns cause preadolescents to begin taking on a new view of self. During the height of inconsistency between behavior and values, the adolescent is attempting to free himself from parental values and to begin the development of values that he wants to use in defining his behavior. During young adulthood, social integration becomes more important and society has a greater influence on value development; during this period, the correspondence between values and behavior is characterized by greater consistency. Although it is very difficult to place these five groups into age brackets, Thornburg uses the following divisions: childhood (8 years and under); preadolescence (9 to 13); adolescence (14 to 19); young adulthood (20 to 26); and adulthood (27 and older). Thornburg also indicates that those who enter college directly from high school may extend the period of behavior inconsistency because of the dominance of peer influence in college life.

The reason for this discussion of values and behavior as a function of developmental stage is that it has a measure of relevancy to professional value development. A question that most students have about their future life in their chosen profession is, "What will it be like?" Such a broad question is beyond the scope of this book. However, it may be worthwhile to consider briefly the values many young professionals find important, keeping in mind that values affect behavior and that behavior affects advancement and happiness in one's career. The profession needs young engineers and scientists who value knowledge, loyalty, honesty, diligence, efficiency, responsibility, performance, and orderliness. These are some of the values that society (i.e., the professional community) will impress upon young engineers and scientists as important. In Thornburg's pattern, the young engineer or scientist will attempt to incorporate these values into his or her value system in order to adjust socially and professionally. The ease with which one adjusts to these value requirements depends in part on the value base one develops during college. A student should not believe that honesty and orderliness may be important after college but that plagiarism and sloppy homework are acceptable during college. Employers in engineering and science place high value on diligence. A student who is late for class or consistently turns in homework late will have greater difficulty adjusting to professional life than a more diligent student. Thus, it is important to view college life as part of one's professional career, not as something entirely separate. Just as one is developing technical skills in design courses during college, one should also be developing value skills. An understanding of value issues is just as important as an understanding of the physical laws.

According to Thornburg's system, the student who has just finished high school falls in the adolescent category. Although readers who fit into this age category may resent being classed as socially adolescent, they should at least recognize that they will have to refine their value system while they become technically knowledgeable during their four years of college. That is a major purpose of this book. General education courses, if properly selected, can help develop the value base that will be important in professional practice. It is not sufficient to develop just the technical aspects of professional life. It is also necessary to advance from the adolescent behavior stage to the young adulthood stage.


## TECHNOLOGY AS A VALUE SOURCE

As noted earlier, Bremer (1971) has identified five traditional value input sources that are environmental in nature: the agricultural society, family, town and community, religion, and education. The traditional mix of these input sources was time- and space-dependent. However, the increased development of a technologically oriented culture, with its increased mobility and affluence, has altered the impact of each of these value input sources. Although Bremer contends that it is the influence of business that has altered the source of values, a reasonably good argument could be made that technology has been partially responsible. There appears to be a better correlation between technological changes and value changes than between changes in business practices and value changes; but this is largely a subjective observation. One might reasonably argue that technology currently has a significant influence on the formation of value systems. If engineers and scientists are largely responsible for much of technology, then it is not unreasonable to conclude that they may have a significant influence on the evolutionary path of human value systems. But it is not just technology that influences behavioral development; there are other forces.

Even though technological advances have helped overcome human suffering, technology has been blamed for many social problems. Because of the primary role that engineers and scientists have played in the growth of technology, they are frequently criticized for their role and blamed for many of the ills that have resulted from technological advances. But are technologists the force responsible for the evil side of technology? A solid case can be made that the responsibility must be shared by many elements of society, including scientists and engineers, courts and judges, politicians and governmental institutions, economists and managers, and, not least, the public. For those who are dissatisfied with the results of technological growth, it is foolish to blame some impersonal, uncontrollable force called technology rather than the values and social structure that are responsible for the past allocation of both human and material resources (Florman, 1976).

## HISTORY AND SOCIETY: THE DETERMINANTS
## OF A PROFESSION'S VALUE SYSTEM

Heredity is believed to be an important determinant of an individual's value system. Similarly, history serves as the corresponding determinant in the formation of a profession's value system. Just as heredity is believed to limit an individual's value capacity, history in the form of social choices has a significant limiting effect on the value capacity of a profession. We will show here that historical forces have had a significant impact on the value system of the engineering and science professions.

Just as environmental factors interact with the genetic determinants to mold an individual's value system, society interacts with historical determinants to mold the value system of a profession. Corresponding to an individual's value input sources, societal factors that have been influential in shaping the value system of the engineering and science professions include (1) the expanding role of government in establishing public policies that control technological growth; (2) the need for organizational changes that separate engineers and scientists from the moral consequences of their work; and (3) the expanding gap between technological growth and the public's understanding of it.

Historical events and the social choices made in past years influence the state of professional values and influence engineering practice today. We will use three examples to illustrate the effects of events and social choices of the past: (1) Francis Bacon, as an example of a "scientist" around the time of the birth of modern science; (2) the loss of life due to explosions of steam engines, as an example that shows the concern of the technologists of the early nineteenth century for human welfare; and (3) resource policy and the social forces that shaped it, as an example of the role of engineers and scientists of past generations in balancing economic growth and human welfare.

### The Birth of Modern Science

Francis Bacon (1561-1626) and Rene Descartes (1596-1650) were two major figures who stood at the turning point between medieval and modern science. Bacon has received more recognition for his role because he preceded Descartes and because the medieval system of thought was less entrenched in England than in France (Bernal, 1971). The scientific climate that existed prior to the sixteenth century had a significant impact on the advancement of science and on the relationship between science and human values; thus, it is of interest to examine the scientific climate that existed prior to Bacon.

*The pre-Bacon scientific climate.* The birth of Christianity represented a drastic change in value input sources. Paganism was replaced by a value system that put man above nature (White, 1967). However, an element of mythology remained. Instead of worshipping the sun, fire, and pagan gods, belief in a single god became the source of values. In addition, saints identified by religious leaders influenced the behavior of individuals.

The scientific period before Bacon was dominated by the Humanists and by Renaissance "Platonists," who interpreted natural science so that it maintained a proper harmony with the revealed dogmas of Christianity; that is, they served as defenders of past tradition rather than as initiators of empirical scientific research. During the fifteenth century, the literary and artistic efforts that were characteristic of the Renaissance absorbed a considerable portion of the time of the best thinkers; the scientific investigation of nature received scant attention. Even into the sixteenth century, the Humanists attempted to suppress development of the scientific method; they gained support by questioning the value of studies of natural science. Erasmus (1466?-1536), like Petrarch (1304-1374) and Boccaccio (1313-1375) before him, implied that it was impossible to understand the natural world through empirical science.

The only writings in the fifteenth century that emphasized the importance of experience and experimental observation were the early works of Leonardo da Vinci (1452-1519); however, although he recognized its value, he did not provide any systematic discussion of the scientific method. But Leonardo's work is evidence that he had a good understanding of the scientific method. Not until the time of Galileo, however, did the scientific method become systematized.

The scientific climate of this period is aptly illustrated by developments in astronomy. Astronomers before the sixteenth century did not believe that empirical evidence was necessary to formulate or prove a theory, and they believed that failure to fit observed measurements was not sufficient reason to reject a theory. Ptolemy (second century A.D.) argued that the simplest plausible theory was the most acceptable; the Ptolemaic system was accepted by many until the fifteenth century. Copernicus (1473-1543) was one of the first to require agreement between a theory and observed phenomena.

The problem of scientific advancement was compounded because of theological constraints. Even Copernicus was censured by the Holy Congregation of the Index because he presented his theory as a physical reality, rather than just a mathematical hypothesis. The movement of celestial bodies was considered to be a theological phenomena, and theologians did not believe that astronomers were justified in examining theological phenomena. As a further constraint, failure to fit the astronomical teachings of the Sacred Scripture was considered sufficient grounds for rejecting a theory.

Although it is important to understand the scientific climate that existed before Bacon and Descartes and its effect on the development of the scientific method, one must realize that the scientific climate also influenced both the evolution of professional values and the relationship between technological growth and human values. The theological constraints directed scientific theories away from the physical world; this limited the ability of science to serve society and encouraged a separation of scientific advancement and professional values. It was an atmosphere that limited the influence of religion as a value input source to professional development. It is recognized that the theological constraints limited scientific investigation; however, it must be emphasized that they also detracted from the professional nature of scientific investigation and thus limited the growth of professional values. Science could not develop as a means of serving human welfare; thus, it served only to tantalize the intellect of a few. This also limited technological growth. It was necessary to overcome this climate before scientific inquiry could proceed properly and before professional values could evolve.

*Francis Bacon and the scientific method.* Francis Bacon and others of his era sensed a change in the existing attitudes toward science and seized the opportunity to refine the methodology by which science advanced. Because of his interest in both scientific inquiry and philosophy, he was quite aware of the link between science and human values. Bacon set much of human knowledge on a new path by (1) freeing science from learning and from the practices and privileges of the learned; (2) separating truth that is humanly discoverable from the dogmas of revealed theology; and (3) propounding a philosophy that is to be achieved by a new sort of scientific investigation, a "modern" interpretation of nature, and the identification of metaphysics with a generalized natural science based on natural history (Anderson, 1971). Bacon thus encouraged science to follow a path of observational and experimental investigation and to disassociate itself from magisterial learning.

Bacon's views on knowledge were in direct opposition to the prevailing Aristotelian philosophy. The key to Bacon's doctrine was his emphasis on inductive investigation, which he detailed in the *Novum organum,* dated 1620. Inductive investigations begin with particulars and proceed to definition; Bacon's philosophy thus emphasized the value of experimental investigation and the identification of truth from the data obtained from observation.

Bacon's inductive approach to scientific investigation was an important factor in technological progress, and his contribution to human welfare is just as important. Bacon preached the doctrine that the true and lawful end of the sciences is that human life be enriched by new discoveries. That is, education must be utility oriented, with the aim of relieving the burdens of life. This new philosophy had a profound impact on society and was used as a model for guidance by many reformers under Cromwell and Charles. It even changed the image of Christ, who came to be regarded as an experimenter who proved himself not by theories but by works (Anderson, 1971). This in itself represents a significant change in the relationship between science and religion, which contributed to the change in attitude about science and human welfare.

### The Steam Engine and Professional Values

The growth of the steam engine provides a historical example of the concern of engineering groups with the social impact of their technology. The steam engine played a significant role in the expansion of the United States during the early nineteenth century. However, the high-pressure, noncondensive steam engine turned out to be an example of uncontrolled technology because of the significant number of fatalities that resulted from boiler explosions. Burke (1966) has detailed the impact of this problem on federal power. In the early 1800s, the city council of Philadelphia appears to have been the first legislative body in the United States to recognize the problem and initiate an investigation. A group of engineers recognized the importance of experimental observation and recommended initial testing and regular proof tests to ensure the safety of all boilers. In June 1830 the Franklin Institute of Philadelphia empowered a committee to conduct experimental investigations to obtain the knowledge necessary to formulate satisfactory regulatory legislation. In addition to following the scientific method that evolved during Bacon's era, the committee also recognized the need to consider public safety; that is, the group believed that public safety should not be endangered by private negligence. This concern reflected Bacon's philosophical doctrine that scientific advancement must reflect upon human values.

Unfortunately, it wasn't until the mid-nineteenth century that engineers were successful in getting legislators to enact legislation that reflected their concern for public safety. It took the engineers and scientists almost fifty years to effect significant changes in public policy. The professional committees emphasized the values of life, security, and public health and safety, but they failed to appreciate the competing value—freedom—which was embedded in the economic system of the early nineteenth century. Just as the engineers and scientists of the late twentieth century have difficulty influencing public policy, the same difficulties limited their effectiveness 150 years ago.

### Resource Policy and the Public Interest

The development of resource policy in the United States is another example of the engineering profession using both Bacon's scientific method and his concern for the public interest. John Wesley Powell is credited with being a pioneer in the development of federal science (Wengert, 1955). At a meeting of the Geological Society of America during the last decade of the nineteenth century, Powell identified two stages in development: a "preliminary" experimental or preparatory stage, and the final or effecting stage. During the first stage, methods are devised, experiments are conducted, scientific apparatus is invented and subjected to trial, and the plan for the work is formulated. During the second stage, the methods and apparatus are employed practically and the plans are carried out. Powell stated: "It is the highest function of systemized knowledge to promote human welfare, . . . the first stage represents the seed-time, the second the harvest-time of science" (Rabbitt, 1969). It is especially noteworthy that this philosophy directly parallels Bacon's two-phased philosophy, with emphasis on human welfare in the second phase. John Wesley Powell applied this philosophy throughout his career as an engineer and statesman. It represented the concern for human welfare that was characteristic of the engineers of his time. Powell's major emphasis was on the use of his observations in the development of public policy that would ensure progress for the human race.

Unfortunately, Powell was dismissed from his post as secretary of the interior in the late nineteenth century in spite of his logical program formulation for national resource policy (Rabbitt, 1969). This parallels the frustration of the engineers investigating the steam boiler explosions in the earlier part of the nineteenth century. Powell failed to appreciate the expansionary forces that existed in the late nineteenth century, and he failed to understand the use of political power and the potential of professional societies to affect public opinion and public policy. It wasn't until many of his followers, such as Gifford Pinchot, became influential in the political process that many of Powell's recommendations on land policy and the role of government in science were institutionalized.

### History as an Evolutionary Force in Professional Value Development

The technological revolution, which had substantial societal influence in the sixteenth and seventeenth centuries, had an effect on human value input sources that rivaled the effect of the birth of Christianity. Individuals no longer prayed for rain; they built dams to store water for irrigation. They no longer prayed for recovery from disease; they used medical research to find a cure. Prayer was still important, but it was used only after scientific inquiry could not discover a cure for the sickness or there was no water left in the dam for irrigation. Thus, the technological society replaced a value system that was almost entirely faith oriented with one that was "human expert" oriented; that is, society went from a faith-oriented value system to one in which man participated in the control of events.

The change in value input sources that was associated with the technological society immediately following Bacon reflected the human responsibility for the control of events. The responsibility that was placed on the technologist created a need for a human value system that was more oriented toward society, and a central element of Bacon's philosophy was that the technologist had such a responsibility.

It is apparent that the philosophy of Francis Bacon had a significant impact on the development of both science and human values. Bacon believed that scientific advancement must have proper respect for human values. This attitude continued in those involved in technological development, including engineers in the United States. In the early stages of technological growth in the United States, engineers adhered to a doctrine that recognized the relationship between scientific advancement (i.e., technological growth) and human welfare. However, the laissez-faire economic philosophy made it difficult for engineers to get approval for public policies that provided the proper balance between technological growth and human welfare. For example, policies that were designed to limit pressures in steam engines were viewed as constraints on free enterprise. Similarly, policies dealing with the conservation of resources and constraints on land use were viewed as constraints on economic expansion, rather than as tools for incorporating human values into technological growth. These examples suggest that early attempts by engineers to incorporate human values into technological decision making were frustrated by other forces. The examples also illustrate that the roots of professional value development lie partly in historical events.

Historical events may have had a significant impact on the engineering profession's role in public policy. As we have indicated, engineers tend to avoid involvement in the formulation of public policy. This is significant because the values of a society are reflected in its public policy (Rosenberg, 1979). In the early period of technological development in the United States, engineers actively participated in efforts to influence public policy; the steam engine and resource policy cases are prime examples. In both cases, the efforts of the engineers were ignored or, at best, were given minimal consideration. One can only speculate whether or not these historical frustrations influenced the apathy of present-day engineers and scientists toward public policy formulation. Given the importance of heredity on the value system of an individual, however, one must acknowledge the potential impact of historical forces on the values of a profession.

Although Bacon's philosophy was certainly valid for the role technology played at that time, there is some question whether it is adequate for the extent and type of technology that exists today. Bacon's philosophy needs to be adapted for the current state of technology. Many believe that there is a moral crisis in both the public and the professional domains. The "me generation" appears to overemphasize the individual and place less emphasis on the community. If one uses the same value system for making professional decisions that is used in making personal decisions, is there any reason to believe that the value input sources of the "me generation" are not applied in professional value judgments? Does the professional in the current technological state give more weight to egoistic concerns than to the concerns of the firm and the profession? If one believes that a moral crisis exists in society, then there is also a basis for believing that there should be an increased concern about professional values. The moral crisis that apparently exists in society is especially critical because individuals affect the lives of others who are beyond their circle of family, friends, and neighbors; this creates a value attitude of indifference toward those outside this closed circle. There is some concern by the public that this attitude of indifference is carried over to the individuals who are responsible for technological advances—namely, engineers and scientists. After all, technologies transcend national borders and cultures; thus, technologists are far removed from the effects of their technology. Such a situation offers the opportunity for increased egoistic value decision making by engineers and scientists. As we recognize the increased involvement of engineers and scientists in technological decision making, there is clearly a need for them to be sensitized to the social effects of their work. It is imperative that they recognize both the philosophy initiated by Bacon and the increased need to be sensitive to the societal impacts of new technologies.

## CONCLUSIONS

The history of science during the critical period of Francis Bacon's era was not the work of one man alone. Yet a failure to appreciate the contributions to the advancement of science by Bacon and his contemporaries limits one's ability to appreciate the effects of engineering, science, and technology in the present scientific period. Although Bacon's abilities as a philosopher and scientist are widely recognized and greatly respected, it is doubtful that the contributions of him and others like him would have been as significant to the advancement of scientific thought if it had not been for their ability to overcome the theological and cultural constraints that existed at the time. These forces had contributed to the suppression of scientific advancement for almost a millennium prior to Bacon's time. Scientific advancement proceeds at a much more rapid pace today, but it would not do so if it were necessary to reverse the entire framework of science, as was necessary for Bacon and his contemporaries. It is especially noteworthy that the progress in both human values and scientific methods occurred almost simultaneously; this reflects the degree to which philosophers participated in the advancement of the scientific method and their realization that science could have a significant impact on human welfare. One might reasonably argue that philosophers need to participate more actively in the technological growth of the last part of the twentieth century. Also, it suggests that the engineering and science professions should make a greater effort to ensure that engineering and science education includes a significant effort toward humanizing the engineering student; this will encourage optimum development of the profession's value system.

## EXERCISES

5.1. Identify courses in your undergraduate course catalog that discuss technology and values.

5.2. Do you agree with Bremer (1971) that television and business have a greater impact on children's values than the value input sources of past generations (i.e., religion, community, farm life, etc.)? Discuss and give examples. Do you believe that this is detrimental to the future of our country? Explain.

5.3. Discuss three value issues associated with space exploration. In each case, identify the values in conflict and your assessment of the best solution.

5.4. Technology creates value conflicts by increasing our options. Nuclear power was not an issue for past generations; now there are those who favor it and those who oppose it. It offers a cheap source of energy, which permits people to use the money saved to express their *freedom* and *pleasure*. Others are concerned with *public health and safety*. Discuss the issue from the standpoint of technology and values.

5.5. Developing countries are concerned that their brightest citizens are emigrating to the more developed countries, such as the United States. This has been referred to as the "brain drain." Discuss the issue from the standpoint of technology and values.

5.6. The assembly line was criticized for its effect on jobs and work quality. Discuss why people were not able to predict that the positive effects would far outweigh the negative effects.

5.7. Develop a "Hippocratic Oath" for those who are developing new technologies.

5.8. Some have argued that science should be "value-free" and that scientists should not get involved in discussions of value issues. They argue that scientists should address the technical issues and that elected legislators and courts should solve the value conflicts. Do you agree or disagree, and why?

5.9. Risk is a major factor in value conflicts. Explain the social responsibilities of engineers and scientists in assessing the risk of new technologies.

5.10. Many people consider population growth to be a major global problem for the future (if it is not already). Discuss types of new technologies that would be most helpful in overcoming the problems associated with the population explosion. What ill effects might accompany these new technologies?

5.11. Robotics is a new technology that is receiving both praise and criticism because of its potential impact on society. Evaluate the benefits and evils of robotics from a value standpoint, and discuss the role that engineers and scientists could play to reduce the negative impacts of this new technology.

5.12. Guns are an example of a technology that is widely criticized. Discuss the benefits and evils of guns from a value standpoint.

5.13. Television is an example of a technology that has drastically changed life in America. From a value standpoint, discuss the benefits and evils of television.

**6**

# History and Leadership

*Rosemarie N. Thomas*

## INTRODUCTION

When the average student thinks of history, he or she usually thinks of courses that involve memorizing facts—names, dates, or places. But a study of history is more than just a review of the timetable of recorded events. Given that the historical record is incomplete, a part of the study of history should involve developing an appreciation for a culture when only a few facts are present. Studying history requires a little bit of detective work and a little bit of imagination. The student of history must recognize the biases of historians and must be sufficiently creative to fill in the gaps where events have not been recorded. Thus, historical study is not just learning the order of events; it requires the ability to synthesize and interpret events. The need to synthesize is also important to the engineer or scientist, and the ability to synthesize is just one characteristic that can be enhanced through a study of history.

A study of history can also develop other skills; it can educate and broaden the student by (1) developing an appreciation and understanding of other cultures, both past and present; (2) showing the causes of the rise and decline of societies; (3) exploring the role of political, economic, and social structures in past cultures; (4) providing examples of the role of engineering, science, and technology in changing world events; and (5) demonstrating the importance of leadership in world events.

Recognizing the importance of leadership to the success and happiness of those in technical professions, this chapter is intended to show that even a limited study of history can enhance one's leadership skills. By observing how historical figures served their societies, one can recognize the important ingredients of leadership: confidence, communication, and creativity. Leadership skills are important to the individual as well as to the professional in meeting his or her social responsibilities. Thus, showing how a study of history can enhance one's ability to be a leader with imagination and values is one step in fulfilling the objective of studying history as part of a general education program—namely, to develop a personal philosophy that is based on the ingredients of leadership. This is not to imply that the other skills that can be enhanced through a study of history are not important, but only that, with limited space, we will discuss leadership because it is especially important, both personally and professionally.

## LEADERSHIP

Leadership could be defined as the ability to direct the activities of others. Yet leadership is more than just effectively managing others' conduct. A true leader is one who establishes an environment that provides guidance in both physical activities and values. As noted in *In Search of Excellence* (Peters and Waterman, 1982), a leader instills values and produces a culture that survives even after the leader has left the organization (or society). Very often, the leader will create an atmosphere of excellence that survives by way of myths, rather than through written rules; the myths inspire the members of the culture when the leader is not present.

Peters and Waterman characterize the qualities of a leader as those of a pathfinder, a decision maker, and an implementer. Intuition and idea generation are important traits of the pathfinder, and these require a creative attitude. The decision maker organizes activities and has good analytical skills. The implementer works well with others and can motivate others to action; organization and motivation require confidence and the ability to communicate. The stereotyped personality of the engineer or scientist enables him or her to function easily in the role of decision maker. To be a true leader in society, however, one should have all three qualities—that of the pathfinder, the decision maker, and the implementer. Those who develop a capacity for all three roles are best able to fulfill their responsibilities to their families, professions, and society.

Engineers and scientists are recognized both for their specialized knowledge and skills and for their organizational and analytical abilities; these characteristics make them good decision makers. To be true leaders, however, those in technology need to develop further the talents of the pathfinder and implementer. Specifically, they need to develop a broader perspective, one that is value oriented and complements the organizational and analytical skills of the decision maker. In a good working atmosphere, the members of the organization work toward excellence. The implementer understands the importance of people to the activities of the organization. Therefore, to develop this element of leadership potential, the individual must understand the importance of motivating others in the organization. Leaders must also be goal oriented. The technical solution provided by the decision maker may not reach its full potential to serve society if the individual does not have the ability to sell the solution to those who will use it; this requires the skills and the abilities of the implementer.

## LEADERS AND LEADERSHIP IN HISTORY

A study of any historical period usually focuses on, among many other things, the leaders of that period. One could easily argue that leaders shape historical events. One could argue just as easily that the reverse is true—that historical conditions create the need for a leader. In any case, leaders obviously play an important role in history. Not everyone possesses the aforementioned qualities of leadership, but an individual can develop these qualities. To do so, however, one must first understand them and their applications. An obvious way to gain this knowledge is to examine the qualities of successful leaders in history. As the following discussion will illustrate, a study of leaders and their roles in history reveals an important quality needed by all leaders: an awareness of one's responsibility to society. We will now examine a potpourri of some famous and some not-so-famous leaders to see how they displayed leadership qualities while fulfilling what they saw as their duty to society.

### Washington A. Roebling

To demonstrate that engineers can be leaders and that their leadership can be recognized, we begin with Washington A. Roebling, a civil engineer. When John A. Roebling died as a result of an accident while doing the final surveys for the Brooklyn Bridge, which he had designed, his son, Washington, took over construction of the bridge. The design of the suspension bridge, using steel cables and underwater concrete foundations, represented a breakthrough in bridge architecture. Upon its completion in May 1883, it was the longest bridge in the world and the only suspension bridge to employ steel cables. Because the design contained such new concepts, however, few engineers were qualified to ensure that the completed bridge would be safe and durable. Washington Roebling realized his responsibility to follow through on his father's design and to utilize his specialized knowledge to supervise the construction of the Brooklyn Bridge.

Even after suffering an accident that left him bedridden, Washington continued to supervise the construction from his bed, using a telescope to view the progress. His "pathfinder" attitude enabled him to create an atmosphere of excellence even though he could not be at the site. His "decision maker" abilities were necessary to organize the construction of a structure based on a new technology. His leadership in this project exemplified an important "implementer" quality—perseverance. He was determined to see the construction completed correctly.

On May 24, 1983, the hundredth anniversary of the completion of the Brooklyn Bridge was celebrated; in that time, no major repairs had been required on the bridge. Thus, the leadership of Washington A. Roebling resulted in an engineering project that has continued to serve society for over 100 years; this service is especially noteworthy because of its classic design and perfect record with respect to public safety.

### Joan of Arc

Joan of Arc (1412-1431) is considered by some historians to be one of the great leaders of the fifteenth century. At a time when France was divided and without a king and the English were threatening to defeat the entire nation, she revived the courage of the French people. Claiming to be acting out of divine guidance, Joan raised an army and fought occupying forces of England. She brought Charles VII, the rightful heir to the French throne, to Reims where he could be crowned. Her complete faith in Charles VII as king of France and her courage in fighting the English served to unite the French people as a nation.

Joan was eventually captured and executed, but even as a martyr, she continued to be an inspiration to her compatriots. In life, she had succeeded in establishing an attitude that continued to provide guidance after her death. Her heroism and leadership seem all the more remarkable when we consider that she was a woman, just a teenager, in a society where women and youth were viewed as inferior. Her leadership qualities were mobilized through the one quality that she most exemplified—her ability to overcome conventional prejudices and restraints and to set her own goals and achieve them.

Her life epitomized the importance of pathfinder traits to leadership. She inspired, she organized, and she instilled an attitude based on values (in a sense, life, liberty, and the pursuit of happiness). Whether or not she was led by divine guidance, Joan believed that she had a responsibility to unite France as one nation to save her country from the invading English, and she subordinated herself completely to the task of achieving success. Although success was achieved only after she had been executed, it was, in part, the myth that grew up about her name that inspired the French soldiers to continue on the path that she so influenced.

### Martin Luther

When one thinks of the Reformation, one thinks of the sixteenth-century professor of divinity, Martin Luther (1483-1546). Luther posted his "Ninety-five Theses" in 1517 and then refused to recant. His writings and actions contributed to the Protestant Reformation. Yet it must be recognized that, just as the Reformation would probably not have occurred without Luther, Luther would not have succeeded if the economic, social, and political conditions had not been as they were at the start of the sixteenth century. At the time, the Turks were advancing up the Danube, the Germans were burdened by the economic demands of Rome and were searching for someone who would develop a nationalistic pride, and the people were socially concerned about the materialistic excess of the Catholic church. Luther organized a personal philosophy that appealed to both the German people and the princes. He set forth a set of values that differed from the Catholic church and that appealed to the spiritual beliefs of the people.

Luther served as a pathfinder by establishing a path toward economic and social freedom. He was able to organize and communicate these beliefs, which is the role of the decision maker. His actions served to motivate the German princes and other leaders to implement the religious doctrine that he proposed. By having these characteristics of a leader, Luther was able to succeed in changing the direction of a culture. Martin Luther started a movement by challenging the standards of his day, which grew beyond the boundaries of religion. The birth and growth of Protestant churches contributed to the start of the Renaissance, which brought Europe out of the Dark Ages and into its modern era.

### Martin Luther King, Jr.

Like his namesake, Martin Luther King, Jr., was also a great leader and a religious man. But King's leadership was felt most strongly in the area of social reform; he was America's most influential civil rights leader of the 1950s and 1960s. While studying for his graduate degree, King was strongly impressed by Mahatma Ghandi's use of peaceful demonstrations. This influence led King to introduce the use of civil disobedience into the struggle for civil rights. He turned the fight for equality for blacks into a mass movement, marked by his march on Washington in 1963. More than 250,000 people attended and it was here that King gave his famous, inspirational, "I have a dream" speech.

King opposed all injustices and fought to end poverty for all races. His social awareness and devotion to society defined his life, and his convictions were so strong that he continued to work toward his goals even though he knew his life was in danger. After his assassination, King remained an inspiration to those fighting for equal rights for all people. Of the many leadership qualities he possessed, he most exemplified the motivating power of an implementer. Like all great leaders, Martin Luther King, Jr., effected changes in society that continued to influence and improve American culture long after his death.

### General Douglas E. MacArthur

As a final example of leadership, one cannot ignore the profession in which the need for leadership is most obvious—the military. General Douglas MacArthur is an exemplary role model. His life was devoted to his military career, and he displayed great leadership characteristics throughout that career. He graduated first in his class from West Point in 1903 and gained notoriety in World War I. In 1933, President Herbert Hoover named him chief of staff of the U.S. Army.

MacArthur retired in 1937, but in 1941, at the age of 61, he was recalled to active duty in the Phillipines. It was as supreme commander of the Southwest Pacific area during World War II that he rose to fame. When Japan surrendered, he was named commander of Japan and led that nation back to recovery to become a strong product supplier. MacArthur also commanded the United Nations forces in the Korean War until his dismissal.

Although his life was full of controversy, none can deny that MacArthur was one of the greatest military leaders of the century. He saw his responsibility to his country and to those he defended as allowing democracy a chance to rule over dictatorship. He possessed a mastery over all aspects of his profession, which earned him the loyalty and affection of the soldiers he led. Although MacArthur was obviously a pathfinder, a decision maker, and an implementer, the leadership quality that he demonstrated most vividly was supreme self-confidence. Some argued that it went beyond self-confidence to arrogance, but the fact that his confidence and courage contributed greatly to his success as a military leader is undeniable. General Douglas MacArthur gave leadership to cultures in both the United States and Japan by continuing to provide guidance and affect society after his departure from active duty.

## LEADERSHIP DEVELOPMENT THROUGH A STUDY OF HISTORY

We have taken a specific, but cursory, look at the leadership skills of an engineer, a civilian "freedom fighter," a religious reformer, a social reformer, and a military officer. In spite of the diversity of their societal involvement, they shared a common characteristic—they were leaders. As students of engineering and science, it should be evident that the engineers and scientists of your generation will have to have these same leadership qualities. As the pulse of technology quickens, the need for the developers of new technologies to incorporate values into their growth and use will be even more critical than it is now. Thus, future technologists must be pathfinders. To ensure that the new technologies are applied as intended, future technologists will also have to be implementers. They cannot meet their social responsibilities as decision makers alone.

How can a study of history help develop these qualities, these leadership skills? Since engineers and scientists feel most comfortable working within the framework of the scientific method (often called the systems process by engineers), we will use this framework to answer this important question. For our purposes here, we will assume that the scientific method consists of four steps: problem identification, hypothesis, reality test, and evaluation.

Problem identification here consists solely in recognizing that leadership is important both for individual engineers or scientists personally and for them to fulfill their social responsibility. The problem is that the technical courses in engineering and science programs are usually oriented toward the decision maker element of leadership; they usually do not develop skills related to the pathfinder and implementer elements.

As the second step, we hypothesize here that leadership skills can be learned by evaluating historical leaders and cultures. The third step of the process involves studying the conditions of the culture that prove fertile for change and the characteristics of the individual that enable him or her to use pathfinding, decision making, and implementation skills. The foregoing case studies provided a very cursory look at this reality testing stage, and it appeared to work.

The fourth step, evaluation, is probably the most important. For the individual, this involves evaluating one's own personality and philosophy by comparing oneself to existing leaders. Does one have a social awareness—that is, a sensitivity to the needs of others and a willingness to place the needs of society above personal needs? Is one interested in value issues as well as technical issues? A pathfinder must have these qualities. A decision maker needs to understand how to incorporate values into decisions; the difficulty of this was clearly illustrated in Chapter 2. An implementer must be able to organize and motivate people; that is, the implementer is a "people" person. A study of the leaders of history and a simultaneous self-evaluation is one way of improving your chances of becoming a leader in your chosen profession.

Besides helping society, the development of leadership traits can enhance your personal life as well as your professional life. You will encounter situations daily in which you are required to take a position of leadership to resolve a conflict. Whether it is making a simple decision such as fighting peer pressure to get involved in illegal drugs or acting as a mediator in a family quarrel, the ability to lead will be required of you. Also, the ability to set your own course instead of blindly following a conventional path can lead to greater satisfaction in both your career and your personal life.

Professionally, the benefits are even more obvious. Whether or not you assume a managerial role, leadership abilities will enhance your job performance. Self-confidence allows you to set your own goals and work toward achieving them despite obstacles you may encounter. Many engineering positions involve teamwork, which makes assertiveness an indispensable trait. It is important that individuals in the group combine their talents synergistically to make the whole more powerful than the individual parts. If and when you do enter a supervisory position, as most engineers do, the ability to direct those who work for you is necessary to attain success for yourself, the firm, the client, and society.

## COURSE RECOMMENDATIONS

It is hoped that the material in this chapter will serve as an inspiration for a study of history. We have attempted to show that a study of history can be beneficial to your career. As mentioned earlier, courses on the history of any period will include discussions of many leaders, from which you can seek to understand the personal and social characteristics that made them leaders. A study of a country over many generations can show the effect of leadership on the rise and fall of the power of that country. In addition to characteristics of individuals, leadership within a group or social organization should be studied; for example, a study of group leadership in engineering firms and professional organizations is important from a professional standpoint. Similarly, leadership within the family and within community organizations can be an important topic in a history course that covers group leadership.

It is unlikely that specific history courses will emphasize the leadership aspect, but a wide variety of courses deal directly with leaders. A course on biography in history would probably be most likely to emphasize leadership. A course that details the roles of women in history and their contributions to social, political, and industrial advancement might also illustrate leadership. Courses on the history of groups (e.g., the Jewish people, American Indians, the Aztecs) would discuss leadership in groups and communities. In each of these courses, students should try to extend the material to their personal lives and their concept of professional life; such reflection will enhance their leadership skills. Also, in each course, students should seek to identify specific factors related to the tasks of pathfinder, decision maker, and implementer; such analysis will emphasize the tasks of every element of leadership and the factors that the students should try to develop personally.

## CONCLUSIONS

In his discussion of history, Florman (1968) identified four uses of history: education, inspiration, pleasure, and a sense of our heritage. The emphasis in this chapter has been on the development of leadership. But such an approach is not independent of Florman's four uses. Past mistakes are not repeated when there is good leadership; good leaders have learned from past mistakes, whether they were mistakes of an entire society or mistakes of the management of an engineering firm. In the former case, we are considering the political history of nations; in the latter case, it is the economic history of engineering firms. It is always hoped that the student of history will obtain pleasure from the material and will develop an enthusiasm for learning about the past. Although the history of engineering and technology may be of special interest to the student of engineering and science, other topics in history also have value. A creative student should seek out these connections; after all, that is what education is about.

Given the important role technology plays in the unfolding of history, future technologists should recognize a need and a desire to study history. As part of a liberal arts education, history has much to offer, including helping one develop one's leadership potential. Although this is only one of the many benefits, it is an obviously important one. Technological professions are in great need of leaders, especially with the ever-rising debate over technology's contributions to society. More and more these days, concerned members of society are questioning whether technologists give sufficient consideration to the possibly dangerous repercussions of their inventions. Individuals who develop into leaders as well as engineers or scientists are better able to control the effects of their technological advances and thus make a positive contribution to society.

It is important to note that human values are an important aspect of leadership. One role of a pathfinder is to establish a value base for the group or society that he or she is leading. Washington Roebling certainly displayed values of diligence, perseverance, and responsibility. Joan of Arc recognized the importance of freedom to her society, and Martin Luther King, Jr., recognized the importance of equality to contemporary American culture. It is important to note that value issues were central to the causes of each of these leaders. This is true of all leaders, whether they lead in the fifteenth or the twentieth century, whether they lead nations or professions, whether they lead large international engineering companies or small local companies. Leadership is effective only when it is working from a strong moral position. As Florman (1968) points out, "But where adequate moral goals have been lacking, technological competence has usually been wasted." This applies to engineering firms as well as to societies. Leaders develop the moral goals that provide the atmosphere in which technical ability can flourish. A primary responsibility of a leader in an engineering firm, from the CEO to the company president to the project manager, is to create the moral climate in which the firm's engineers can practice properly.

## EXERCISES

**6.1.** Review the book *In Search of Excellence*. Identify and discuss the characteristics of a pathfinder, a decision maker, and an implementer.

**6.2.** Three elements of leadership were identified: pathfinding, decision making, and implementation. Discuss how the engineering personality (see Chapters 1 and 2) serves as a constraint on each of these elements, and discuss how a strong background in general education can help overcome these personality limitations.

**6.3.** Describe characteristics that would determine whether or not a student was a good leader of a student organization. What types of activities, or lack of such activities, would distinguish the good leaders from the moderate or poor leaders?

**6.4.** If a professional society for engineers or scientists is to provide leadership for the profession, describe the types of activities that would fulfill the tasks of pathfinding, decision making, and implementation.

**6.5.** Assume that you are starting your own company. The company will market a new technology or a service associated with a new technology. You wish to emphasize to all new employees, both professional and technical/service personnel, that your company has high value standards. Discuss what you could do to provide the necessary leadership.

**6.6.** Identify an individual who is currently a leader in your local engineering or science community. Meet with this individual and discuss the importance of leadership and values to the professional engineer or scientist.

**6.7.** Review a brief biography of George Washington and provide examples to illustrate his role as a pathfinder, a decision maker, and an implementer.

**6.8.** Select an American leader and review one or more biographies of the leader to determine the characteristics that made him or her a leader.

**6.9.** Other chapters in this book emphasize the importance of an appreciation of other cultures. Select a non-American historical figure who is considered to be a leader of a past culture and review one or more biographies of the leader to determine the characteristics that made him or her a leader.

**6.10.** Any initial study of history and culture indicates the importance of objectivity and a lack of bias in historical study. Explain why these characteristics are important (a) to the historian and (b) to the engineer or scientist. What are possible results of bias and lack of objectivity in historical reporting and in reports by engineers and scientists?

**6.11.** History deals with issues involving value conflicts. For example, the opening of the West led to value conflicts as well as physical conflicts with the American Indians. Also, the history of the growth of machines during the Industrial Revolution is an example of values in conflict. Pick a historical event in which values were in conflict, identify the values, and discuss a process by which such value conflicts could be resolved. Could the same process be used to solve value conflicts in engineering and science?

**6.12.** If you have participated in a group activity such as a sports team, high school yearbook committee, church youth group, or Boy Scout/Girl Scout troop, discuss the individuals who provided group leadership and the characteristics that best exemplify their leadership skills. Discuss how such leadership characteristics might be beneficial to the operation of a small business, such as an engineering firm.

**6.13.** What types of general education courses might help develop leadership skills? Identify courses in your undergraduate course catalog that would be appropriate.

**6.14.** For many periods of history, few facts are available. The historian must therefore use his or her imagination to put the facts into an organized form. Such reconstructed history may even be considered a hypothesis. Identify courses from your undergraduate course catalog that deal with the reconstruction of history. Discuss why imagination is important to the engineer or scientist and how such history courses could develop imaginative powers.

7

# Issues in Contemporary Culture

*Patricia J. Gaynor*

## INTRODUCTION

Social and behavioral scientists continue to debate how to define the term *culture*. For our purposes here, culture consists of all things that are socially learned and shared by members of a society. That is, culture is the acquired knowledge of members of a society that generates behavior and is used to interpret behavior. It includes those aspects of the environment that are not in the form provided by nature, and it includes acquired, but not hereditary, traits that members of a society share. Thus, culture can be divided into material and nonmaterial culture. Engineers and scientists contribute to material culture with computers, lasers, buildings, and other physical objects that are not in their natural form. Engineers and scientists also contribute to the nonmaterial culture with technical jargon and strategies for solving problems.

Culture has many aspects; it is learned, relative, dynamic, taken for granted, tacit and explicit, limiting, and liberating. Traditional culture can be studied, however indirectly, through the study of art, literature, languages, anthropology, history, and philosophy. Art and anthropology reflect culture to the extent that the values and beliefs of a given period of time are revealed in the physical art works produced at the time. For example, the art of Peter Paul Rubens (1577–1640), a Flemish painter, shows women as full-bodied, reflecting the aesthetic and erotic ideals of the culture of his period. The art of contemporary artists, such as Frank Frazetta, show women as slender but busty, reflecting the perceptions and ideals of our current culture. Literature reveals culture by describing the rules of behavior as well as the values and the beliefs of the society it represents. The language of a society is evidence of the thought processes and concepts inherent in the culture of those who speak it. (For example, differences between English and the Hopi Indian language are discussed in Chapter 10.) Even though people of different cultures use the same physical apparatus to produce and hear the patterns of sounds, they develop different speech and auditory skills; the resulting forms of communication are part of the social training that preserves social structures.

Our definition of culture used the word *society,* so it may be worthwhile to make a distinction between the concepts of culture and society. There are cultural differences among people within a society, yet two different societies may have common cultural elements. A society is a group of people who share a common value system and many other social characteristics. We might speak of a professional society, the Hopi Indian society, or the American society. Each society has a culture, which is reflected in the behavioral patterns of individuals and groups within it. For the purpose of this chapter, it is important to recognize that subcultures develop within a culture. In some cases, these subcultures develop because the overall culture is less objective than it should be and thus is not meeting the needs of all its members. By developing an understanding of a subculture, an overall culture can grow to incorporate the behavior and needs of the subculture, thus forming a more refined culture—that is, a culture with greater objectivity and a better sense of its own behavior and values. The resulting culture will have a slightly different form and pattern to reflect the changes in ideas, purpose, or goals of the society.

Studies in contemporary culture tend to be specific and oriented toward a particular perspective of a segment of a society. College programs that discuss issues in contemporary culture include Afro-American studies, American studies, Jewish studies, women's studies, and urban studies. These are relatively new programs, but their interdisciplinary methodologies are not new.

Studies in contemporary culture arise because of problems associated with groups in a society. These problems may be created by new technologies, or new technologies may be able to help alleviate the burden on these groups. Because of the role of engineers and scientists in developing new technologies, a study of issues in contemporary culture may help engineering and science students develop an awareness of the effects of new technologies on specific segments of society. The students may then be able to view the profession in the context of society, rather than just as a set of physical laws, assumptions, and simplifications that led to technological development. Studies in contemporary culture are relevant in many aspects of professional as well as personal life. On a professional level, engineers and scientists, who most certainly come away from their academic endeavors with the technical skill required to solve social problems, may acquire a social awareness of their responsibilities for guiding the implementation of technology. It is assumed here that those who provide technology in an attempt to solve social problems are at least partially responsible for the social impact of those solutions.

## AMERICAN STUDIES

American studies courses focus on the variety in American culture. The theories and methods of this discipline are borrowed from anthropology, sociology, and other social sciences. The theories of American studies are based on the idea that American society is marked more by contrast than by consensus, although this does not mean that there is not a national character that applies to the entire population. The ultimate objective of such studies is to develop a "connecting habit of mind"; that is, because of the diversity of our culture, it is important for students to have the ability to recognize the interrelationships between the elements that comprise culture. Such an ability should give students of American studies intellectual leverage on their culture by stimulating them to connect from the present back to the past, from the personal out to the wider culture, from the aesthetic down to the social structure, and from the intimate out to the abstract. A connecting habit of mind is important to students in engineering and science. They need to recognize the role of science and technology in their culture, and they need to accept the restrictions that culture may place on the expansion of their technological work. Our culture affects all aspects of our lives and behavior, and the components of American culture can be explored to the extent that this pervasive nature of culture is made clear. These components consist of values and beliefs, rules and recipes for behavior, and symbols and rituals. Introductory courses in American studies include an examination of value systems in America, and contemporary American autobiographies may be used as the vehicle for this exercise. Such autobiographies are written by ordinary Americans, not great thinkers or great writers. American studies courses are grounded on the assumption that people are citizens of the world and their own culture before they are doctors, or lawyers, or accountants, or engineers, and that an education that proposes to train students for that world must be based on cultural understanding as well as technical understanding.

Some of the topics covered by American studies courses are material aspects of American life, contemporary American culture, popular music, film, critics of American culture, race in American culture, and mental disorders in modern America. All of these topics are relevant in the sense that they reflect the diversity of contemporary lifestyles in America. Students will find course work in popular culture or youth culture interesting because these topics reflect the attitudes and values of themselves and their peers.

The professions of engineering and science involve many issues of deep moral and human concern. Advanced military weapons systems and genetic engineering are just two examples. Engineers and scientists share common values and attitudes that often differ from those in other professions and, even more, from those of the general public. These values and attitudes can create biases in their actions, such that the work of the engineers and scientists will not reflect the values and attitudes of the mainstream of American culture. When an engineer uses a factor of safety in a design, he or she should use objective criteria in selecting the factor of safety so that it reflects the user's value assessment of public safety. Social stress may result from engineering designs that do not reflect the values of the users of the engineering works. The engineer or scientist thus must be capable of making objective assessments of social needs and wants. American studies courses promote objectivity and a cosmopolitan perspective through the recognition of cultural bias. Once cultural bias is recognized, connections between it and other types of bias may be realized.

## WOMEN'S STUDIES

Women's studies programs are concerned with a different form of bias. Courses in such programs attempt to educate students about sex biases in our culture so that they may be free not only from sexism but also from racism, class bias, ageism, heterosexual bias, and all the ideologies and attitudes that constrict our understanding of reality. These courses are thus supplements to traditional curricula, which have often ignored or distorted the roles of women in society. Some of the topics include women in art, literature, economic life, politics, and history. This supplementary aspect of women's studies provides evidence that women have made significant, if not always influential, contributions in these areas. Sex roles, socialization, and women in sports, in the mass media, and in various cultures may also be studied. Class formats vary from seminars and experimental labs to standard lecture classes and discussion groups.

Courses that deal with sex role conditioning and socialization can be very helpful to engineers and scientists in a professional context, as well as providing diverse personal benefits. One of the most noteworthy social changes in this country is the influx of women into nontraditional careers. Women in engineering and science are often taken by surprise when they encounter sexism in the work place. Emerging from the academic cocoon, these women are often not prepared to deal with such problems, just as men are often unprepared to deal with women in these roles. Sexism becomes less of a threat to both victim and perpetrator when the roots of such behavior are known. An understanding of sex role conditioning may develop a woman's capacity to explore her potential more positively. Nowhere is the plight of women more clearly in evidence than in construction management. Women graduates with degrees in construction management must spend several years working in the field among male workers who doubt their capabilities. This doubt is often expressed in the form of ridicule and, sometimes, contempt. The female construction manager not only must gain the respect of her co-workers but also must funnel these negative energies into productive ends. Given an understanding of the roots of such aggression, women can more easily get beyond the negative emotions such behavior may cause and can work more effectively. Women's studies discussion groups also include discussion of how to handle sexism in many contexts. This is particularly helpful for women entering male-dominated occupations, in which sexism is most likely to occur and women are least likely to get cooperation or encouragement from their co-workers.

Male students can also benefit from women's studies courses. The two-career family is a reality, and stress in both the home and the work place is often a result of such a lifestyle. Courses in women's studies may develop an awareness of the roots of the problem and thus minimize the stress. Men who choose to adopt nontraditional roles, such as a part-time househusband, may also face sexism. In women's studies courses, men may discover the origins of sexist attitudes of both women and other men toward men in such roles. They may also gain an understanding of the problems women face when confronted with sexism. Such knowledge may also enable a husband to help his wife overcome sexism in her work place.

Students of women's studies are also made aware of biases other than sexism in our society and in themselves. This awareness can go a long way toward helping people peacefully co-exist with others who choose alternative lifestyles, thereby increasing social effectiveness and on-the-job efficiency.

## URBAN STUDIES

Urban studies programs are devoted to the understanding of urban cultures and the issues involved in urban crisis. Some of the issues studied are pollution, crime, transportation, deteriorating health, educational, and welfare services, slums and poor housing conditions, and violence in minority relations. Courses in urban studies demonstrate that cities are multidimensional. In introductory courses, the evolution and development of metropolitan areas are examined, along with current social trends and urban problems. These classes may include field trips to nearby cities so that students can obtain a view of an emerging urban world. Such field studies add realism and relevance to course material. Urban studies programs are also interdisciplinary in methodology. Topics may include urban design, social influences on the environment, environmental studies, transportation, communities, human ecology, public administration, and public policy. Some of the more relevant courses for engineers and scientists are those that cover the behavioral and social dimensions of the urban community as well as the environmental and technological dimensions. Such courses help students learn how to integrate social responsibility with technical knowledge.

In the most tangible sense, urban studies are relevant for most students in that most people will live or work in a city at some time in their lives. Anyone with an interest in some aspect of urban life should find urban studies applicable. Useful courses may also be found in related disciplines, such as architecture, ecology, health, and sociology.

The contributions of engineers and scientists to the solution of urban problems are a function of their knowledge of urban life and culture. Engineers often have problems because of their reluctance to incorporate sociological, political, and aesthetic considerations in their quantitative analyses. Students of engineering and science also should learn about the need for major experiments and the ambiguity in meaningful experimental results. Engineering and science education is designed around well-defined experiments, which is unlike real-world practice. Urban studies courses can introduce the student to problems for which well-defined, single-objective experiments are not possible.

In solving urban problems, engineers must take into account such values as beauty, safety, efficiency, and reliability in designing and in implementing their designs. For example, in the interest of beauty, engineers must realize that a city takes on character according to the enduring structures contained in it. To ignore this fact is surely to create disharmony. Cities and their problems arise out of human social needs, and engineers cannot hope to solve these problems by simply applying technology without understanding these often conflicting needs.

## COURSE SELECTION

Topics in American culture may be found in a number of programs, and entire programs on American studies are often available. Where a single program on American studies is not available, courses may be found within such departments as history, anthropology, sociology, physical education, and geography. Diverse topics are covered, such as the historical forces that shape culture, geographic features that serve as cultural barriers, and the impact of American sport on the national culture; these show the diversity of the American culture. In studying such topics, students should keep in mind the possible impacts of engineering and science on the American culture as well as the constraints that our culture imposes on professional practice.

Courses in women's studies that might help develop value awareness can be found in sociology, history, nutrition, and literature, as well as in programs that deal entirely with issues related to women's roles in our society. A course on women's health might deal with the stressful effects of two-career families and the problems involved in serving as both a parent and a professional. A history course that deals with women's role in industrialization would discuss the contributions of women to technological growth and the constraints that culture has imposed on women to limit their direct participation in industrialization. It is commonly believed that women do not seek careers in engineering and science because they are "masculine" careers; a physical education course that discusses the development of masculinity and femininity in children through early play experiences may enlighten students on the cultural constraints placed on women. History courses that cover the change in women's roles in economic, political, and family life might be used to illustrate social change and value changes. Courses in other disciplines such as journalism and business management may illustrate the changing social status of women in other professions; these can be of particular value because courses on the role of women in engineering and science are rare, if they exist at all.

Courses in urban studies can be found in any number of programs, even where an entire program on urban studies does not exist. Such departments as geography, architecture, sociology, recreation, and economics might include courses that discuss aspects of culture and society that are particular to urban environments. A course might be available that defines the emerging national culture of urban environments as contained in values, ideas, and moral standards. A course that discusses the architect's role in the social and political dynamics of decision-making processes in urban environmental design would certainly be of value to an engineering or science student who is interested in learning about the social responsibilities of professionals. A geography course that describes the effects of economic and social changes on the cultural evolution of cities would also be valuable, as would a sociology course on population, which would discuss the migration of people to urban areas and the resulting social problems. Such courses may point up the importance of participation by engineers and scientists in public policy formulation.

In choosing courses to meet liberal arts requirements, students are encouraged to take a minimum of three courses in contemporary culture. One course should include an examination of our own culture as it is applied to everyday behaviors and attitudes. In such a course, students can identify with much of what is being presented—more so than in studies of fine arts, great literature, or abstract philosophy. The second course should be a study of a society that is foreign to the student—perhaps one that constitutes a subculture in America that is particularly vocal about some common attitudes or behaviors in American society. The third course should be problem oriented and thus relevant to contemporary cultural phenomena. A student should come away from such a course not only with some knowledge of current problems but also with an ability to identify future problems according to techniques presented in the course. Students are encouraged to take such contemporary culture courses above and beyond degree requirements, as these courses deal with the hard-to-quantify human factors that are involved in the advent of any technology.

## CONCLUSIONS

Culture studies are studies of human groups. Contemporary culture studies incorporate the various perspectives of cultural groups in relation to the environment from which the problems of contemporary society arise. Engineers and scientists are often called upon to help solve these problems, and in doing so, they have to make value decisions. Individuals cannot make such value decisions until they are aware of not only their own value system but also how it relates to the value systems of those who are most affected by their inventions. It is not responsible conduct to provide technical solutions when no consideration has been given to the impact of those solutions on society. The impact of technology cannot be estimated until the social content of the problems has been evaluated, and such evaluation cannot be accurate if the technologist is not in touch with contemporary society. Contemporary culture studies can give students this requisite knowledge and perspective.

Culture studies are often considered irrelevant to or unimportant in the pursuit of a technical education and life in a highly technical society. Nothing could be further from the truth. Culture studies are an exercise in self-development. As one examines one's own culture, one can identify the influence that culture exerts in generating behaviors and attitudes. A technically oriented society can be gauged and predicted more accurately by urban planners and transportation system managers who understand the high value Americans place on efficiency. Thus, the need for time-efficient transportation systems would be of prime concern to these professionals.

As students study other cultures, their awareness is expanded to the extent that behaviors in their own society, even those most taken for granted, can be altered to include factors outside their culture. Students become more self-aware when comparisons are made between themselves and others who either share their culture or are shaped by another. Such examinations are conducive to open-mindedness and objectivity and thus contain the rudiments of wisdom

## EXERCISES

7.1. In your undergraduate college catalog, identify courses in the fields of sociology and community development that would enhance an engineering or science student's understanding of the following description of a professional: "One who recognizes a service motive to society in vital and honorable activities."

7.2. Technology is an important factor in the growth and change of cultures. Discuss how technologies such as the space program and computers have changed American culture.

7.3. In sociological studies of the family, the oral ideals that give the family its distinctive and identifying characteristic are the basis for cultural analyses of the family. Identify fundamental values important to family cohesiveness and draw analogies between the role of the individual in the family and in a profession. Discuss how a study of the family could help students develop a better understanding of the importance of values to a profession.

7.4. Some historians have suggested that a decline in values and morality has contributed to the decline in power of societies. For example, the decline of the Roman empire has been attributed to a decline in values. Discuss value issues in contemporary American culture that could contribute to a decline in our society.

7.5. Read autobiographies by one of your heroes—a musician, athlete, political figure, or artist. Evaluate the influence of culture on the individual's career, and evaluate the effect of the individual's work on the culture of the society.

7.6. Visit an art museum and examine the works of artists from different periods and cultures, taking note of the varying concepts of beauty as reflected in the portrayal of people, architecture, technology, and so forth. Write an essay on your impression of art as a medium for reflecting a culture.

**7.7.** Attend a festival put on by people of some other nationality to observe the differences in clothing, food, dance, and music. Write an essay that describes the cultural differences.

**7.8.** Attend the functions of a minority student group to gain an understanding of their particular concerns and problems and how they fit into American society. Write an essay on the experience.

**7.9.** Plan trips to both rural and urban areas to see how people live and work. Write an essay reflecting on how the environment affects our attitudes and values.

**8**

# Culture, Society, and Values

*Richard H. McCuen*

## INTRODUCTION

How can studying the social sciences benefit an engineer or scientist? It does *not* teach the student of chemistry about chemical reactions. It does *not* teach the aerospace engineer about lift and drag coefficients for the design of airplanes. But these are technical details that are taught in specialty courses within engineering and science. Social science can benefit students in other, equally important ways. An education should expand one's horizons, not just develop skills in a narrow specialty. In addition to the technical details of a professional discipline, education should teach students about themselves, their communities, and the role their profession plays independent of technical skills. Education should make students aware of their own capacities and prejudices, of the values that are important to them, and of the criteria that they use in making moral decisions; these are benefits of education that pertain to the student's personal life. With respect to society, education should develop an awareness of social problems, of the origins of our culture, and of the institutions in which we function. Finally, a profession functions within a society and is subject to the constraints of that society; this was clearly illustrated in Chapter 5 in the discussion of Francis Bacon and the scientific and cultural climate that existed in the fifteenth and sixteenth centuries. Education should develop an awareness of the relationship between a profession and society in a way that is removed from the technical details of the profession.

In summary, besides developing the technical skills that are necessary to function within a profession, education should develop three other important concepts in students:

1. An understanding of self, of human nature, and of the individual's responsibilities as a citizen;
2. An understanding of communities and society, of social problems, and of the effectiveness of alternative solutions to these social problems; and
3. An understanding of the role of their professions in society.

A study of the social sciences will serve to increase students' understanding of all three of these important areas of concern.

## SOCIOLOGY

From a geological time standpoint, the study of humans and their environment is a relatively new endeavor. As noted in Chapter 5, the scientific climate prior to the seventeenth century was not conducive to scientific study. Just as astronomers were discouraged from studying the motion of the planets, the study of humans was discouraged. Despite the torturing, burning, and disemboweling that was widely practiced in the Middle Ages, anyone who was involved in human dissections for the purpose of learning about anatomical functions was considered a heretic. With the rise of the Industrial Revolution, the mechanical universe was studied far more intensively than the human body and the social universe. Scientifically speaking, even today we know more about space than we do about the social institutions that encourage and support space exploration. Also, we know more about space vehicles than we do about the astronauts who pilot them. Is this lack of understanding about ourselves, our cultures, and our social institutions a contributing factor in the inability of new technologies to solve our social problems? One could reasonably argue that those involved in developing new technologies should know more about the users of the new technologies and the social institutions governing human behavior. Such knowledge would better enable them to meet their social responsibilities.

Sociology is the study of human social behavior, especially the origins, organization, institutions, and development of human society. It is concerned with the relationships between humans rather than with the biological functioning of humans. This somewhat abstract, dictionary-type definition may be better understood if we consider the topics that are typically studied by sociologists. In very general terms, sociology can be divided into the study of culture; socialization, or social change; and collective behavior (groups and social institutions). Although this subdivision could be debated, it should be evident that engineers and scientists need to have an understanding of such topics. We will discuss each of these topics briefly and illustrate the value of a knowledge of such sociological concepts and methods to engineers and scientists.

### Culture

Knowledge of one's culture facilitates personal integration into that culture and professional functioning within the society. A culture survives by being passed on to the next generation. Actions, both personal and professional, are judged, in part, on how they help a society preserve that culture. If some segments of a society, such as professional engineers or scientists, do not exhibit behavior patterns that reflect the values of the culture, then they are not helping that society preserve its culture. This is why professional codes of ethics must reflect the values of society; they represent a contribution to society by professionals in preserving the culture. Thus, for engineers and scientists to fully appreciate the intent of their professional codes of ethics, they must understand their culture. Courses in sociology that discuss culture can provide engineers or scientists with an understanding of the social fabric in which the codes of ethics are meant to apply.

An understanding of culture provides an understanding of many human values. A society has personal *freedom* because the culture defines acceptable behavior patterns, freedom is lost when behavior patterns cause the culture to become fragmented. Language is characteristic of a culture; it is used to transmit *knowledge* and it can be applied in obtaining *pleasure*. Communication through language skills also helps public *safety* and *security,* as well as enhancing public *health.* The habits that we acquire from our culture allow us to use our time to acquire *knowledge* and to perform acts of *creativity.* Through an understanding of culture, we can predict the behavior of others, which increases the *efficiency* of social efforts and reduces the possibility of conflicts, thus increasing our sense of *security.* These are just a few of the ways that culture is related to values. Values are an important part of a culture, and different cultures place different importance on different values. Developing a knowledge of a culture provides insights into the values that a culture considers important.

A knowledge of one's culture also provides a basis for understanding the unacceptability of unprofessional behavior such as kickbacks, bid-rigging, and cheating. Such beliefs are part of our culture, and a failure to understand the culture makes it difficult to understand that these examples of unprofessional conduct are wrong. Someone who lacks an understanding of the culture can view such unprofessional conduct only from a behavior-punishment perspective; that is, it is wrong only when one gets caught, and the risk of punishment determines whether or not the unacceptable action should be performed. When individuals have a knowledge of their culture, their behavioral patterns, both personal and professional, are more likely to be sensitive to social values. Their conduct will have an altruistic direction, not only an egoistic one. To move from an egoistic stage of moral development to an altruistic stage requires an appreciation for the culture. Moreover, professional codes of ethics are written at an altruistic level, and they cannot be fully appreciated unless one understands the cultural framework in which the codes are embedded.

## Socialization

The nature-versus-nurture controversy, introduced in Chapter 5, has important implications here because it is central to the culture concept. Humans differ from other animals in that a design for living is not transferred genetically in humans; we are unique in that we can learn from the experiences of others. It is our culture that we learn; culture is transmitted to us, and it shapes our personalities. Our capacities for socialization are roughly set by biological processes, but personality is formed by society. This is not to imply that certain drives are not inborn, only that the shape and direction of these drives is socially learned.

The development of individual value systems, an important theme of this book, takes place as part of the socialization process. There is no society in which materialistic accumulation is the only goal of its people. Nonquantifiable goals are evident in every society. These value goals are shaped by culture and by subcultures, and the transmission of these value goals is part of the socialization process. Very often, whole societies are thought to be characterized by certain values. For example, industriousness and efficiency are highly valued in modern-day America. The American Indian of the nineteenth century is usually portrayed as self-reliant and individualistic. In contrast, the Japanese are thought to place high value on loyalty. Even within a society, however, there are groups that place different weights on different values. And even within these groups or communities, individuals show marked variations in value preferences. One child may prefer an ice cream cone, while another prefers a comic book. One employer may prefer engineers who are creative and act with professional freedom, while another employer may discourage such qualities and encourage diligence and efficiency. These value preferences are not inborn; they are shaped by experience—they are part of our socialization. The socialization process continues throughout life, although many values are shaped in childhood. An end result of the socialization process, at least with respect to values, is a society that has many shared values, that rewards behavior patterns that are consistent with these values, and that expects communities to respect these values.

The implications of such social values for professional practice should be evident from the discussions in earlier chapters of this book. American culture has many values, and the engineering and science communities are expected to respect these values. When any professional community consistently shows a lack of respect for them, the society places restrictions on the professional community. Professional societies, recognizing that these restrictions decrease the efficiency of the professional community, attempt to reduce the likelihood of antisocial behavior by setting professional guidelines to practice that reflect the values of the culture and by educating their membership about these social responsibilities. Codes of ethics and related documents represent the values of a society that members are expected to follow. A professional community that fails to discipline members who violate these codes may be subject to legal restrictions.

How do professional communities attempt to educate their members about their social responsibilities? In other words, how is a culture transmitted to members of a professional community? The first approach is through education. Just as parents educate their children that stealing other children's toys is wrong, professional communities educate their young members about shared values and social responsibility. This is the intent of the GERs as well as courses on professional ethics. Second, professional communities publish journals that include discussions of the social responsibilities of their members. Third, members who fail to respect the social values embedded within the professional code of ethics are disciplined; expulsion from the community is the most severe form of professional discipline. Finally, discussions of social responsibilities are encouraged at professional meetings.

Members of a professional community must understand and respect the culture in which they practice. Thus, value socialization is necessary. Engineers and scientists must recognize the extent to which variations in social behavior are permitted. They must seek a continued understanding of their culture, especially as their professional responsibilities increase. Socialization is a process that continues throughout one's career, just as the individual continues to learn about the personal community in which he or she resides.

### Collective Behavior

In addition to culture and socialization, a study of sociology involves concepts related to behavioral patterns of groups and institutions. People do not function solely as individuals; they also function as members of groups. For example, the family is a primary group; church groups, athletic groups, and school groups are other groupings that affect individual behavior patterns. Individuals also are involved in professional groups, referred to here as professional societies.

Simply stated, a group consists of two or more individuals who are joined together in a social framework and who work with a common goal. They are joined together because of common interests and social purpose. For our purposes here, it is important to recognize that group behavior can affect both society and the actions of the individuals who make up the group.

Each group is a strand in the social fabric of society. A study of sociology would emphasize how groups meet their cultural objectives and the socialization of group members. With respect to professional societies, a study of group behavior would provide the student of engineering or science with the knowledge necessary to understand how professional societies fit into the social fabric of society. An understanding of sociological concepts and methods would enable students who seek to belong to one of these professions (i.e., groups) to understand the effects of group actions on society; this is central to their understanding of their social responsibilities as engineers and scientists.

A knowledge of group behavior can also enhance one's ability to understand other professional concepts. Professional misconduct often originates from group behavior rather than from individual decision making. For example, when an engineer is confronted by a kickback proposal, the decision to participate may emanate from a discussion with partners in the firm. In this case, the partners are a group, and their behavior will clearly affect society. They may try to justify the action by stating that if their firm had not made the kickback, someone else would have; they argue that it is a "common business practice." The implication is that everybody is doing it and, therefore, it is acceptable. Such an attitude is a rationalization, even though individuals often believe that improper professional behavior truly is a common business practice. Psychology or philosophy courses may deal with the concept of rationalization, but a sociology course will help students understand the social effects of behavior.

A study of sociology will show that collective behavior is influenced by cultural characteristics and that culture can be influenced by collective behavior. A culture determines both the nature and the intensity of collective behavioral patterns and prescribes limits to these patterns. As subcultures, professions work to maintain bounds on the conduct of their members. Professional codes of ethics are the visible instruments for describing these bounds. When individuals or subgroups within a larger group exhibit behavioral patterns that violate cultural norms, the group seeks to rid itself of these members. In this sense, collective professional behavior is influenced by the cultural characteristics of the society in which it functions.

## ANTHROPOLOGY

Anthropology is the scientific study of the origin and the physical, social, and cultural development and behavior of humans. Its ties to sociology should be evident. Both disciplines deal with culture, patterns of behavior, and social development. Social changes are also central to both. There are a number of subdisciplines within the broad category of anthropology, including archaeology; physical, cultural, and social anthropology; and anthropological linguistics. Even within these subdisciplines, further subdivision is possible. For example, physical anthropology can be subdivided into population genetics, molecular biology, human ecology, embryology, primatology, and so on. Subdivisions of cultural anthropology include economic anthropology, political anthropology, and the anthropology of education.

A study of anthropology would be of particular interest to anyone who has visited the ruins of past cultures. The cliff dwellings of Mesa Verde National Park in southwestern Colorado provide a good example. The archaeological ruins there are the result of cultures that flourished in that area from about 550 A.D. to 1300 A.D. During the first two centuries of this period, the inhabitants constructed dwellings on the mesa tops, and both pottery and the bow and arrow were introduced. Pueblo architecture began about 750 A.D. and cliff dwellings became the rule after 1200 A.D. Anthropologists are not sure exactly why the people moved their dwellings from the mesa tops to the cliffs, but security from roaming bands of Indians is believed to be the reason. The culture died out after about 1300 A.D.; again, the actual cause is unknown, but severe drought over a ten- to twenty-five-year period is believed to be the cause. Whether they were studying the ruins of pithouses from the Modified Basketmaker period (550-750 A.D.) or the ruins of the great cliff dwellings of the Great Pueblo period, anthropologists would seek to synthesize a picture of the entire Anasazi culture from the remains found during excavations of these areas. The available evidence includes grave sites, pottery remains, remains of tools, and the remains of the physical facilities (e.g., cliff dwellings, religious ceremonial sites). A medical anthropologist would try to determine the types of diseases, injuries, and abnormalities that existed among the people. Bones and teeth are the primary pieces of evidence. A religion anthropologist would review the remains of ceremonial sites to try to piece together a picture of the religious life of the Indians.

Anthropologists must use incomplete data to put together a picture of a culture, and in this respect, engineers and scientists are much like anthropologists. An astronomer tries to synthesize an explanation of the origin of the universe using a few measurements made with our crude telescopes. A flood hydrologist tries to synthesize a model of flood behavior at a site using a few measurements of past floods, often with only a few years' records. A structural engineer tries to predict how a proposed 100-story high-rise building will function during a hurricane or massive earthquake using results from a few laboratory studies and, possibly, measurements taken on other buildings during less severe events. Thus, just as anthropologists work with incomplete evidence, engineers and scientists also must synthesize pictures of reality from incomplete and uncertain data. A knowledge of anthropology can develop an appreciation for such a task.

Why did the Anasazi culture of the Great Pueblo period disintegrate? Was it because of drought or a lack of security from marauders? Or was it from a disintegration of the moral basis of the society and the social harmony within it? Did a new technological development have disastrous side effects, or was the culture unable to develop new technologies to solve existing problems? Similar questions could be asked about other cultures that have declined or disappeared. Are there lessons to be learned from a study of other cultures that can teach us about our own culture? Will the importance of engineers and scientists to the growth of our own culture increase or decline in the coming decades? These are not just idle questions, nor should they be left to the anthropologists to answer. Engineers and scientists also need to think about social issues, and a study of anthropology can be illuminating.

## COURSE SELECTION

It should be evident that courses in the social sciences serve many purposes, both personal and professional. Two disciplines (sociology and anthropology) were discussed in this chapter, and others were discussed in Chapter 7. It should also be evident that there are links between these topics and other topics discussed in this book. In our examination of sociology, we discussed the values that are inherent in a culture. Values and moral decision-making are also taught in philosophy and theology courses. A course in economics might discuss the economic aspects of social welfare; this is also taught in sociology courses that cover the institutional aspects of society. Bureaucratic and institutional power issues are central to courses in government and politics; they are also studied by sociologists. The relationship between language and culture is studied both in language courses and in such social science courses as sociology and anthropology. Social changes are a major part of sociology, and many history courses also deal with these issues. The point is that knowledge gained from sociology, anthropology, and other closely related social science courses provides a basis for understanding many other disciplines. Social science courses provide a broad perspective for many other courses, and variety and breadth should be one objective of any individual's general education program.

## CONCLUSIONS

Three general reasons for studying the social sciences were given in the introduction to this chapter. Having discussed two specific disciplines that represent the social sciences, we can state more specific reasons for selecting social science courses to fulfill the GERs:

1. To develop an understanding of the tasks of social scientists;
2. To obtain some basic knowledge that social scientists have developed;
3. To understand the elements of social science thinking and to learn the strategies social scientists use in developing knowledge of culture;
4. To understand behavioral patterns within a society and differences in behavioral patterns between societies;
5. To place the functioning of one's chosen profession into the framework of society;
6. To understand the need for the professional to make decisions within a broader social framework; and
7. To understand the past so that better social decisions can be made in the future.

The knowledge students gain from such courses is of value both personally and professionally. Through an understanding of culture, they are better able to understand their own value system and how it compares with society's expectations. Such knowledge should reduce the likelihood of value conflicts in both personal and professional actions. Recognizing that individuals and groups develop consistent behavioral patterns, knowledge of culture can both explain others' past actions and help predict their future behavior. Knowledge of the elements of social science thinking and research methods is useful to engineers and scientists as a guide to obtaining knowledge in the face of uncertainty and with incomplete data.

There is a synergistic benefit to a study of culture. It provides knowledge of history, art, economics, religion, politics, and other disciplines in a broader perspective—a perspective that would not be possible without a knowledge of culture. This is especially important in meeting the objective that underlies this book—developing an awareness of social responsibilities in students of engineering and science. These responsibilities cannot be met if engineers and scientists do not have a knowledge of their culture.

## EXERCISES

**8.1.** What should students expect to learn from a study of social sciences?

**8.2.** How can a knowledge of sociology develop an awareness of the importance of human welfare to the professional engineer or scientist?

**8.3.** Discuss the cultural characteristics that permit science to advance more rapidly in a free, open society. Is this also true of the arts? Why?

**8.4.** Social science research is conducted according to the scientific method that is used by scientists and engineers in solving their problems. Outline the steps of the scientific method and illustrate the steps using one example from sociological or anthropological research and one example from the engineering or science discipline you will major in.

**8.5.** Identify subcultures to which you belong, which might include religious, political, social, and athletic groups. What values do each of these subcultures feel are important? Rank the values in their order of importance to you.

**8.6.** Why do students who belong to fraternities and sororities feel more comfortable socializing with others in fraternities and sororities? Explain using the concept of culture. Identify differences in the subcultures of those who are fraternity or sorority members and those who are not.

**8.7.** Characterize the cultures of urban and rural living. What are the primary differences? Why would a student from an urban area be more likely to choose friends from urban areas rather than rural areas?

**8.8.** Students often believe that there is a generation gap between their culture and their parents' culture. Discuss the primary differences in these subcultures.

**8.9.** From a cultural standpoint, explain why engineers and scientists have an obligation to participate in the formulation of public policies.

**8.10.** Characterize the culture of a professional ice hockey team and identify the values it would consider important.

**8.11.** Explain why, without culture, humans would be worse off than other animals.

**8.12.** Identify courses in sociology that appear to address cultural issues that would be of importance to engineers and scientists.

**8.13.** Identify courses in anthropology and archaeology that would discuss the methods social scientists use to draw inferences from incomplete information.

**9**

# Philosophy, Social Experience, and Values

*Michael Gould*
*James M. Wallace*

## INTRODUCTION

Unlike most disciplines studied in a university, philosophy is usually unknown to the entering college student. Although high school students are intellectually capable of studying philosophy, high school curricula seldom provide them with the opportunity. Furthermore, the impressions that students acquire about philosophy are apt to be distorted; it is sometimes confused with religion, with psychology, and even with mystical experience. Thus, undergraduate students are commonly uninformed or misinformed about the nature of philosophy much more than about the nature of other academic subjects.

## WHAT IS PHILOSOPHY?

The origin of the word *philosopher* is both interesting and instructive. It came from the Greek thinker, Pythagoras (572-497 B.C.), whose famous theorem you know from geometry. When he was asked whether he regarded himself as a wise man, he modestly replied that he was not wise, but merely a lover of wisdom. The Greek word for "lover of wisdom," *philosophos,* became our word, *philosopher.*

Philosophy grows out of both wonder and intellectual curiosity about the nature and purpose of human life. In the description provided by Plato, the defense given by Socrates at his trial was that "the unexamined life is not worth living." This reflective examination of life is the essence of philosophy. It is the examination of what we can know and how we can know it—the branches of philosophy known as *logic* and *epistomology*. It is the examination of the various kinds of possible existence and their relationships, known as *ontology*. It is the exploration of the general features of the universe, known as *cosmology*. It is the study of the nature of value, known as *ethics* and *aesthetics*. Inquiries into these subjects can be very abstract, but the questions raised are always rooted in real concerns of real life. None of us find it very satisfying to plunge headlong into action without thinking about what our goals are or why those goals are desirable. And even if we take enough time to address these two issues, we still will need to determine the best means to obtain our goals. These are philosophical questions with a very practical importance.

In contrast to most analytical forms of human inquiry, such as the natural and biological sciences, the social sciences (history, anthropology, economics, political science, sociology, and psychology), and the analysis of literature and art, philosophy is concerned more with synthesis. The word *synthesis* comes from the Greek *syntithenai,* which means "to put together." Although philosophy also utilizes detailed analysis, particularly analysis of the use of language, its larger concern is with how parts are related. In searching for meaning, philosophers want to discover how the individually analyzed parts of a question fit into the larger whole.

At this point, it may be worthwhile to recognize that the concept of synthesis is important to the engineer or scientist. The structural engineer synthesizes, or designs, a high-rise building by "putting together" the necessary beams, columns, foundations, and so forth. The computer scientist synthesizes a new computer algorithm to solve a complex problem or to simulate a real-world system. An understanding of the philosophical concept of synthesis can enhance your understanding of the role of synthesis in engineering or science.

All forms of human inquiry involve a search for meaning, but in philosophy, this search is distinctive. In literature, music, and art we search for meaning in terms of feeling and imagination; in religion, the search is in terms of personal encounter. In the study of anatomy, we determine the various structures of the human body; and in physiology, we determine how these structures function. Psychology examines human behavior in terms of emotions and perceptions, whereas sociology and anthropology interpret group behavior in terms of various forms of relationships. Physics and chemistry inquire into the basic nature of matter. In all of these disciplines, we discover and report facts obtained from observation and experiment. In philosophy, however, the search for meaning is carried out by reflective, rational thought alone. We don't employ empirical knowledge gained from the scientific method or the formal logic of mathematical equations.

Since our thinking is always done in terms of language, as noted in Chapter 10, philosophy pays a great deal of attention to the uses and misuses of language. Thus, a philosopher will look carefully at someone's claims of truth to see if there are logical flaws in the way these claims are expressed. Linguistic analysis is the dominant form of philosophy practiced by professionals today.

Philosophy is concerned with ultimate or final questions. In a sense, it deepens rather than widens our knowledge. In philosophy, we push questions back to their ultimate sources until we reach something that explains other things but cannot itself be explained.

To summarize, there are three characteristics of philosophical problems (Thompson, 1961). First, they are problems that can be examined by thought alone. As we have made clear, this is not the only form of knowledge, but it is the exclusive tool of philosophy. Philosophers not only use their thoughts, they also use a test for truth. The truth that philosophy seeks is obtained by the unrelenting application of the requirements of necessity and universality. Thus, when philosophers claim that something is true, they are claiming that anyone who makes the same assumptions and logically follows through the consequences of these assumptions will come to the same conclusions. Second, the philosophical search for truth is concerned not only with what we know but also with how we know it. Thus, mathematics, physics, history, and sociology use philosophy as a means of examining their methods. The third characteristic is that philosophy is concerned with ultimates. We encounter many serious questions in our daily lives—questions about where we should go to college, what jobs we should take when we graduate, and whom we should marry. Such questions involve important choices that will shape the course of our lives. But they are not ultimate questions. Ultimate questions ask such things as "How should I *best* live my life?" or "Does life have meaning?" Such questions are not so abstract and remote as they may seem. They often arise in times of crisis when we are forced to examine who we are and where we are heading.

In the time of Plato (428-348 B.C.), philosophy encompassed all facets of intellectual life. Today, however, professional philosophers have only a minor effect on the intellectual climate of our age. Once, truth was sought in the branch of philosophy known as logic. Today, when we wish to increase our knowledge of "truth," we turn to the scientist or the mathematician for guidance. An understanding of beauty was once pursued in the branch of philosophy known as aesthetics. Today, artists and art critics define beauty with little attention to philosophers. Goodness was once sought in the branch of philosophy known as ethics. Today, religious leaders, novelists, poets, social scientists, doctors, lawyers, and even journalists—just about everyone except professional philosophers—are looked to for the definitions of right and wrong in their specialties. Ultimate principles and causes, the nature of reality, and the essence of the universe were once speculated about in the branch of philosophy known as metaphysics. Today, the word *metaphysics* is rarely heard except as an object of derision.

When the universe was an almost total mystery, philosophy—the science of explanation—flourished. Thus, it is regarded as the most universal and oldest science. Perhaps it would be worthwhile to pause and look a little more closely at what we have lost by neglecting philosophy in our headlong pursuit of "what works."

## WHY STUDY PHILOSOPHY?

As a freshman engineering or science student, you probably wonder why you should study philosophy. Is there any reason to believe that it will be valuable to you? There are many reasons. Indirect results of studying philosophy are increased levels of competence in expository clarity, logical rigor, articulateness, and analytical skill. A direct benefit of philosophy is that it makes available to you a significant portion of the world's great literature. When you are introduced to the writings of such masters of philosophical thinking as Plato, Descartes, Mill, Dewey, and Sartre, you will become aware of the extent to which scientists, artists, poets, statespersons, educators, and theologians have been influenced by the work of philosophers in the course of their own development.

Creativity is a necessary quality of scientists and engineers. The problems you will face as professionals in these fields will not be like the "canned" laboratory experiments or homework exercises that you face as students. They will require well-developed, logically rigorous analysis and innovative solutions. By enabling engineering or science students to see beyond the world as it presently exists, philosophy can help them develop a controlled but imaginative awareness of how things might be. In addition, philosophy enriches students' understanding of conceptual scientific ideas and phenomena, such as electromagnetic field theory, relativity, or quantum mechanics. After all, natural science is a branch of philosophy; it is still called natural philosophy in some of the great European universities. The study of philosophy helps students grapple intelligently with such basic, yet elusive questions as "What is a person?" "Why should I do what society tells me to do?" "Can we be sure of any of our beliefs?" and "Is there a God?" Seriously struggling with and satisfactorily coming to terms with such questions invests our lives with greater meaning.

Philosophy develops students' ability to distinguish between good and bad reasoning in decisions that are not quantitative, such as value judgments. Values—the principles, standards, or qualities that we consider worthwhile—derive from various sources, and we need to examine what those sources are to critically evaluate our values and those of others. The study of philosophy can be invaluable in this undertaking. It helps us place our perceptions, opinions, and actions within an ethical framework.

## UNIVERSAL RULES FOR HUMANKIND

The establishment of moral laws has long been a dominant human concern. Human beings seem to have sought absolute moral laws from the beginnings of ethical introspection. Although human beings have individual awareness of certain rights and wrongs, difficulties arise in stating definitive moral laws that are satisfactory for all and acceptable to all. Moral laws that are adequate for modern city dwellers will not do for a stone-age tribe in the jungles of New Guinea, and vice versa. Moral laws are inextricably subject to the needs of local conditions. Unless the laws reduce to a few simple human basics, the instinctive dos and don'ts of the human race, moral codes often prove impossible to impart successfully and to implement in different environments and cultures. Perhaps the point is that technology and the ambition for modern progress are easier to transfer than ideas of good and bad. History provides innumerable examples of desperate conflicts resulting from a confrontation of different moralities; the brutal meeting of Indians and Europeans in North America is a sad example.

Religions have offered variations on these basic moral laws, expressed in different words but with the meaning substantially the same. Endeavoring to fit the Golden Rule and similar moral guides into the formal corpus of philosophical thought, the German philosopher Immanuel Kant introduced the "categorical imperative," which describes rules that can be considered ethically mandatory in human conduct: "Act only on that maxim whereby you can at the same time will that it should become a universal law."

As we saw in the earlier chapters of this book, after graduation you will be enmeshed in technological and scientific projects that will inevitably bring values—yours and those of others affected by your work—into conflict. If your personal and social values are only vaguely held or remain unexamined, you will be ill prepared to apply your work toward the human good. One of the major tasks of philosophy is just this: a systematic examination of the bases of human values, which is the branch of philosophy known as ethics.

## SOURCES OF VALUES

As discussed in Chapter 5, heredity and environment shape individual reactions to situations in life through the value systems they jointly influence people to develop and adopt. Many factors contribute to the value systems of each individual. Thinking processes and habits are influenced by parents, peers, teachers, public figures we admire, and achievers we seek to emulate. Thus, as individuals mature, they develop, consciously or unconsciously, their own individual value systems. The process is inescapable and inevitable, but the resulting system often appears sketchy and contradictory, with fuzzy boundaries and a lack of precise definition. Individual value systems may be mirrors of the society in which we live, but they sometimes reflect some of its worst qualities rather than its best.

The possessors of flawed or unexamined value systems are sometimes shocked into critical consideration of their values by personal or social crises. For example, many students in the mid-1960s were forced to examine their allegiance to American government policy as the war in Vietnam escalated and threatened to personally involve them or their friends. For some of these students, that experience, which forced them to critically examine their values, continues to influence the way they live today. From that generation of students came countless social workers and community organizers and even some notable political figures.

The happiest individuals are those who possess distinct value systems that have been consciously and methodically appraised and have been brought into harmonious relationship with their lives. Such systems, openly arrived at and actively maintained, are easier to adjust and alter when necessary. Ideally, of course, values provide the stable foundation stones on which we build our lives. When they are solidly fixed in place, they are altered only after long contemplation. The formation of a reliable value system is a person's most important task, and there are numerous elements to consider, from one's view of nature to one's ideologies and philosophies. Very often, individuals' value systems undergo considerable change and development when they are college students. This development occurs because it is often the first time the students are away from home and are not subjected to the constraints of parents. Instead of relying on the rules of conduct dictated by parents, students must make decisions for themselves. Since many of these decisions involve values, the students are forced to recognize just what it is that they value and to develop guidelines for solving value conflicts in their personal lives. In addition, the students reassess past value decisions and use these experiences to better define their own value systems. Certainly, knowledge of the value rules proposed by the great philosophers and the guidelines provided in philosophy courses for synthesizing solutions to value questions can be of tremendous personal benefit.

As members and promoters of the technological/scientific culture, we engineers and scientists often have not examined our value systems very closely. We become so preoccupied with immediate tasks—the experiment to be done, the building to design, or the paper to write—that we often choose no particular philosophy at all, at least not in a formal sense. Engineers in particular often take the physical world much as they find it, with no questions asked. If they are pressed to verbalize their intuitive aversion to philosophy, they echo Francis Bacon, the father of the scientific method, who proclaimed 300 years ago: "That rule which is most effective in practice is also most true in theory. Whatever works best is most true." Although this pragmatism has an active, "can-do," creative side, it can engender a special kind of passivity with regard to radically different concepts. In its extreme form, it is a mentality that decides, at a certain point of development, that it knows "enough" and does not care to look further. Here, "enough" is the immediately given, directly perceivable concretes of our past and present experience, as though they were formed in stone. The anticonceptual mentality takes most things as irreducible primaries and regards them as self-evident. It treats concepts as if they were memorized precepts; it treats abstractions as if they were perceptual concretes. To such a mentality, everything is the given. The two cardinal questions—the prime movers of the human mind—"Why?" and "What for?" are alien to an anticonceptual mentality. The absence of concern with the "What for?" eliminates long-range purpose and cuts off the future. Thus, only the present is fully real to an anticonceptual mentality, and misguided values naturally result from a lack of concern with past and future.

## COURSE SELECTION

Philosophy courses often resemble courses in English literature. Reading material is assigned and discussed; parallels, contrasts, or influences of philosophy in different civilizations are pointed out. For example, a class may read Karl Marx's *Das Kapital* and discuss the differences and similarities between his philosophies and those practiced in the Soviet Union today. Typically, tests are in the form of thought-provoking essay questions that seek to extract personal observations or interpretations of the assigned material.

An introductory course in philosophy at the freshman level would be ideal for the beginner. It will introduce the student to the literature, problems, and methods of philosophy through assignments of classical philosophical texts by such giants as Plato, Descartes, Berkeley, Hume, or Sartre.

The second of a three-course sequence could be a course in the philosophy of science. A background in science is neither necessary nor expected. The obvious theme of such a course is the ways in which science and philosophy interact. Some questions that might be addressed include:

- What are the differences between science and nonscience?
- How do scientists come up with their results and their reasons for belief?
- Why are theories important?
- What is observation?
- What goals do the sciences have, and how are they chosen?
- How does scientific knowledge develop?
- How does scientific knowledge influence culture and way of life?

The final course could be one on decision making. Such a course would provide an examination of various approaches to decision making in several different contexts. This will help in personal decisions, conflict resolutions, moral or ethical dilemmas, human value judgments, and public choice.

This sequence of course selection would be most effective if the courses are taken one per year, commencing at the freshman level. This would facilitate gradual and more permanent learning, as well as providing an opportunity to compare and contrast the reality of the modern world with various types of philosophy.

## CONCLUSIONS

We emphasize in this book the need for engineers and scientists to develop their understanding of the social role they play in unleashing science and shaping technology for good or ill. To accomplish this goal, we must be much more conscious than our predecessors of our own values and of the values of others who are affected by our work. As we clarify which values are at stake and how they may be in conflict through new developments in science or through the implementation of a particular technology, we may be able to contribute to the making of more beneficial choices. Perhaps no other academic discipline can help us develop these abilities more directly than philosophy can. With its search for the sources of values, with its insistence on clarity of language and logical rigor, and with its forceful differentiation of the questions at issue, it can help us immeasurably in sorting out our own values and determining their bases, in altering them when necessary, and in acting on them in the interest of human welfare.

Thinking through and grounding our own philosophy is satisfying in itself. The old dictum of Plato—that "the unconsidered life is not worth living"—is still true and will always be true. Your life will be greatly enriched by encountering and grappling with the questions that have engaged philosophers for centuries. You will surely not be able to arrive at definitive answers to these questions, but the intellectual pursuit we call philosophy will strengthen your mind, deepen your sympathy, and anchor your values.

### EXERCISES

**9.1.** How could the study of philosophy be valuable to you? Discuss why it does or does not appeal to you.

**9.2.** Do you see any similarity between the skills required for the study of science or engineering and those required for the study of philosophy? Explain.

**9.3.** List the five things you most value. Try to determine how you arrived at these values. Did they develop from your parents, from church or synagogue, from school, from your own reflection, or from some combination of these? Is there anything you wish you valued more? Is there anything you want to value less?

**9.4.** Describe your personal ethics and clarify how you obtained them.

**9.5.** Describe three of the types of ethics explained by philosophy. Give examples from your personal experience of each type.

**9.6.** In deciding whether or not to work on a weapons system for a military contractor as an engineer or scientist, what ethical questions should you consider? Would any of the ethical theories in philosophy be of help?

**9.7.** When deciding for whom you will vote in the next presidential election, what ethical questions will be of importance to you?

**9.8.** Do you believe that science and technology are "value-free"? Justify your view.

**9.9.** In your undergraduate course catalog, identify courses in philosophy that would meet both the objectives discussed in this chapter and the general education requirements that you must fulfill for your degree.

**9.10.** If you were part of a building or bridge design team, how would you decide whether your design is beautiful? Would the study of aesthetics be of help?

**9.11.** Describe what you think is meant by a scientific law. What makes it a *law*?

**9.12.** Find out what is meant by ontology and define it. Describe one ontological question you have thought about. Of what value is it to ask such questions?

**10**

# Language, Communication, and Values

*Kenyon R. Miller*

## INTRODUCTION

In all the animal kingdom, only human beings have been endowed with the ability to reason and to formulate abstract ideas. This ability is inseparably bound to human expressions through language. To illustrate this point, try to conceptualize the concept that "liberty is a natural right of all people" solely by means of mental pictures. You can easily picture "people," and perhaps you can even conjure up images associated with "liberty," but what image do you use for "natural right"? The statement itself is an abstract idea that requires the use of language. Mental pictures alone are incapable of containing the complex thoughts that can be formulated in the human mind.

Although language, the meanings of words, and their grammatical relations form the basis of communication, few of us fully appreciate their importance to society. The engineer or scientist who is aware of the value of a broad education will likely appreciate the many personal and professional benefits deriving from studies of language and communication. The relation of creative problem solving, computer science, and artificial intelligence to the structure of language, and the

need for language and communication skills in international business, engineering, and science are more than sufficient reasons for students training in these fields to have a special professional motivation. But professional self-interest is by no means the only good reason to learn another language and to sharpen your ability to express yourself in your native tongue.

Studying a second language will give you access to another culture that you could otherwise experience only superficially. You only have to travel in another country whose language you cannot speak to realize how much you are missing. At the very least, you need to be able to read a menu and reserve a hotel room. As your facility with a foreign language improves, you will first be able to understand signs in stores and on the street. Then you will be able to follow the gist of conversations before you are able to haltingly form sentences yourself. When you are finally able to hold up your end of a conversation with someone in another language, you will experience an unimagined thrill, and you will discover that the door to a completely different culture has opened.

The value of another language is not only limited to modern, "living" languages. The classical languages, Latin and Greek, lead back to the origin of our own grammar and vocabulary as well as the origin of Western civilization and culture. Modern mathematics, science, and technology have deep roots in Greek and Roman societies; they were developed in medieval Europe, where the learned used these languages.

One of the regrettable aspects of modern American education, with its increasing emphasis on providing students with marketable skills, is a lack of appreciation for language studies, particularly foreign language studies. Enrollment of high school students in foreign language courses declined from 24 percent in 1965 to 15 percent in 1979, according to an article in *Today's Education* ("A Call to Arms," 1980). Only one out of twenty high school students studies French, German, or Russian beyond the second year. This is indicative of the trend toward specialized technological training instead of a broad liberal arts education. As a beginning engineering or science student, you may not have studied a second language, or if you have, you very likely have not mastered it. Did the educators of past generations prize the value of second languages too highly, or have modern educators failed to comprehend their value? In 1979, the President's Commission on Foreign Language and International Studies urged that foreign language be reinstated as a requirement either for college admission or for college graduation. Although you may now believe that a second language is an unnecessary luxury, you will certainly discover later in your personal life and career that it will give you much personal pleasure and serve you well professionally.

Even more fundamental than the value of learning a second language is the need for students of engineering and science to sharpen their abilities in their native tongue. It is not an exaggeration to note that the single greatest deficiency of scientific/technical education is its consistent failure to produce graduates who are able to express themselves effectively in spoken and written form. As will be pointe

out in this chapter, this lack inevitably has a crippling effect on one's professional and personal life.


## THE BENEFITS OF LANGUAGE SKILLS

### Communication and Creative Problem Solving

Problem solving is perhaps the most basic skill of engineers and scientists, and both creativity and good communication ability are essential ingredients of effective problem solving. Solving problems involves looking at them logically and thinking about them in clear and precise language. It also requires communication skills that enable engineers or scientists to engage their own ideas with those of their colleagues. Rarely are difficult problems cracked by flashes of isolated genius. Much more often they are solved through the interplay of ideas in a team. New technologies often emerge from creative solutions to perceived problems. Company managers value employees who have this flair more highly, since it obviously gives the company a competitive advantage.

But just what do we mean by creative problem solving? It involves four steps: preparation, incubation, illumination, and verification. In the preparatory stage, the problem is identified and goals are formulated. The incubation stage is when you put the problem aside, to reduce the pressure for an immediate answer, and call upon past experiences and associations that give clues about how to find a solution. Illumination is often referred to as the "aha" stage; it is at this point that an idea is conceptualized and translated into a workable solution. The verification stage involves both inference and decision to test the validity of the solution. Although you are probably not so consciously aware of these four stages as you solve problems at school and in your personal life, notice how your problem-solving efforts usually follow the pattern.

Communication and language skills are important at all stages of creative problem solving. Language difficulties that result in an inability to comprehend the problem statement make further effort useless. Similarly, in goal formulation, the inability to define objectives precisely can be the result of poor language skills and can lead to redundant or diffused work. A broad education that includes studies of other languages and cultures provides a rich set of experiences that enhance one's ability to transfer experiences from one situation to another. This is essential in the incubation phase, because creative problem solving often involves a transfer of knowledge between two dissimilar situations. To translate an idea into a useful solution often involves teamwork, for which good communication is essential. Finally, creative solutions must be sold to the user. The power to convince the user that the new solution is the best one requires good communication skills; without them the solution, good as it may be, may not be accepted. Engineers or scientists who want to be able to solve more than just routine problems are at a great disadvantage if they do not have well-developed language and communication abilities.

**Career Advancement**

Having a strong command of language may prove crucial to you in obtaining an interesting job and advancing within it. Most engineers move into management after about seven years, and most employers are looking for engineers who can express themselves clearly and communicate effectively. Scientists must be able to read the international literature, speak effectively about their work at conferences, and write about it in journals. Intelligence alone will not guarantee success or a good job. You surely have met bright people who simply are inarticulate. Are they likely to get job opportunities equal to their intellectual abilities? It is the rare employer who will overlook this skill deficiency. Effective communication skills may well be the single most important factor in career advancement. If you are unable to present the results of your work verbally, your work is of little use to anyone else, no matter how original and innovative you are.

Learning the grammar and vocabulary of a second language forces you to examine your native tongue in ways you probably would not otherwise consider. As you learn a foreign grammar, you naturally compare it with English and thus are forced to better understand the grammatical structure of English. As you learn the subtle shades of word meanings in Spanish or German, you will discover that they have close similarities but often not exact equivalence with words in English. In this process, the precise meanings of English words can become clearer. This indirect development of your command of English grammar and vocabulary will undoubtedly serve you well in your professional career.

**Language and Computers**

Language and communication should not be viewed solely in terms of natural languages. Technology has created the need for new forms of communication as well as new symbols and jargon. Computer languages form an essential part of the education of scientists and engineers. These languages vary widely in their structure and in the applications for which they are useful. At first glance, they might not seem to have a very close relation to natural languages—that is, the languages with which people communicate. However, researchers in the field of artificial intelligence are studying the problem of making computers "think." Some look forward to a day when a conversation with a computer will be indistinguishable from a conversation with a person. The importance of natural language in making progress toward this end should be apparent. After all, researchers must have a firm grasp of the nature and structure of natural language if they are to impart such language to a computer. Already languages like PROLOG, which are based on the object language of first-order logic, have been developed. Such languages facilitate logical inference in much the same way that people construct logical arguments in natural language.

Another application of language is in the design of intelligent man-machine interfaces. To make a computer "user-friendly," one must understand how a user will respond to various actions of the computer; that is, can the user understand what the computer is doing and respond in such a way that the computer will understand what the user wants? You have probably had the experience of sitting before a computer terminal and not knowing what to do with its message, or the converse experience of typing in a command that is indecipherable to the computer. Designers are aiming toward making computers that respond to normal human modes of communication.

Learning a second natural language can develop a deeper understanding of human thought and of the logical structures of language. Studies in linguistics and philosophy are also very useful in other areas of science and technology, but especially in computer science. Philosophers and psychologists have laid much of the foundation upon which artificial intelligence and related fields are based.

### Language and the Growing Internationalism of Business

Foreign languages can be useful to the engineer or scientist employed in industry because of the growing internationalism of business. In a speech delivered at the National Association for Bilingual Education Conference in 1983, Harris (1983) stated:

> The trend toward internationalism and concern with cultural issues has been apparent at multinational corporations since the sixties. Now there is also a growing number of medium-sized companies doing business abroad or planning overseas ventures.

Although many engineers and scientists may never live abroad for an extended period, there is a good chance that they will travel to other countries in the course of their work. There is an offensive cultural arrogance in the assumption that everyone else in the world should speak your language, but most Americans make this assumption in dealing with foreigners. What if the shoe was on the other foot? How would you feel? When someone makes the effort to speak in your language, it makes you sense how seriously they are treating you and your concerns. With the simple sentence, "Ich bin ein Berliner," President John F. Kennedy won the trust and endearment of his German audience in a way nothing else could have done. It had the immediate effect of increasing his power and influence. In most Northern European countries such as Denmark, the Netherlands, and West Germany, seven to nine years of English instruction is required in school. Persons in commerce in these countries have little difficulty when they need to carry out business within the United States. Their positions in business meetings are significantly strengthened because they do not require a translator. Imagine trying to conduct delicate negotiations through a third party. You would always be afraid that you were missing the most important point or that your own precise intentions were being lost in translation.

## Cultural Understanding

The cultural advantages of learning a second language extend far deeper than technical and commercial utility. In the process of learning a second language, you encounter the thought forms of another culture. Just as history and geography introduce students to various world views, so languages expose them to new ways of thinking about the world. Language is more than just a carrier of content. Language *is* content, revealing the ideology and world view of the culture that uses the language. The proverbs and idioms of a language reveal much about the way the people who speak it think. Fyle (1983) has concluded that the vocabulary of the language of a people is the sum total of all the objects, actions, and ideas that affect them or that they need to know in their environment. A good example of this is Tzeltal, a Maya language of Mexico. Tzeltal includes twenty-five different terms to represent variations of our word *carry*. Carrying things is such an integral part of the people's lives that a single term does not suffice; all the subtly different ways of carrying things require distinctively different words.

The ways in which different peoples structure their thought and interpret their experiences is largely determined by their language. Virtually all languages commonly taught in the United States are part of the Indo-European language group. Slavic languages, such as Russian, and Germanic languages, such as Dutch and German, are part of this group. Languages in this group that are much more distantly related to English are Iranian and Sanskrit. French, Spanish, and Italian, among others, are referred to as Romance languages because they descend directly from Latin, itself an Indo-European language. These languages have grammatical structures that are very similar to those of the English language; English itself is Germanic, but it was greatly influenced by French, which was spoken by the English court for 200 years.

However, many languages are not at all like English. The Hopi Indian language, for example, uses no aggregate nouns for things that cannot be observed simultaneously, such as "ten days." Nor does it use a three-tense verb system, as we do. Its "validity forms" indicate that an event is present or past, that an event is expected but not sure, or that a statement is generally recognized to be true. Whereas English employs spatial metaphors to express duration, intensity, or tendency, the Hopi language uses no such metaphors, as pointed out by Brown et al. (1966). Differences between languages are not always so profound, but subtle differences will always emerge to show variations in the way people categorize their experiences.

As you begin to penetrate the thought and expression forms of other peoples, you will find yourself developing quite different ways of experiencing life. Many people find that they develop a heightened awareness of what is going on around them when they are living in another culture and attempting to think and speak in another language. People live much more self-consciously and are enriched by the effort exerted to express themselves in another language.

### The Value of Learning Classical Languages

Machail (1968) cites three things that have been handed down to us by the Romans and the Greeks. First, we have the classical languages themselves—Latin and Greek—as models of precise expression. Second, we have a rich tradition of literature, which reveals much of our own history. Third, we have much of the Roman and Greek cultures embedded in our own. Latin and Greek are thus windows to the past that reveal the philosophies and beliefs that permeate much of Western culture.

Learning Latin is an excellent way to understand the English language and thus develop effective communication skills. A 1928 report of the British Prime Minister's Committee on the Classics in Education states: "We regard Latin as of great and almost irreplaceable value as a means of promoting the proper use of the English language, both in speech and writing, by all classes of the community" (Machail, 1968). Latin grammar forms the foundation for English grammar, so a knowledge of Latin will increase one's awareness of proper grammar in English. Furthermore, as Fodor and Katz (1964) have noted, a fluent speaker is not someone who can imitate previously heard sentences but rather someone who can produce and understand sentences never before encountered. Learning a second language, particularly the one upon which the grammar of our native language is based, increases a person's ability to express ideas in new ways.

In the past, knowledge of Latin and Greek was considered essential to a complete education. Machail (1968) recalls:

> In Scotland fifty years ago, when I was a schoolboy there, the question we are considering was seldom if ever asked. The value of Greek was taken for granted. Education was prized, no doubt, for its own results in market value. But it was prized higher, and more widely, for itself. It was recognized as enabling human beings, not perhaps to be successful in the ordinary sense, but to realize their moral powers and intellectual capacities; thus giving its possessors self-respect and entitling them to respect from others, furnishing them with a surer hold on life, with sources of lasting strength and inward happiness.

A revolution in educational philosophy has taken place since that time; now, to be considered worthwhile, most human pursuits must have immediate material utility.

Such a narrow view of human activity is precisely what a broad education will help to dispel. The "Rennaissance" woman or man who has a firm grasp of many disciplines is unusual indeed. Learning a classical language can provide a personal satisfaction and confidence that the material gain from a merely utilitarian education does not provide. Perhaps it is time to learn from the past and to see the value of education and cultural refinement for their own sake and for the intangible benefits they bring. The person who exerts the effort to become truly educated and to develop character will likely surpass the pragmatist who tries to take a shortcut to success.

### The Philosophy of Language

A final discipline related to language use is the philosophy of language. Although language is taken for granted by most of us, it poses some very interesting philosophical questions. As noted earlier, these questions become particularly important as computers are made increasingly more intelligent. The problem of language acquisition, for example, poses many perplexing questions. If adults must learn a second language by translating from their first language, how can children acquire a language without the benefit of translation?

Some philosophers and logicians have proposed that an artificial language be developed to replace natural language. Fodor and Katz (1964) note that the motivations for constructing artificial languages include the desire to eliminate ambiguity, vagueness, and imprecision of terms. However, philosophers of natural language do not regard these features of language as inherently undesirable. Rather, they think of them as maintaining the expressive power of language by holding meanings relatively constant while our knowledge of the world changes. The issues raised by logic, language, philosophy, and linguistics help us understand how we think and how our thoughts can be effectively shared with others.

## COURSE SUGGESTIONS

Many courses in language and communication are available that will satisfy the general education requirements of undergraduate students in engineering and science at most universities. If one is interested in learning a second language, and thereby learning about the culture of the people who speak that language, courses are offered in many languages and at various levels of advancement. Although taking a single introductory course in a language by no means makes a person literate in it, the value of this endeavor should not be underestimated. There is a great difference between a little knowledge of a language and no knowledge at all. For instance, a person visiting France would be able to function much better if he or she had previously taken even a one-semester course in French. Technical schools normally offer courses in French, Spanish, Russian, and German, and larger universities may also offer such languages as Chinese, Greek, Latin, Hebrew, Italian, and Japanese.

The value of Latin and Greek in understanding English grammar and vocabulary has already been mentioned. Moreover, some schools offer courses that analyze Latin words in law and medicine, which could be of particular use to someone in these fields. Many foreign language departments also offer courses in which foreign culture or literature can be studied in English translation. Students who already have some knowledge of a language may find it valuable to take a course of readings in various aspects of the culture.

Courses of an interdisciplinary nature may also be available to satisfy general education requirements. A course in sociolinguistics would study language from a sociological perspective. Similarly, a course in psycholinguistics would look at language from a psychological perspective. An anthropology course may be available that looks at language in relation to development of a culture. Other courses might be available in linguistics and language philosophy. A course in linguistics would investigate .the theoretical issues surrounding the structure of language. Such a course could be very useful in theoretical computer science, especially artificial intelligence, as mentioned earlier. Other courses may also be available that investigate philosophical issues inherent in language. The point is that one should not only study a foreign language but should view language study in all its many ramifications.

Finally, courses in communication can be very valuable to engineers or scientists. Good communication skills will likely result in faster job advancement. An introductory course in communication theory can point out aspects of the theory that ought to be considered in human communication. A course in speech can develop invaluable skills in public speaking.

## SUMMARY AND CONCLUSIONS

The advantages of acquiring good language and communication skills are diverse. Clear thinking and good communication are an integral part of the creative problem-solving process, which is the heart of science and engineering. Language is particularly important in the field of computer science, especially in artificial intelligence applications. Communication skills are essential for rapid career advancement, and the growing internationalism in business relations gives a decided advantage to the engineer or scientist who has mastered a second modern language. Culturally, many benefits come from learning a second language. A language can open up a culture just as history and anthropology can. The classical languages in particular provide a clearer understanding of the grammar and vocabulary of our own language as well as an understanding of the civilization and ideas upon which our own civilization is built. Finally, a student inclined toward philosophical questions will find that the philosophy of language poses some fascinating questions about the language people use every day.

If you are like most American students, you have not learned a second language or, at best, you have had the minimum required two years of high school Spanish or French. You probably think the effort required to master the language you began or to start a new one, such as German or Russian, is not justified. After all, many foreigners speak some English, so why bother? Learning one of the classical languages probably seems even more useless. You have a difficult enough course of study ahead of you as a beginning engineering or science student without taking on this extra, seemingly irrelevant burden. It is hoped that the discussion of the value of languages in this chapter has raised some questions in your mind about this utilitarian approach to your education. Even from the point of view of utility, however, learning a second language is justified. But language is much more than a means to career advancement and international business negotiation. It opens up the past and present thought and culture of your world and that of others. Mastery of language is indispensable to the process of becoming an educated, civilized person.

## EXERCISES

10.1. Have you learned a second language? If not, why not? List the reasons you think studying another language would or would not be valuable to you. List the obstacles in your way.

10.2. Identify and discuss the four stages of creative problem solving described in this chapter for a problem you recently encountered and solved. Discuss particularly the role communication and language played.

10.3. Describe some ways that a computer language you know, such as BASIC, is different from the logical structure of the way you think and speak.

10.4. Create an imaginary business meeting scenario in which negotiations break down because of language miscommunication.

10.5. Identify a word in another language that has no exact equivalent word in English. Attempt to express the meaning of the word.

10.6. What do you consider to be the primary purpose of your education? Would learning a second language foster that purpose? Would learning Latin or Greek be helpful to your educational goals?

10.7. Describe one question about human nature that is raised by the way we frame our thoughts in language.

10.8. Identify specific courses that could be used to fulfill the general education requirements from each of the following disciplines: (a) foreign languages, (b) linguistics, (c) communication arts, (d) others, such as philosophy or journalism. Discuss the benefits of each course.

10.9. Describe at least four situations in which a scientist or engineer would have a particular need for a good command of language. What might be some negative results of poor communication skills and imprecision in the technical environment?

10.10. For any computer language with which you are familiar, list the sequence control structures and describe in English what they do in the language. *If . . . then . . . else* is an example of a control structure.

10.11. What advantages might there be in conducting business in foreign markets? How might ignorance of the language hinder business relations?

10.12. Using a college catalog or similar source of information, list all foreign languages offered at your school.

10.13. Considering the topics discussed in this chapter, what studies in language and communication would be of most benefit to you personally?

10.14. Using a college catalog or similar source of information, list as many courses as you can that emphasize cultural aspects of a language.

10.15. List all of the ways you can take courses in language and communication to satisfy your particular degree requirements.

**11**

# Literature
# for the Professions

*Julie Ann Tarr*

## INTRODUCTION

Literature is the written artistic expression of the best and worst of life; it is the communication of action, emotion, and thought through written words. It presents, through fact or fiction, a slice of life and asks us to suspend disbelief if necessary. Through literature, we vicariously experience the actions and emotions of the author and the characters, and come to understand their values. We are exposed at different levels to events and experiences, but also to reflections and thoughts as well as word usage and artistic use of the language of others. For engineering and science majors, this exposure may cultivate many abilities and qualities that can be beneficial to both their professional capacity and their personal life. Literature also allows engineers or scientists to view technology and science from broader, non-technical perspectives. In sum. literature can both expand and focus engineering or science students' perceptions of themselves, the profession, and its relationship to society.

Engineering and science students who are interested in exploring literature could very easily be frightened away from a valuable experience by reading the course catalog. What is "The Modern Novel 1900 to Present" about? Would such a course require that you read what critics say about one very long novel in progress or about all novels that claim to be modern? What could an entire course on Hemingway or Hawthorne be like? How could you possibly read all of Russia's literature? And why would you want to? To answer these questions, let us look at what it means to study literature and at how literature courses are organized.

## THE STUDY OF LITERATURE

The study of literature involves reading, analyzing, and interpreting existing writings. The reading is often entertaining and easy, but what is analysis? That may be a little harder. It consists of asking and answering key questions: What is the author trying to do? How was it accomplished? What does it tell us about ourselves and our world?

It is the interpretation of literature, however, that is often most rewarding. After reading a work and figuring out what the author is doing and saying, it is time to decide what it means to you personally. Do you agree? Do you disagree? Have you been exposed to something you have never felt or thought before? Since literature usually reflects some portion of the thoughts and culture of the author, it provides you with a new experience; then you can decide the worth and value of the writing to you. You may disagree with what others think about its merit, art, or significance, but the survivability of a piece of literature is conditioned not only on your interpretation of its value, but also on its creative, perceptive, and universal portrayal of people, ideas, and themes.

## THE ORGANIZATION OF LITERATURE COURSES

The study of literature is organized in several basic formats: (1) writings of a specified time period; (2) literature of ethnic cultures; (3) genre; (4) major authors; and (5) writings of topical similarity.

### Time Period

Literature contains an artistic history of civilized thinking, captured in the fiction or essays of different time periods. This allows the reader to trace the evolution of values, philosophy, society, and human understanding as well as changes in language use and writing style. When literature is coupled with information about the historical events and the cultural and political forces of a time period, students can gain exciting insights into how similar yet different we all are, into what is lasting and important, into the causes and effects of life. For instance, the romantic period, championing harmony in spirit and nature, grew out of the tremendous disruptions—social, economic, and philosophical—of the beginning of the nineteenth century in England. The significant literary form of the age of reason, the essay, gave way to poems about daffodils or Grecian urns.

### Cultures

Culture-grouped writings mirror the customs and thoughts of a particular people. Studying the literature of different societies takes us inside a culture, gives us a fresh perspective, and, through vicarious experience, helps us feel another community's values and way of thinking. We are able, without self-consciousness or expensive travel, to compare and contrast who we are, how we think, what we value. Of course, the relationship between literary style and content can also lead to new understandings.

### Genre

Approaching literature by looking at one type of writing—one genre—is another common technique of study. Some of the genres of literature are the short story, the novel, poetry, and drama. Specific, identifying characteristics distinguish each genre. These characteristics, once identified, give us a handle on the artistic accomplishments of a writer and help us understand what feelings, thoughts, impressions, and ideas or messages are being conveyed. Because form and content are interrelated, we are better able to feel and understand what the artist wishes to convey once we are familiar with the characteristics of the form. For instance, the genre of Haiku poetry requires that a poem be three lines long and that the lines contain five, seven, and five syllables, respectively. In such poems, one clear picture or image is created, and the brevity and clarity of so few words arouses a distinct emotion or suggests a specific insight. In twenty words, Ezra Pound captured the feelings or impressions of the experience of watching one beautiful face after another come out of a Paris METRO subway, where he wrote:

In a station of the METRO

The apparition of these faces in the crowd
Petals on a wet, black bough.

### Major Authors

Reading the works of the major authors is yet another way in which literature classes are organized. Students read a significant sampling of one author's novels, short stores, or poems and learn a great deal about that writer's concerns and style. The works of William Shakespeare, for example, show us a man who knew a great deal about his Elizabethan England. His writings contain detailed references to wars, botany, religion, games, myths, history, geography, and politics. Perhaps more important, however, this man had profound insight into human nature. He understood people so well that he could make his hundreds of characters—from Julius Caesar and Cleopatra to kings, princes, grave diggers, and fools—stand out as unique individuals and speak in a language and manner befitting each one's personality and class. At the same time, Shakespeare teaches us about such things as the dangers of extreme ambition, greed, pride, jealousy, and indecisiveness or about the value of humor, modesty, loyalty, compassion, and love. When Lady Macbeth says "smile and smile but be the serpent under it," or when Lear casts off the daughter who truly loves him because she will not observe the superficial conventions of a dutiful child, we learn that the appearance is not always the reality. Shakespeare's style also heightens our appreciation for his insight. Using a special rhyme scheme called iambic pentameter, this author wrote tragedies, histories, comedies, romances, and poems.

### Topics

One final organizational methodology of literature is clustering by topic. In such courses, students can expect to find different authors, from different time periods, writing in various genres, but united in similar topics. For instance, a black literature course might include works by Africans, American slaves, and present-day black politicians or professors. Women's literature classes might contain readings spanning several centuries, continents, and genres.

### Summary

However it is organized, the study of literature involves the themes, thoughts, feelings, and values of people and how they are expressed. The payoff for this kind of study, both personally and professionally, is high. From reading and discussion we learn appreciation for language and its art; we learn how to express our own thoughts and feelings; we develop compassion and understanding for others; we learn more about our personal tastes, motives, values, and feelings; we develop thinking and analyzing skills; and we learn about cultural differences and the universal truths and verities of the human mind and heart. Now we will consider a few of these skills and insights and see why they are useful to the engineering or science student.

## THE VALUE OF LITERATURE TO THE ENGINEERING OR SCIENCE STUDENT

### Language Usage

Since language is the medium of literature, the study of literature usually includes the study of language. The writings of the ages provide innumerable examples of compelling, effective, and creative uses of language. To read these art forms gives us a heightened awareness of how language can be used. Through this exposure, we can develop better precision of expression and organization of thought, an increased vocabulary and capacity for expression, a sensitivity toward language, and an expanded facility of communication.

Poetry especially exemplifies precision of expression. The following poem by Emily Dickinson illustrates the concise word use found in poetry:

*Success Is Counted Sweetest*

Success is counted sweetest
By those who ne'er succeed.
To comprehend a nectar
Requires sorest need.

Not one of all the purple Host
Who took the Flag today
Can tell the definition
So clear of Victory

As he defeated—dying—
On whose forbidden ear
The distant strains of triumph
Burst agonized and clear!

In twelve short lines, this poem makes us feel how bitter and anguishing the longing for success can be for those who have failed. As we investigate how so few words can convey so much thought and feeling, we increase our own ability to write concisely and with precision.

Literature also requires form or organization to carry its meaning. Writing can be organized in hundreds of different structures, but each imposes certain limits and boundaries on expression. For example, the following lines by William Shakespeare (Sonnet 73) show the organization of thought in the form of an English sonnet, a form composed of three quatrains or "paragraphs" of four lines each and a concluding couplet of two rhyming lines:

That time of year thou mayst in me behold
When yellow leaves, or none, or few, do hang
Upon those boughs which shake against the cold,
Bare ruined choirs where late the sweet birds sang.

In me thou see'st the twilight of such day
As after sunset fadeth in the west,
Which by and by black night doth take away,
Death's second self, that seals up all in rest.

In me thou see'st the glowing of such fire,
That on the ashes of his youth doth lie
As the deathbed whereon it must expire,
Consumed with that which it was nourished by

This thou perceivest, which makes thy love more strong,
To love that well which thou must leave ere long.

Shakespeare presents a different image of impending death in each quatrain—images of late fall, deep twilight, and a dying fire—and then uses the couplet to sum up these images and explain his love's intensity. We can appreciate three units of foundation-laying images capped off in two lines by the pith of his feelings and thought. Such organization, leading to an insightful conclusion, feels dramatic and vital and helps the student recognize the role that structure and organization play in creating effect and meaning.

The study of literature also increases our vocabulary and language sensitivity. Language sensitivity is the sense or feeling of correctness or effectiveness in written communication. Of course, communication is an absolutely essential element in the engineer's or scientist's professional and personal life. On the job, engineers and scientists must be able to say and write what they mean effectively. Surveys have shown that most employers consider communication skills the most sought-after quality, and studying literature is the best and certainly the most interesting way to improve one's communication skills.

### Empathy

Empathy is the conduit that leads us to understand and feel the experiences of others. When we pick up a book, suspend disbelief, and "get into" the characters, we experience empathy and its counterparts—imagination and identification. Literature obviously provides a great deal of opportunity to "walk a mile in someone else's shoes."

For example, if we read William Styron's novel *Sophie's Choice,* we don't have to be present in a concentration camp to know and feel the horror, the excruciating, almost unbelievable anguish Sophie experiences when she is forced to make her choice. Sophie and her two young children, with thousands of others, had been transported to Auschwitz by train, and after many hours their car is unloaded. They are all lined up for review. Suddenly, Sophie realizes that she and the children are undergoing the ordeal she had heard about—a selection. The suspense is high as Sophie advances in the line. The reviewing doctor accuses her, saying that although she is not Jewish, she is communist. To reinforce her case, she blurts helplessly, "I'm not Jewish! Or my children—they're not Jewish either. . . . They are racially pure. . . . I'm a Christian. I'm a devout Catholic." The doctor, however, seems to hate Christians as well as Jews and communists, and he mocks, "Did he not say, 'Suffer the little children to come unto Me?' . . . You may keep one of your children."

> "You mean, I have to choose?" asked Sophie. . . . Her thought processes dwindled, ceased. Then she felt her legs crumple. "I can't choose! I can't choose!" She began to scream.

The doctor threatened to take both children, however, if Sophie didn't choose quickly.

> She could not believe that she was now kneeling on the hurtful, abrading concrete, drawing her children toward her so smotheringly tight that she felt

that their flesh might be engrafted to hers even through layers of clothes. Her disbelief was total, deranged. . . . "Don't make me choose," she heard herself plead in a whisper, "I can't choose."

When the doctor snapped an order for the death of both children, Sophie "rose from the concrete with a clumsy stumbling motion. 'Take the baby!' she called out. 'Take my little girl!'"

This touching, terrifying scene—the event that provides insight into Sophie's complex neurotic character and into why she allows herself to be a victim years after she has left Auschwitz—makes us feel her nightmare, know the burden of her choice, and empathize with her pain. Empathy makes it possible for us to enter Sophie's reality and see life as a mother, as a victim, as another human being.

Why does relating or empathizing matter to someone who is going to be doing mathematical calculations, computer modeling, and plotting of graphs? First, remember that scientists and engineers, far from being isolated, solitary workers, must be able to interact with many types of people in the course of their careers— from clients and supervisors to support personnel and fellow employees. But being able to interact in a professional yet personal manner requires the ability to feel the other person's reality. Interacting effectively requires knowing where the other person is "coming from." Communication on the job that does not connect with or carry the appropriate information to colleagues and nontechnically oriented fellow workers can lead to misunderstanding, stress, and job inefficiency.

Second, in our personal lives, we need to relate with compassion and understanding to loved ones, family members, neighbors, and friends. These relationships in particular make life rich and meaningful and even affect the quality and productivity of our work.

Finally, empathy is the key to perception. Through empathy, we practice seeing and feeling what we may not have understood from an abstraction. This approach to knowledge—often about people's needs, motives, and desires—yields insights and intuitions that are not available to those who have not had practice in honing their perceptive abilities. By studying literature, engineering and science students can better develop their perceptive, empathetic capacities.

### Cultural Perspectives

Much of literature deals with the lives of people of different cultures, countries, and eras. Even though we can't travel to all the different countries, nor can we live in another time period, by reading we can at least escape the limitations of experience and the provincialism of knowing only what we have personally experienced. In addition, literature gives us an author's concept of a culture, thus adding the dimension of another person's perceptions and thoughts. For example, E.M. Forster's *A Passage to India* not only depicts the Indian culture, its customs and practices, but forces readers to see reality from both Western and Eastern perspectives, leaving them more modest and tolerant.

Understanding other cultures can prove valuable to engineering and scientific professionals. International projects will require that the successful professional relate to and understand the needs, habits, and values of other cultures. Ignorance of another culture's customs can be embarrassing—even dangerous, since some countries have strict laws and prohibitions concerning such things as dress and appearance. A minimum knowledge and acceptance is needed before we can accommodate foreign customs. However, a deeper, more integrated knowledge of another culture is mandatory for the engineer who will presume to design and build the technologies of that country. Similarly, scientists are continually called on to relate to colleagues from other cultures at international conferences. And increasingly we are asked to incorporate foreign aesthetics and principles into American life and environs. How better can one become aware of another people than through their literature?

### Value Conflicts

Literature often deals with conflicts of thoughts, values, and ethical standards. The dramatic moment of a literary work is frequently the high point of a conflict followed by its resolution. The author's values and judgment are presented through the thoughts and actions of characters in plays, novels, or poetic reflections. By studying the values of others and analyzing their relevance and importance, our own values and moral judgments are engaged; reaction to another's actions and thoughts forces us to evaluate our own beliefs. As we agonize with Paul in Kurt Vonnegut's (1952) *Player Piano,* in his position as chief engineer of a large industry that has laid off most of its workers because of automation, we also struggle with ourselves:

> Paul did a complicated sum in his mind—his savings account plus his securities plus his house plus his cars—and wondered if he didn't have enough to enable him simply to quit, to stop being the instrument of any set of beliefs or any whim of history that might raise hell with somebody's life. To live in a house by the side of a road . . .

Imaginatively engaging yourself in the value conflicts of literary characters will develop your capacity to make the socially responsible decisions you will inevitably be faced with in both your professional and your personal life. For example, if you become a design engineer who values honesty and integrity, you will be confronted with the decision of whether to inform the client of all risks associated with a design, despite the additional work and loss of profit this might entail. If you are a research scientist, you might be tempted to underplay some uncertainty in your experimental results in order to secure a grant or have an article published. If you have struggled with decisions and temptations artistically created by great writers, you will be much better prepared to face the real ones that will determine the course of your life.

### Creativity

Another helpful by-product of studying literature is the opportunity to observe, evaluate, and respond to creativity. Writing is the output of an author's creative process. A writer combines his or her experiences and observations of life with
the creative powers of feeling, thinking, and expression to generate literature. In
short, creativity is part and parcel of literature.

Appreciative reading of literature also requires a kind of creativity or imagination on the part of the reader. He or she must bring to literature an imagination
composed of sensitivity to impressions, acute receptivity, and the ability and willingness to respond to and be involved in the writer's suggestions. Reading literature
demands and promotes imagination, and imagination stimulates creativity. Thus,
reading and studying literature stimulates the growth of our own creative abilities.
Understandably, the more we study literature, the more we develop these abilities.

An example of literature that is creative in itself and demands imagination
and creativity from the reader is E.E. Cummings's poetry. In the following poem,
Cummings (1972) laughs, through both the form and the content of his poem, at
those who worry too much about the structure and format of life and forsake the
living out of feelings:

> since feeling is first
> who pays any attention
> to the syntax of things
> will never wholly kiss you
> wholly to be a fool
> while Spring is in the world
>
> my blood approves,
> and kisses are a better fate
> than wisdom
> lady i swear by all flowers. Don't cry
> the best gesture of my brain is less than
> your eyelid's flutter which says
>
> we are for each other: then
> laugh, leaning back in my arms
> for life's not a paragraph
>
> And death i think is no parenthesis

Creativity is also inherent in an engineer's work. All the components of engineering research and development, design, analysis, problem recognition, writing,
and speaking demand a creative and original approach. How can someone who has
little experience in appreciating or recognizing the fresh, the creative, be or even
become creative? We begin to become creative by exposing ourselves to the creative
process, which for many involves the study of creative literature.

### Analytical Ability

The one skill every college graduate is expected to have mastered is the ability to analyze. Unfortunately, far too many graduates confess to having learned how to organize, memorize, and regurgitate, but not how to think. Developing an understanding of literature, however, also involves developing an ability to analyze—to answer questions concerning the style as well as the meaning of a work. Learning to think, to analyze, to take apart and perceive elements and relationships is a skill that can be transferred. Thus, the analytical skills developed in the study of literature will not be lost when you are probing engineering problems and concepts.

### Technology and Literature

Literature allows the engineer or scientist to view technology and science from perspectives other than merely those of their proponents. Many respected authors have offered their views of technology and science. Some have presented them as miraculous and wonderful, others have seen them as dangerous and threatening. In the following passage from Herman Melville's (1855) "The Tartarus of Maids," machinery has usurped mankind.

> Not a syllable was breathed. Nothing was heard but the low, steady, overruling hum of the iron animals. The human voice was banished from the spot. Machinery, that vaulted slave of humanity, here stood menially served by human beings, who served mutely and cringingly as the slave serves the Sultan. The girls did not so much seem accessory wheels to the general machinery as mere cogs to the wheel.

Charles Dickens, writing in the midst of the Industrial Revolution, also held a negative view of machinery and automation. Other authors, however, seem to have held different views at different times. For instance, in the *Time Machine*, H.G. Wells saw the potential for good in the technological invention that permitted one man to travel through time to view the mistakes made by the human race and attempt to correct or prevent them. But in Wells's *Invisible Man*, the technology that made solid bodies invisible seemed nefarious when it was corrupted into an instrument of crime and violence and used for bank robberies and murders.

Most authors, of course, do not hold a simple, good/bad view of technology. Other aspects are also raised, such as technology's effect on morality, human compassion, concern for the environment, tradition, and equality. For example, Mary Shelley's *Frankenstein* explores the difficult moral task of mediating scientific knowledge and the uses to which it is put. And a work already cited, Kurt Vonnegut's *Player Piano*, presents an ironic view of technology. The automatic manufacturing systems discussed in the novel are efficient, productive, and perfect, but they have supplanted man's reason to live. We realize how absurd things have become when one character speaks:

"If only it weren't for the people, the goddamned people," said Finnerty, "always getting tangled up in the machinery. If it weren't for them, earth would be an engineer's paradise."

Technology is intended for the use of man, not man for the use of technology.

Although we may not be comfortable reading the varying views held by society toward technology and science, we can be sensitized to the range of opinions about them as well as to their possibly negative uses or positive effects. These readings may help educate us about the need for responsible and moral handling of technological/scientific advances. Gaining a sense of others' views of technology and science will help us design products that do not initiate fear or revulsion in the public eye. The design of a robot, for example, must take into consideration the fears, the feelings, and the reality of uselessness that these mechanical workers engender. Finally, reading will help us sort out our values and address for ourselves our moral responsibility to society.


## COURSE SELECTION

The literature departments at most universities and colleges are large and diverse. An engineering or science student would do well to select one or two introductory or survey courses to get an overview of who wrote what kind of literature during which time period. Then, such courses as "Introduction to the Novel," "Introduction to Poetry," or "Introduction to Drama" can give you a chance to begin investigating some of the themes and techniques of a genre. From there, a more advanced course—perhaps covering one author, topic, or theme—would provide an opportunity to explore new interests and experience new challenges. Courses in literary criticism are especially useful for developing analytical skills. Of special interest to engineering students may be the interdisciplinary courses that focus on readings combining science and literature, such as science fiction and fantasy classes. These courses, besides entertaining engineering or science students, may educate them about the consequences of advanced scientific technology and the need for responsible and moral handling of these advances.


## CONCLUSIONS

For freshmen who intend to become professional scientists and engineers after college, a few courses in literature are a must. No other set of classes offered at a university, with the possible exception of a drama department's courses, allows us to live other people's lives one step removed. Literature classes, it could be said, double the speed at which we learn about ourselves by learning about others. But this does not happen pedantically or passively; rather it happens through vicarious experience. Looking at life over the shoulders of the main characters in fiction, we feel new feelings, see new people and new worlds, take new risks, and sometimes escape our small worlds and painful limitations.

With such information in hand, engineering or science majors will be better prepared to face the challenges to creativity, the need for empathy and tolerance, and the conflicts that are sure to arise as the values of technology meet and clash with those of religion, nature, preservation, and community. Faced with a demanding curriculum of calculus, physics, thermodynamics, circuit theory, and power plant design, you will be tempted to satisfy your general education requirements with less demanding courses. You may think that the study of literature is useful only to liberal arts majors and to those who want to teach English at the high school or college level. Nothing could be further from the truth. If you want to be more than a narrow "formula-plugger" or "computer-jock," some study of the world's great literature is essential. It will help you become a scientist or engineer who is aware of the larger ethical issues of our time and, above all, is a more civilized, interesting person.

## EXERCISES

**11.1.** Discuss the organization of the Shakespeare sonnet presented in the chapter ("That time of year . . ."). What are the ideas and images presented in each of the three quatrains? How is the couplet the theme of the poem?

**11.2.** In Mary Shelley's *Frankenstein,* the engineer/scientist is portrayed as socially irresponsible. Discuss how the study of antitechnology literature can be of value to engineers and scientists.

**11.3.** Is Vonnegut's *Player Piano* antitechnology? How can the study of this novel be beneficial to an engineer or scientist?

**11.4.** Discuss how a novel that you have read reflects the social and political forces and events occurring at the time the author wrote it. How does the author transform these forces and events into art? Did you learn something about the period that you might not have learned as well in other ways?

**11.5.** Give examples of literary works you have read that represent each of the genres mentioned in this chapter. Which genre do you like most and which least? Why?

**11.6.** Discuss what you have learned from an author whose works you have read (more than one piece). Has his or her writing affected the way you view yourself and life about you? How does the literary form chosen by this author enhance what he or she attempts to say?

**11.7.** Do you think your writing and speaking skills are sufficiently effective? If not, do you think this deficiency will hamper you in your professional and personal life? How can you begin to correct the deficiencies you perceive?

**11.8.** What are some of the ways increasing your capacity for human empathy could help you in the future? Construct and describe a home situation and a work situation in which a well-developed empathetic capacity would be required.

**11.9.** Discuss an insight you have obtained through literature into the customs and ways of thinking of another culture.

**11.10.** Describe the most intense moral conflict you have ever encountered in literature. How did the author develop it? What do you think he or she was trying to say? What did you learn that you can apply to ethical decisions in your own life?

**11.11.** What capabilities do you think you will need to become an engineer or scientist who is able to tackle original problems? Do you believe the study of literature can help you develop these capabilities? Why or why not?

**11.12.** How has technology or science been treated in literature you have studied? Discuss an example. Do you share the author's viewpoint?

# 12

# The Value of
# the Performing Arts

*Barbara K. Pequet*
*Richard H. McCuen*

## INTRODUCTION

What art form invades our thoughts hundreds of times every day? Advertisements! What images do these works of art present, and what are they appealing to? The aesthetic appeal of these images seeks to arouse certain emotions, feelings, or value needs. Cigarette advertisements often show healthy, young adults having fun. Are the advertisers trying to develop through an "economic art" form an association between their product and the viewer's desire for health and pleasure? Automobile advertisements often show the cars parked in exotic settings. Are they appealing to our need for variety and freedom? Advertisements for photocopiers emphasize the speed and reliability of the manufacturer's products. Do these advertisements appeal to our need for efficiency and a stress-free life? Travel advertisements show deserted beaches with cloud-free skies and clear, clean water. Do these advertisements seek to encourage us to travel to pleasurable surroundings and enjoy our freedom in a healthy environment? It appears that this "economic art" has a unique and strong relationship to our emotions and values.

This relationship is also evident in the other more common art forms. Some people value a night at the ballet or at a poetry recital. Wall murals in inner-city housing projects are intended to inspire and reflect community spirit. A wall mural in a mass transit station in Philadelphia received very favorable responses from citizens, possibly because it represented a social renewal of their urban environment. The photograph of the Earth taken as the Apollo 8 spacecraft emerged from the far side of the moon symbolizes the value of technology to society. A continuous stream of examples could be presented to illustrate the relationship between social values and the arts.

The performing and fine arts attempt to communicate ideas, feelings, and emotions through sensory perception. By affecting people's emotions and feelings, the arts influence their actions. Advertisements appeal to the emotions and feelings of potential consumers, and the advertisers hope that the advertisements are successful in influencing the actions of the potential consumers. Similarly, a ballet performance, a poetry recital, an opera, or an art showing can affect the emotions of those who view it. A curtain call is evidence that the performing artists have affected the emotions of those in the audience. It is thus evident that the arts serve social needs. They provide social pleasure with humorous and aesthetically pleasing art forms. They provide knowledge by communicating the gravity of social problems. And they provide variety, which can reduce personal as well as social stress.

Just as scientists and engineers seek technological solutions to the problems of society, artists attempt to reflect social problems and solutions through their creative media. After recognizing the existence of a social problem, the artist seeks a way of artistically portraying the problem. In primitive cultures of the past, witch doctors devised ceremonial dances and artistic masks that were viewed as having magical powers to help overcome social crises. The paintings, literature, poetry, and dances of the Industrial Revolution reflected the social concerns of the artists of that period. According to the English poet P.B. Shelley (1792-1822) the scientific advancements of the Industrial Revolution "tainted the literature of the age with the hopelessness of the minds from which it flows." Shelley's wife, Mary Wollstonecraft Shelley (1797-1851), wrote *Frankenstein,* a novel in which the monster reflects the ills of the industrialized society; just as the monster brought about the ruin of its creator, industrialization was viewed as the downfall of the culture. The irrationality of Dada art and literature (1916-1923) reflected the artists' concern for the irrationality of the war and social upheaval of that period. The stage production *Hair* was an artistic expression of the social problems of the 1960s.

This chapter has a number of objectives. First, we discuss values and the arts. This discussion is intended to show that a study of the arts can enhance your understanding of values, which are important to engineers and scientists who must make decisions in which human values are important decision criteria. Second, we discuss problem solving and creativity, both of which are inherent in the arts as well as in engineering and science. A study of problem solving and creativity through the arts can broaden your perspective on these topics as they are applied in engineering and science. Third, we discuss the value of the performing arts to students of engineering and science; this is the central theme of the chapter. Finally, throughout the chapter we discuss the types of courses in the performing arts that can develop the skills and knowledge introduced here. (Chapter 13 will explore the value of the fine arts.)

## VALUES AND THE ARTS

In Chapter 2, we stated that values represent feelings or attitudes. In the introduction to this chapter, we state that the arts are a means of communicating ideas, feelings, and emotions. Thus, it follows that there is an intimate relationship between values and the arts. Whether we are discussing the performing arts or the fine arts, we should not lose sight of one objective of a study of the arts: to understand which values are communicated by those in the arts and how they are communicated.

Art is a form of communication; we might even be able to identify some similarities between language and the arts. However, instead of written communication, we are concerned here with the sensory elements of artistic communication. Instead of written words, artists and performers use lines, shapes, light, color, movement, and spoken words to form the images needed to transmit the artist's feelings. For example, color provides *pleasure*. Color televisions are certainly more popular than black-and-white models because of the pleasure derived from the greater sense of reality. Interior decorators use various color schemes in professional offices to create a favorable image of the firm and to make the surroundings more pleasurable for employees. Color also is a reflection of *health*. A child's color is used by a mother as an indication of the child's health. The color of the air is an indirect indicator of the level of air pollution and, therefore, its healthfulness. Color also provides *variety*. Grayish stage settings are often used in plays about urban areas to indicate the lack of variety in such areas. Computer scientists develop color graphics software because of the greater variety it gives the output. A lack of variety in the color of office furniture can cause employee boredom.

The use of light also affects social and biological feelings. An artist might use shadows to indicate a lack of *freedom,* whereas firelight generates feelings of *love.* A picture of a roaring fire in a fireplace might remind someone of the *security* of homelife. Lighting is important professionally, too. Adequate street lighting provides a sense of *public safety.* Knowledge of lighting is important in the design of office space and computer workstations, since poor lighting can affect worker *efficiency.*

A study of the basics of the arts can increase one's knowledge of lighting and color. Line and shape are also used in the arts to focus attention on the central theme of the artwork or performance. Ballet dancers form lines and shapes using their bodies, and the way the choreographer elects to present these lines and shapes will significantly influence the viewers' perception of the performance. These lines and shapes formed by the dancers can cause a subliminal communication of values such as *freedom, security,* and *pleasure.* Thus, the arts do communicate values, and knowledge of the arts can enhance the ability of engineers and scientists to incorporate these values into their work.


## PROBLEM SOLVING IN ART AND SCIENCE

Chapter 5 discussed Francis Bacon's contribution to science. Although Bacon did not invent or discover the scientific method, he and his contemporaries, such as Descartes, formalized the method of inquiry into a generalized framework that could be used in the advancement of all sciences. For our purposes here, the problem-solving process will be separated into four elements: concept formation, hypothesis, experiment, and evaluation. Very briefly, concept formation is the step in which the scientist formalizes the problem and develops an understanding of the variable factors that influence the phenomenon. Based on this background, the scientist formalizes the problem into an experiment that he or she believes will provide the data needed to prove the hypothesis and solve the problem. In the third stage, the experiment is performed and the hypothesis is tested against the data. Finally, the experimentally verified hypothesis must undergo an evaluation for rationality to ensure that it provides rational predictions and does not violate other accepted principles. These four steps of scientific investigation are often undertaken by scientists to solve a social problem, and human value issues are often at the base of the social problem. By developing a solution to such problems, scientists are meeting their social responsibilities.

The artist and scientist are complementary parts of a culture (Cassidy, 1962). Artists—whether they are painters, musicians, dancers, or poets—also have social responsibilities. It is interesting and important to recognize the similarities in the way scientists and artists approach their efforts in contributing to a culture. For the scientist, concept formation often occurs in a creative flash; Newton is reported to have developed his law while sitting under an apple tree, and the concept formation that made Archimedes famous occurred while he was in the bath at the public bathhouse. This is not unlike the artist, who may conceive an idea for a work of art while involved in leisure activities. For example, Mozart got many of his ideas for melodies either while walking after eating or at night when he could not go to sleep. Once an idea is conceived, the artist must develop the idea in much the same way that the scientist struggles to formulate the hypothesis.

Preliminary sketches by such artists as Rembrandt and Picasso are evidence that an idea conceived is not the solution. The artist develops the concept and experiments with shape, texture, color, and the use of space. The dancer experiments with form, content, structure, and the music in choreographing a creative effort. The poet experiments with words, rhythm, and content in the development of a poem. After artists have created their works of art, they must evaluate them to ensure that they fulfill the original intent. The artistic performance or display is one test of an artist's hypothesis. A successful work of art will meet the social need that inspired the work.

The point here is that the scientist and the artist follow a similar process in meeting their social responsibilities. Although there are a few real differences in the processes used in science and art, there are important similarities. A study of topics in the arts can develop and broaden the problem-solving skills that are important to engineers and scientists in meeting their social responsibilities. It should also be evident that the problem-solving process referred to as the scientific method is actually a process that can be used in one's personal life. Whether people are trying to get into a car when they have locked the doors and left the key in the ignition or trying to train a new kitten, the systematic process of experimentation, including a period of idea illumination, can be very useful. A study of the arts will reinforce your understanding of the process and develop an awareness of the generality of the process.

## CREATIVITY IN ART AND SCIENCE

When we think of creativity in the arts, we think of the great painters, poets, singers, and dancers. But to illustrate a point about creativity, we will use humor as the art form. Consider Koestler's (1964) humorous simile:

> Statistics are like a bikini. What they reveal is suggestive. What they conceal is vital.

Such humor, although it may not produce loud laughter, usually results in a smile. Why does humor generate such a response? According to Kestin (1970) it is because humor requires the listener to be creative. The punchline requires the listener to assimilate facts from two frames of reference. In the foregoing humorous simile, the receiver of the humor must combine the technical discipline of statistics with a piece of wearing apparel. In doing so, the listener creates an association between these two frames of reference and the smile is a response that indicates the pleasure the receiver of the humor derives from creating the association. Consider another example of Koestler's humor:

> Some time ago, the following joke circulated in many of the Russian satellite countries:
> "Tell me, Comrade, what is capitalism?"
> "The exploitation of man by man."
> "And what is Communism?"
> "The reverse."

Why does such a joke provoke laughter from some listeners, a smile from others, and no response at all from others? It is because different listeners have different experiences; thus, they attempt to associate different frames of reference. Some listeners fail to laugh or even smile because the joke fails to cause an association between disjointed frames of reference and does not make the listener feel creative.

Such an individual may not have experience or knowledge of different political systems or possibly may fail to see that the inversion of the phrase "exploitation of man by man" produces an identical phrase. The creative act of inversion itself may cause a smile. Someone else may laugh because the joke elicits a creative association between two types of political systems. As with any art form, the response to humor depends, in part, on the ability of the listener or viewer to create. Thus, a piece of modern art may not elicit a favorable response if the viewer does not have the experience or ability to recognize the creative idea behind the art work.

If creativity is a collision of two disjointed ideas, then we limit our creative ability by confining ourselves within a single frame of reference (Kestin, 1970). This is why proponents of creative thinking recommend that brainstorming sessions include people with highly different backgrounds. Although creativity is an individual act, the association of individuals who have dissimilar experiences increases the possibility that different frames of reference will collide. Individuals can enhance their creative potential by developing interests in a variety of reference frames.

This brings us to a reason for including a study of the arts in the education of engineers and scientists. The implication should be obvious: The arts represent one frame of reference, and technical knowledge and skills are a second frame of reference. The possibility of creative development increases when one has knowledge of both frames of reference. Before discussing how creativity can be enhanced through a study of the arts, it may be useful to examine how the creative act fits into the broader framework of problem solving.

The concept formulation part of problem solving often involves a moment of creative development. This is true in art as well as science. This momentary flash of insight to the problem is sometimes called illumination. The examples of Newton and Archimedes illustrate the point, as does the moment of illumination that comes from combining frames of reference in humor. But this moment of illumination is just one part of the creative idea generation act. Knowledge of creative development is of interest here because the arts are believed to be a valuable source of experience in enhancing creative ability. A study of the arts provides an opportunity to enhance creative talents, and such knowledge can provide many personal and professional benefits.

What is creativity? According to Arnold (1956), "it is that mental process by which man combines and recombines his past experience, possibly with some distortion, in such a way that he arrives at new patterns, new configurations, and arrangements that better solve some need of mankind." For our purposes here, creative concept formation will be separated into four phases: preparation, incubation, illumination, and implementation. Preparation involves both the general experiences of life that have provided a framework for incubation and the knowledge about the specific problem that enables one to think about and solve the specific problem. Preparation also requires self-confidence in one's ability to solve problems, whether by invention, discovery, or innovation. Incubation is a period—sometimes short and sometimes long—in which the individual diverts his or her attention from the problem to the other tasks of life. During this period, some believe the mind unconsciously combines and recombines past experience in pursuit of a solution. Mozart's after-dinner walks and Archimedes' relaxation in the public bath were periods of creative incubation. In the creative process, the illumination period is often brief, such as when one responds to a joke; it is the momentary point in time when a possible solution is identified. This is sometimes referred to as an "aha" event. Finally, the creative process leads to implementation of the creative idea. In terms of the scientific process discussed earlier, implementation is the final act of concept formation that leads one to hypothesize.

Alexander Graham Bell's telephone, the electronic computer, and television are evidence that engineers and scientists are and need to be creative. However, many people consider new operas, poems, sculpture, or modern dances as better examples of creativity at work. Artists, not engineers and scientists, are frequently viewed as the exemplars of creativity. If there is some truth to this, perhaps students in engineering and science can enhance their creativity through a study of the arts.

How does a study of the arts transmit an understanding of creativity and its role in problem solving? An underlying theme of this book is that variety is an important human value. Variety in experience is a factor in creative problem solving, whether in the arts or in creative engineering design. As noted by Munro (1967), the musical composer thinks in terms of sound images, discriminating between rhythm, pitch, timbre, and other qualities. The composer must also be aware of sound patterns and must be able to translate experiences into auditory symbols and to transmit social concerns through the suggestive power of musical sound. The playwright uses words as the medium but cannot create without knowledge of lighting, sound, and stage action. The choreographer can be creative only when he or she understands the variety of factors that affect the ability to translate life experiences into a dance performance. The choreographer must thus have knowledge of lighting, body kinetics, music for accompaniment, the relation of dance movement patterns to life activities, and rhythm consciousness. All of these factors are necessary for the development of a creative translation of social concerns to a consciously created art form that satisfies the viewer's aesthetic sense.

Similarly, creative engineering problem solving requires more than just knowledge of physical laws. Variety in experience and knowledge is important. Knowledge of the suggestive power of music sounds, which can result from a study of musical composition or performance, could lead to a design that would minimize stress-causing noise and emphasize aesthetically pleasing sounds. A study of the creative talents of playwrights could certainly improve the writing skills of students in engineering and science. The creative translation of words by a playwright into a social statement might serve as a model for translating the physical laws behind engineering and science into a creative solution of a social problem. The ballet choreographer's creative use of lines and space through body movement could illuminate the creative design of aesthetically pleasing engineering structures or computer workstations. Observations of creative problem solving in the arts thus serve to illustrate the creative process as well as to provide vicarious experiences that are important in concept formation in engineering and science. In addition, knowledge of the way artists creatively communicate social values to their audience can serve as a guide for students of engineering or science for communicating social values in their designs.


## THE PERFORMING ARTS

A specific objective of this chapter is to explore the value of the performing arts, not only to society but, more specifically, to you. To a freshman who has chosen a major in engineering or science because you enjoy working with mechanical objects, such as automobiles or machines, or thinking through mathematical problems and studying physical phenomena, the performing arts probably seem a very unlikely area to study. In fact, your high school acquaintances who have chosen to major in the performing arts may seem to be very different from you. It may be hard for you to imagine yourself as a dancer or an actor or to identify at all with people who have chosen to pursue those professions. After all, aren't all performers extroverts, class clowns, or people who don't mind appearing in makeup or tights? The entire realm of theater, dance, and music seems so different. Why should an engineering or science student be interested in these subjects? Wouldn't taking one of these classes be a waste of valuable elective course time, time that could be used in classes to make your degree stronger or to make you more marketable upon graduation? If you believe this is so, let's explore the performing arts to see if there is something for you in these courses.

How often do you take part in a performance? If you respond "never," you may be thinking of the conventional performances required in theater, symphony, opera, ballet, pantomime, circuses, stand-up comedy, even puppet shows. But what about your participation in football or tennis or karate competitions? And what about speeches, toasts, or public remarks you have made? After all, we perform every time we make a public presentation or exhibition.

You may be aware that the performing arts have many qualities in common with sports. The performing athlete trains for years to develop skills and to coordinate technique and strategy. In spite of this preparation, however, the actual game or competition requires that the player respond spontaneously to the flow of events in an unpredictable and irreversible manner. Like artists, the quarterback on a football team and the gymnast in the Olympics seek to hone their skills to a fine perfection so that they can produce repeatable movements and results. To shine, however, they must go beyond the purely technical and invest their performance with an inspired individuality. The truly great performances for actors, dancers, concert instrumentalists, or athletes occur when the performers push beyond what is easily achieved and take risks by exploring and moving past their limits. When this occurs before a live audience, the performing moment can be electrifying. When we watch Julius Erving leaping from the foul line on a basketball court to make a reverse slam dunk, or witness Mary Lou Retton completing her soaring double back-flip half-twist on the gym floor, or experience Sir Lawrence Olivier playing Shakespeare's *Othello,* we are seeing exquisite performances.

A mere performance, of course, is not necessarily a demonstration of a performing art. There are many different individual performing arts, and each art form has unique techniques, dynamics, and history. In general, performing arts are live performances before an audience, usually executed by professionals who have trained intensively and systematically to deliver planned or rehearsed presentations. Before becoming professionals, many of these artists studied in universities and took the same courses leading to performance that are available to you as a freshman.

Nonetheless, the thought of a class in the performing arts may still make you feel awkward. It is likely that these studies seem more different from science or engineering than any other discipline.

### Differences

The performing artist, closely identified with his or her work, is publicly exposed with every performance and risks immediate, repeated public rejection. By contrast, the engineer or scientist often works in the privacy and solitude of the laboratory or design office and is accountable to the public only with the end product, discovery, or theory.

The work product of the actor, cellist, or ballerina is ephemeral and impermanent. It provides immediate aesthetic, emotional, and intellectual pleasure, but when it is completed, nothing tangible remains. In fact, it ceases to exist unless it is recorded the moment it is born. The work of the engineer or scientist, on the other hand, is designed to last. A new bridge, airplane, or heat exchanger—or even the solution to a previously intractable differential equation—are the material results of hard work.

Consider, also, the personality differences between people in the two disciplines. Performing artists are notoriously individualistic. Only in the arts do we have not only stars but "superstars." Our culture idolizes performing stars, not only for their talent and accomplishments but also for their showmanship and bravado. Even members of a symphony orchestra, movie team, or ensemble theater troup try to express their art individually and are lauded for distinguished supporting work. Although there are stars of science who make the front pages when the Nobel Prizes are awarded, the vast majority of scientists and engineers are self-effacing people who seek satisfaction by working as part of a team. Their egos are rarely affirmed by public acclaim.

The approaches to work of the two professions are also very dissimilar. Although analysis and interpretation are essential ingredients for the performing arts, much of the preparatory work involves memorization of large amounts of material. The actor must memorize lines, the instrumentalist notes, and the dancer movements and counts. Rote memorization plays only a minor role in engineering and science, where analysis of information is most important.

Finally, the very purposes of performing arts and engineering and science differ. The performing arts attempt to express subjective realities and evoke feelings in the audience. Each performer strives to communicate in a well-composed and well-executed format—through the lines of the play, the arrangement of the notes, or the movements of the dance. Performing arts seek to entertain, stimulate, and challenge. Engineering and science fill a more utilitarian, pragmatic purpose and follow rational, seemingly nonsubjective processes. These professions contribute to society by creating products, tools, or inventions that are useful in people's lives.

### Similarities

In spite of these differences, there are significant ways in which the performing arts and engineering and science are alike. In fact, they are much more alike than you might initially think. First, they both require years of disciplined training. We know that the training of skilled professional engineers and scientists involves four or five years of very demanding undergraduate education. Furthermore, most professionals today earn at least one graduate degree, which often involves further polishing of basic skills in such areas as mathematics and the physical sciences or in such engineering sciences as thermodynamics, fluid mechanics, and mechanics of materials. Because performing artists are involved in entertainment, it is easy to overlook how rigorous their training is. Most professionals in the performing arts begin their training at a very early age—particularly dancers, vocalists, and musicians. Often, students of the performing arts pursue additional training, after they have completed a liberal arts education, with a master or leader in their field.

A second similarity is that having acquired their skills, both performing artists and engineers and scientists must work continually to maintain and improve them. New scientific methods and techniques are available through professional literature, and refresher courses and retraining experiences are often necessary for the engineering or science professional to remain current. The actor, musician, and dancer have a lifetime of continual practice to keep their skills sharp. In addition, since control of the body and voice is crucial for them, such artists must fight against time, age, and even gravity.

Third, performing artists and scientists and engineers are similar in their expression of creativity within constraints. For example, the actor who interprets *Hamlet* night after night on the stage is confined by the demands for literalness and accuracy in following Shakespeare's words, not his own. However, these constraints do not prevent different actors from presenting the character of Hamlet in radically different ways. For example, Nicol Williamson's Hamlet is wilder, perhaps more cynical, than Christopher Plummer's or Sam Waterson's. Similarly, an actor may change the interpretation of a character at a different stage in his or her career. For instance, the young Olivier acting in *King Lear* certainly projected different dimensions than he did in the same performance at age 76.

The engineer or scientist works creatively within the constraints of the known laws of mathematics and science. Engineers bring their knowledge of scientific principles, properties of materials, and economic considerations to bear on new problems of technical design. Scientists strive for unconventional ways of viewing physical reality while relying on the time-tested scientific method. For example, in solving the differential equations describing the motion of fluids past an airplane wing, the engineer may try fresh approaches but must not contradict the law of conservation of mass.

Fourth, although the individual performer in the performing arts often receives much recognition and adulation, there are almost always large backup crews and many supporting performers who make individual success possible. Bruce Springsteen, for instance, needs a team of musicians, sound artists, and road crews for each concert. Luciano Pavarotti relies on choreographers, makeup and costume designers, stage hands, and the orchestra and conductor to make his operatic contributions. Similar cooperation in the laboratory or research office is the crux of your profession. For example, the teamwork needed in the scientific research and design of a building by an architectural engineering firm makes an engineer's success possible.

Finally, both disciplines build on the past to make a contribution to the future. The "cutting edge" concept is familiar to both science and engineering and performing arts professions. Leaders in each field see new possibilities, strive to do what hasn't been done, take risks, and define success in ways not always obvious to the average citizen.

If you consider these similarities between the two areas, you may feel more open to further exploration of the performing arts.

### Technology in the Performing Arts

There is yet another kind of bridge between these professions that, at first glance, seem to be poles apart. That bridge is the enormous impact modern technology has had on the shape and delivery of the performing arts. For example, the development of technological innovations in the mass media—the press, radio, film, and television—has made the performing arts accessible to a wider public. Prior to the development of broadcasting systems, concerts, dance, and theater were primarily experiences for rich people or other artists. Now all classes of people can enjoy the highest levels of performance of, for example, Rossini's operas or O'Neill's plays. Because of the invention of electronic sound devices, we are literally surrounded by music. Engineering innovations are wholly responsible for the development of a new second-tier performing arts industry, the recording. Artists now produce and sell reproductions of their performances in large quantities through phonograph records, compact discs, high-fidelity tapes, and videotapes.

The impact of technology and science in this area has been to generate a heightened awareness of our need of the live arts. Because the performing arts communicate human emotion and because they powerfully express and provoke feelings, we turn to them as a release from the more rational, stressful, or noncreative functions of mundane life. For example, when we are driving our cars—observing traffic rules and making split-second decisions about safety—a soothing sonata over the car radio can create peaceful or harmonious feelings. Although some people argue that the development of technology has deprived people of the chance to release and express emotions, others feel that, in fact, some aspects of technology, particularly those that facilitate and advance the rendering of performing arts, increase our opportunities to experience the range of emotions available to us through a transcendent performance.

Science and technology have directly affected the development of the individual arts. Consider the impact of technology on music alone. Instruments have evolved over the centuries to incorporate new understandings of sound, vibration, and resonance dynamics. The piano, in particular, has evolved tremendously. In the sixteenth century, harpsichords were very popular instruments. However, as the solo piano became a feature of the symphony orchestra in large concert halls, piano designers had to develop an instrument that could capture the delicacy of the sound and note range over the several octaves of the harpsichord but could powerfully project its tone. Today, the concert piano is capable of filling large concert halls with beautiful, clear, resonating sound.

Engineering developments in acoustics are also laudable. In Paris, for example, the Pompidou Arts Center houses an acoustic research concert hall to promote the study of the quality of musical sound. There, engineers and others experiment with movable walls, floors, and ceilings and with various absorbing and reflecting materials to design the best possible concert hall facilities for fine listening.

In dance, the movement of the body has long been enhanced by the evolving state of the art in lighting, stage construction, and prop development. Today, we think nothing of seeing a 200-foot Christmas tree rise up from beneath the stage in the ballet, *The Nutcracker.* We take for granted the nylon and lycra leotards that make the human body and its form in movement highly visible. Clearly, dance, music, and the other performing arts are often closely intertwined with developments made possible by engineers and scientists.

Now we begin to see that what may seem far afield in your conception of your profession may, in fact, be directly applicable to the work you will later do as an engineer or scientist. If your interest has been whetted, you may be wondering how to begin choosing a course in which to learn more about the performing arts. A quick check of a course catalog will show two basic types of classes. As you might expect, one group will be classes that require actual performance or participation by class members; this group would include dance, acting, or vocalization classes. Such courses offer hands-on, active learning experiences. In some instances, a background of study or an audition will be required for admission. Fortunately, many opportunities for first-hand performing experience do exist.

The second approach to learning more about the performing arts is through courses that do not require that you put yourself on the line but, rather, encourage you to stand back, observe, and appreciate the history, development, and accomplishments of the live arts.

## PERFORMANCE AND APPRECIATION

You may recall, as a child, being encouraged by your parents to try out your performing skills before relatives or guests in your home by doing skits or playing some musical instrument. Perhaps you remember being dressed in your best clothes and taken to public places to watch older people entertain and even show off. Now it's your turn to explore the challenges of live communication before unknown individuals. But if it's not a matter of instinct, how does one learn to perform?

### Learning to Perform

The first step in learning to perform is to select an instrument. You may feel most comfortable working with what you already have. For instance, you may decide you would like to explore the uses of voice, either in song and choral work or in expository speech or drama. Perhaps you regard yourself as at least normally agile and athletic and could use your own body as your performing instrument, through dance, mime, or feats of dexterity such as those required in juggling or gymnastics.

Once you have identified the appropriate instrument for you, you need to find a forum. Begin by selecting a course that will train you in the specific techniques of the performance type you have selected. In dance, for instance, you might choose modern dance for nonmajors, dance production, improvisation, or dance fundamentals of performing. Similar courses exist for voice, musical instruments, acting, play directing, mime, speech, and creative expression.

The next step is to structure your approach to study. The basic skills-building classes are often called "technique" classes. Such courses are designed to give the basic action principles of the specific performance type and structured exercises to develop experience, confidence, and understanding through participation and then study. The technique classes are perhaps the most engaging and, as a result, the most exciting, because they demand an involvement of both the mind and body, they force us out of our "safe" seats, and they require us to sweat often and to risk always. These courses are dynamic because we participate fully and learn from our actions, successes, and failures.

Another kind of course that is available—in some cases with no prior experience required—is the repertory or workshop class. Such courses often consist of rehearsal and practice leading to a production or performance. A reader's theater class, for example, will work on the interpretation and directing abilities of students and structure an end-of-the-semester reading for each participant. Or a beginning dance class may teach movements throughout the semester and then reorganize and choreograph them into a short piece for performance for either the class or the campus community near the end of the semester. Such classes provide the safest approach for a blossoming performing artist, since they progress in a step-by-step manner, guiding the student toward the exciting finale of being a performer.

### Benefits of Performance

There are both personal and professional payoffs for taking the risk of exploring the performing arts. First, you are quite likely to grow in self-confidence. Because there is no teacher like experience, what better way is there to overcome stage fright, fear of attention, or shyness than to practice, with help, in presenting yourself to others? Succeeding at one kind of performance gives a basis for believing in yourself, for knowing that you have done it before and you can succeed again in other, even unpredictable, command performances.

Second, the very process of acting or doing enlivens us and makes us feel. When so much of studying is passive or sedentary, performing arts classes not only can be educational, enriching, and challenging but also can help break the tedium of the "active mind, dead body" approach to learning.

Furthermore, recent studies in the acting arts and performances that convey emotions show that acting or portraying an emotion can actually trigger the corresponding feeling in the actor. Dr. Ekman of the University of California at San Francisco recently reported on studies showing that there is a link between the part of the brain controlling the facial muscles and the part where the emotions arise. Thus, through performance, we are given permission to act out and, therefore, to feel a wider range of experiences than is often available in an average day. Although it is the human capacity for reason that marks us from other animals, it is our capacity to emote that makes us feel alive. And obviously the enhanced possibility, through acting, of getting in touch with our emotions, understanding them, and being comfortable with our feelings is something we all need and desire.

Finally, our capacity for self-expression and communication grows as we become competent in a variety of forums. Some social scientists contend that many of today's problems, such as drug abuse and violence, are part of a destructive rebellion or a rupture of human emotion that has been wounded and suppressed for a long time. The outbursts are seen as attempts to escape the prison of logic, rules, convention, alienation, and misunderstanding. Whether this is true or not, the ability to understand and to be understood is a strong, universal need, and people who are better skilled in expression and communication have happier, better-adjusted lives. Performance courses help us feel comfortable with a wider range of communication modes and styles.

The same benefits apply professionally. As a practicing engineer or scientist, you will need the self-confidence to believe in the assessment of your work, to conduct yourself with authority in a laboratory or office, and to make presentations before clients, professional societies, and other peer groups. The shy, timid, nervous professional makes others feel ill at ease and uncertain. Familiarity with the skills and techniques of developing a stage presence can help you put aside self-consciousness and the mannerisms that call attention to inexperience and let your authentic and likable personality come through.

Finally, as in your personal life, self-expression and communication is a necessity for professional growth and advancement. The inarticulate and incommunicative employee is hindered greatly in opportunities for advancement and in the success of daily work. These are only a few of the many benefits that can re-bound to you from participating in theater or dance or learning to play a musical instrument.

### Learning How to Appreciate

Most universities offer a second type of course to educate students in the performing arts. These courses, appearing under different names and organizational themes, are directed toward advancing an awareness of a particular art, an appreciation of its various facets, and, frequently, an understanding of its historical context. Performing arts appreciation courses are structured much like other courses outside the engineering or science departments with which you are familiar, such as American history courses, English literature surveys, and reading seminars. Students are allowed to study without having to participate physically. Most arts appreciation courses are organized under one of three types of approaches.

Almost every performing art department will have a basic course entitled "Introduction to . . . "—for instance, dance, film, or drama. Introductory classes explore some of the major components of the art and discuss a selected number of famous artists in that medium through history and perhaps forms and styles that comprise basic movements or eras of the art. For example, in an introduction to dance course, students study dance as a form of communication and as an art form, survey the theories in styles of dance, and relate dance to other art forms. With the help of films and other media and the re-creation of famous dances that were performed years before moving cameras were invented, students can see and discuss the characteristics and advances of the many schools of dance. To illustrate, an introductory dance class might explore the contribution of Martha Graham—her theories of "contraction and release" and their effects on modern dance. Films of Graham herself in a number of her dances—such as "Oedipus," "Appalachian Spring," and "Projects for a Divine Comedy"—might be seen in such a class. Her fantastically intense delivery, her severe and dramatic presentations, and her willingness to explore the psychological and complex are signatures for all her works. Because she is considered the "grandmother" of modern dance, it could be expected that an introductory course would define these characteristics and trace Graham's influence on later schools of the dance and such artists as Eric Hawkins, José Limon, and Merce Cunningham.

In a music department, you may find an introductory course to advanced appreciation with a title such as "The Art of the Performer." Here students learn by observing performers in recitals and lectures. For example, soloists, ensemble performers, conductors, listeners, even members of the media might make presentations to the class to discuss and show what they do, how they perceive, and what they think is important or valuable in the art. These classes can be very enjoyable because we rarely have the opportunity to hear from the experts involved with performance.

A second approach to organizing appreciation classes is the history survey class. Courses such as the history of music, film, or opera move chronologically to define the various eras or periods and to help students see the evolution of the performing art form. For example, in a course entitled "History of Theater," students would survey the developments of theater in the Western world. The course would probably begin by looking at theater in Greece around 500 B.C. Theater was well developed that long ago. In festivals honoring the God Dionysus, plays by Aeschylus, Sophocles, and Euripedes explored the range of human experience through tragedy and comedy. We study these plays today not only for an appreciation of the times but for what they convey that is universal. After the Greeks came the Romans, and theater continued to flourish; but with the fall of the Roman empire, theater almost died in the West. When it was revived in the tenth century A.D., it was much less sophisticated and universal. In the Dark Ages, theater was strictly limited to religious themes expressed in mystery or mysticism, often performed in front of a church.

It wasn't until the Renaissance and the renewed awareness of Greek and Roman theater that this art form came back and exceeded its past successes. In fact, in the fifty years from 1580 to 1630, a significant body of English drama—much of it Shakespeare's, which some say is still unequaled in language use, character insight, and scope—was created. Of course, these plays are still performed today around the world. The next significant era in theater arrived a century later, when the giants of French literature, Racine and Moliere, appeared on the scene. Although the eighteenth century was not a time of exciting new plays, new changes in the production process occurred, such as movable scenery and the use of women to play female roles. Theater in North America probably began in Philadelphia and New York in the late 1760s. In this century, we have seen the flowering of autobiographical writing in Eugene O'Neill's plays; the exploration of sexual complexity and human interaction in Tennessee Williams's plays, such as *Streetcar Named Desire* and *Cat on a Hot Tin Roof*; and the unique use of language in Beckett's or Stoppard's plays. In such courses, students read *about* drama as often as they read drama.

The third approach to understanding the performing arts is the literature survey class. Here, masterpieces of artists are selectively studied, often chronologically. For instance, in a music literature course, you might study the symphonic or operatic repertory of Bach, Mozart, Brahms, Beethoven, Verdi, or Debussy. Or you might study a specialized repertory, such as Handel's sonatas, Scubert's lieder, or Bartok's string quartets. The distinguishing organizing characteristic of such classes is that they provide in-depth work with specific important artists in a given period.

A study of the masters is also possible in most performing arts departments. Whole courses in Beethoven's works, Balanchine's dances, or Orson Welles's films might be available. Such focused courses may not provide for broad overviews, but they can give a more thorough understanding and familiarity with one great performing artist.

Finally, a more abstract or intellectual option for thinking about live art is provided in philosophy courses. Frequently, a performing arts department will offer one philosophy course, such as theatrical theory and criticism, film theory and criticism, or the philosophy of dance. Such courses explore the philosophical basis of theater, film, or dance and discuss important theorists and the practical application of their theories in the specific performing art.

A philosophy of beauty, or aesthetics, class may provide the greatest insight into the performing arts while allowing you to develop your own sense of beauty and enjoyment. Beauty is usually a significant part of performing art. Classical vocalists spend hours training their voices to produce a wide range of pure notes; the better they succeed, the more beautiful we find their achievement. Ballet dancers try to implement with their bodies the lovely movements created in the imagination of the choreographer. Instrumental musicians practice hours every day, not only to reproduce notes with technical accuracy but also to realize through their instrument what their artistic imagination knows to be beautiful. Actors, through makeup, costume, vocal inflection, and facial and body gestures—placed in the light, color, and furnishings of a stage set—bring their own powerful, sometimes disturbing beauty to a dramatist's words.

But what is beauty and what is beautiful? Is beauty an intrinsic quality that we need only have the capacity to recognize? Or is it simply a matter of taste? Does beauty exist in the eye of the beholder? A course in aesthetics will help you explore these questions and come to your own conclusions about what you value in the arts.

Although there are varying philosophical views, it is generally accepted in human life that beauty lifts us out of our littleness to an understanding of the meaning of existence. Without a sense of beauty, human life can seem drab and monotonous, colorless, and humdrum. Food, clothing, and housing can simply provide us with nutrition, warmth, and protection, or they can excite our senses of taste, sight, and smell. We find greater pleasure in living when they do so.

It may be unfair to say that many engineers undervalue beauty. It is true, however, that the concern for function and performance in the design of products can overshadow attention to aesthetic qualities. For example, consider two types of bridges. The bridges over the autostrada in the northern Italian Alps are soaring, graceful, and artistic. Their American counterparts—and you have seen hundreds of them on the interstate highways—are often squat, functional, conventional bridges. Although all of these bridges serve the same function, the Italian bridges, in harmony with their natural environment, please as well as serve. A course in aesthetics—the philosophy of beauty—will help you develop your aesthetic judgment by analyzing aesthetic theories and experience.

## COURSE SELECTION

It should be easy to identify courses in the performing and fine arts that can be used to fulfill general education requirements. From such courses, you might develop a better understanding of the relationship between emotions and social action. Furthermore, these courses may enhance your creative and problem-solving skills while providing variety to educational programs that are largely technical-skill-oriented. Such courses can provide pleasure and can develop interests that might last long after you have left college. These new interests may help relieve stress and can provide a basis for social interactions. It is these qualities that should be considered in selecting courses in the arts.

It is important to recognize that the arts are not independent of other disciplines. Given the importance of perception to the arts, a psychology course that emphasizes the psychological, anatomical, physiological, and environmental factors that influence perception may be of interest and of value. Psychology courses on learning theory or thinking would also be useful for those who want to enhance their understanding of the creative problem-solving process; some of these courses discuss strategies for improving students' thinking processes and problem-solving behavior.

In addition to philosophy courses that deal with moral and ethical decision making, which are of general value, a number of philosophy courses could be used to reinforce concepts that are important with respect to the value of the arts to the engineer or scientist. Courses may be available in the philosophy of art, the philosophy of beauty, the philosophy of music, the philosophy of language, and the theory of knowledge. A theory of knowledge course would include a discussion of perception and how it affects the accumulation of knowledge; it may also discuss problems of induction that relate to problem solving. A course in the philosophy of beauty would introduce topics dealing with theories of aesthetic experience and judgment. In courses on the philosophy of music or art, the meaning and purpose of these art forms would be discussed; such courses might also discuss how art or music transmits emotion and feelings as well as how it influences action.

Education courses that discuss learning theories and creativity are usually available. A course in educational psychology, for example, would examine specific topics such as learning, problem solving, and communicating knowledge. Education courses that deal with perceptual learning problems can reinforce the material learned in more basic courses on perception.

## CONCLUSION

Learning to appreciate the performing arts, whether through first-hand, performance-based experience, objective, observational study, or philosophical, aesthetic appreciation, is one of the major ways to develop an individual sense of beauty. Through the study of the theater, ballet, music, cinema, and even athletics, we can train and refine our aesthetic sensibilities, expand our experiences, broaden our understanding, and increase our communication skills. As our senses grow, as creativity is viewed and considered, and as our perceptions expand, our world opens and we are made richer.

## EXERCISES

**12.1.** Think of some way in which you have been required to *perform*. What was difficult about the experience? How did you benefit?

**12.2.** List all the performing arts courses at your college or university that you have the prerequisites to take. Which three would most benefit you personally? Which three would most benefit you professionally? What would prevent you from taking one of these courses?

**12.3.** List examples (other than those mentioned in this chapter) of links between technology and the performing arts. What future links with new technology can you anticipate?

**12.4.** Which of your personality characteristics do you think could be altered or enhanced through a performing arts class?

**12.5.** How does aesthetics come into engineering and science? Is it undervalued in these disciplines? If so, why, and how could it be valued more?

**12.6.** How might you benefit from studying the history of a performing art form?

**12.7.** Describe the evolution of the staging of theater. How have developments in technology affected this evolution?

**12.8.** Try to identify what keeps you from performing in some art form. Explain why you think your reasons are adequate or inadequate.

**13**

# The Value of the Fine Arts

*Margaret B. Martin*

## INTRODUCTION

Not many entering college students have been exposed to art in an organized way during their high school years. At best, you may have had one art studio class, and you likely have no idea what art history is about. Without previous exposure to the study of fine arts—that is, studio art and the history of art—you can hardly be expected to have an interest in these or related subjects.

Entering freshmen who are majoring in engineering or the sciences are probably most concerned with taking the necessary courses for their particular technical field. The academic demands of these majors are formidable. The nonengineering, nonscience course requirements seem less important and usually receive little consideration. It is not uncommon for engineering students to regard the requirement for humanities courses as medicine—a necessary but unpleasant part of the "cure" of college. Such students hope that the required humanities courses are at least not difficult and that they fit conveniently into their class schedules.

This chapter intends to demonstrate to the freshman that these "other courses"—the fine arts in particular—can be of value, both professionally and personally. We shall look at three basic questions. First, *what* is included in the study of art? For both art history and studio art courses, we will define the subject, discuss the scope of the subject material, and outline the method of presentation and instruction. Second, *why* should you take an art course? Through examples, we will provide insight into why an engineering or science major might take these courses and what can be learned from them. Finally, *how* should you choose an art course?

We will provide practical suggestions about how to begin to learn about the fine arts, and we will mention a few beginning courses in both art history and studio art. Those are the questions—now on to the answers!

## ART HISTORY

### What Is Art History?

Art history is the study and interpretation of existing works of art. It consists of following the development of art through the ages as well as learning to appreciate the artist behind the creation. Studying art history is an intellectual pursuit rather than a creative one. The approach is much the same as that of most engineering and science courses; analysis, interpretation, and synthesis comprise the heart of the learning process.

The history of art reflects the history of humankind. The subject matter is as broad as the spectrum of human events. Of course, art does not concern itself solely with issues of humankind; its scope is even more varied and extensive. When we study history, we study human events, which are characterized by names, dates, places, and issues of politics, economics, philosophy, and religion. The study of the history of art is analogous; it involves names, dates, the subject matter of works of art, and the significance of the works and their contribution to the world of art.

Facts taken individually or out of context may seem to have little importance. Studied as a whole, however, the development of events or of a work of art takes on real meaning and gives a true appreciation for the subject. To illustrate, consider the Statue of Liberty. To the uninformed tourist, its most notable characteristics are its size, its location in the middle of the New York harbor, and the fact that people can climb to the crown. Learning its history gives us a greater appreciation of the statue's significance. When we learn that the Statue of Liberty was a gift from the French to commemorate the birth of the United States and the friendship between the peoples of the two countries, or that the iron-and-steel framework was designed by the famed French engineer, Gustave Eiffel, who also designed the Eiffel Tower, we appreciate the work even more. Knowing the history of the work adds social meaning and cultural significance to the innate artistic qualities of this massive metal structure.

### The Scope of Study

The material for studying art history can be organized and presented in several different ways. Examples of some common groupings are (1) cultural orientation, (2) movements, (3) the Masters, and (4) form. These categories are tools used by the art historian to order the flood of material, thereby facilitating understanding and interpretation.

*Cultural orientation.* Material organized by cultural orientation might include such headings as folk art, Eskimo art, New Mexican art, or African art. Culturally organized art allows us to study and learn about the art of a particular culture. In doing so, we gain insight into that culture—how economic, social, or religious forces influenced its development and decline. The art of a culture often reflects what that society values and portrays the life and times of the people. For example, the paintings of the American "primitives" show us eighteenth-century life in a pastoral America before the Industrial Revolution, when 90 percent of the population lived on small family farms. We can garner from these paintings how houses were constructed, what farm implements the people used, how they dressed, and what their economic station in life was. Religious scenes tell us how they worshipped. This body of work powerfully expresses the agrarian ideal of Thomas Jefferson, which dominated American politics until the mid-nineteenth century.

Art may be generalized to reflect a specific time period, although this is not always easily separable from the culture, as we saw in the preceding example. Many freshmen, through their grandparents or other older relatives, have had some exposure to the events of the 1930s, known as the Great Depression. We can see the effects of the economic collapse of the United States in the poignant photographs of Walker Evans, who captured a slice of social history in his work. Seeing a small unwashed boy in tattered clothes blankly staring out from a broken-down front porch of a shack is a heart-wrenching expression of the poverty, despair, and helplessness of a nation. Evans recorded the degradation rural America experienced, particularly in the Midwest and the South. Farmlands had been scoured and ruined by lack of soil conservation and by drought. With the general economic collapse of the nation, banks that had not been forced to close themselves foreclosed on unpaid mortgages, forcing the rural poor off the land. The technology of modern farm machinery, well advanced by this time, was of no use to people without the wherewithal to meet their monthly payments.

An example of the technical civilization of twentieth-century America is depicted in an entire room of the Detroit Art Museum. In the hub of the automobile industry, a mural by Diego Rivera depicts automobile manufacturing in all its many social faces. Chemists and metallurgists are shown next to miners and assembly-line workers. The convenient mobility that this technical miracle has provided us is contrasted with the monotony of the assembly work.

*Movements.* Another method of art history organization is by movements, particularly for modern art. A movement in art usually represents a specific style of art. Examples include Impressionism, Fauvism, Dada, and Abstract Expressionism. These movements are not restricted to a particular locale or country. Instead, they grew out of specific artistic characteristics in the art of a specific time period. The development of movements and their continuing rise and fall reflect the transitory state of the times. An art movement often begins with a reaction to the current sociopolitical environment. Dada is a good example. The Dada movement began in Zurich during World War I as a reaction to the atrocities and madness of the times. The style was anti-art and anti-sense. Artists relied on whimsy, chance, and irrationality as their guiding principles. Parallel to this movement in art were the short stories, novels, and poems of the "Lost Generation" of writers who had lived through the senseless, nationalistic, mass destruction of the war. Hemingway's *A Farewell to Arms* expressed in language some of what Dada artists attempted to say with their whimsical creations.

In a very different movement, Impressionist artists in the late nineteenth and early twentieth centuries concerned themselves with the physiological act of "seeing" all that was in a landscape or a face. Breaking with centuries of artistic tradition that had concerned itself with formal composition, psychological expression, and even statements about moral issues, Impressionism limited its scope to the *effects* light and color have on us. It is surely no accident that the development of a science-based technology in the nineteenth century, which viewed itself as value-neutral, was occurring while Impressionist painters were thinking and experimenting with what it means for us to "see." Of course, in limiting themselves to the optical impression, they removed the cultural, social, and moral filters that influence what we see. No one better illustrates this amoral, almost technocratic approach to painting than Seurat. His pointalist paintings, utilizing tiny dots of color, give the grainy effect of a color photograph. He painted these works just after a new understanding of optics and chemical processes had resulted in the invention of the camera.

*The Masters.*   Another way to approach the study of art history is by learning about individual artists. Courses organized in this fashion usually study one "Master." The Masters are those artists who have had a significant influence on the development of art and other artists. A few of the Masters include Leonardo da Vinci, Michelangelo, Rembrandt, Monet, and Picasso. An afternoon spent in a room full of Rembrandt portraits in a major museum will leave you with an unforgettable insight into human character and personality. His paintings of his neighbors, his wife, and himself are studies in human psychology that speak volumes. By taking apart the elements of an object, or even a person, and reconstructing them in an odd juxtaposition, Picasso, one of the founders of Cubism, jars us into seeing what we might otherwise overlook.

*Form.*   Works of art can also be studied by their form—such as painting, sculpture, architecture, or a combination of these forms. Each of these forms has its own history, technique, Masters, and criteria—usually more information than can be studied in one course.

### Why Study Art History?

What can you hope to gain by taking an art history course? We all know, of course, that what we get out of something is what we put into it. But what, exactly, would we be getting?

Most important, the art of a culture often reflects the values of that culture. Thus, studying a particular culture's art can afford us greater insight into what different people consider important and unimportant. For both engineers and scientists, professional opportunities could require that we work with foreigners in distant countries. Our Western values are not universal. The ways in which we conduct ourselves and our business may be well recognized around the world, but these ways may not always be readily accepted by others in their own homelands. Knowing the values and culture of a host country establishes a bridge of understanding and mutual respect between visitors and natives.

For example, an engineer might have an overseas assignment in Africa. The study of the art of Africa would be an enormously useful way to learn about the customs and values of the African people. African art, an essential aspect of African society, represents the major cultural, social, and religious beliefs of the people as well as their revered values. Their sculpture and masks are sacred and are an integral part of tribal entertainment and all religious ceremonies, such as celebrations marking a new stage in life or a change in status. Although the ways of Africa are slowly changing through institutionalized education of the young, the ancient traditions are still a living part of today's generations. To know Africa's art is to see the values of those people and to gain an understanding of their ways.

In addition to deriving cultural understanding from studying art history, there is another more immediate reward. Everyone is likely to travel at some time, whether locally or to foreign countries, and knowing a region's art and architecture gives us an immediate familiarity with the surroundings. This may seem trivial to someone who has not had the experience of traveling in foreign lands. The experienced traveler, however, knows that the discomfort and general weariness of being in unfamiliar cities and being ignorant of what the area has to offer can be overwhelming. Travel should be an exciting learning experience, and understanding something of the art of our destinations can give us a greater appreciation for the environment as well as a welcome peace of mind.

## STUDIO ART

### What Is Studio Art?

The fine arts include not only the study of art but also the creation of works of art. Studio art is the physical, immediate act of creating. To some, it is the physical representation of ideas and emotions in such forms as oil on canvas, carved stone, or welded steel. To others, studio art is a release and freedom, an activity that opens up a greater self-awareness. And to still others, creating art serves other purposes. It is a very personal act. The artist and the scientist or engineer both know the immediate experiential, tactile satisfaction that results from personal, creative control. Both do hands-on work—students of engineering and science through research and lab work, art majors through studio courses. Professionals in both fields, who have great freedom in problem solving, can find this aspect of their work very challenging, creative, and rewarding.

Even the creative process is similar for the art student and the engineering or science student. Each begins with an idea, or concept, that sets the direction for the creation of the project. The ideas then propel both students to try new ways of approaching old problems. What is labeled "creativity" for the artist is called "ingenuity" for the engineer and scientist, but both are creating.

### The Scope of Study

Art forms vary greatly. To simplify study, courses are separated into two-dimensional and three-dimensional subject matter. Two-dimensional art encompasses design, drawing, printmaking, photography, and painting, including watercolors, oil, and acrylics. Three-dimensional art is sculpture in various media, including stone, clay, marble, metal, and wood. The kinds of materials used in sculpture are limited only by the sculptor's preference and imagination.

Two-dimensional art is more familiar to most people than three-dimensional art. We constantly see photographs, drawings, maps, and illustrations. In fact, much of our textbook and printed educational material is two-dimensional, even when a three-dimensional subject is being represented. To overcome this limitation, various techniques are used, such as color variation, lighting, shading, and the manipulation of form and composition.

The focus of study in two-dimensional art classes is working with color, light, and composition. Each course is a variation on the same theme, differing only in the medium and the level of study. Students are usually introduced to studio art by taking a basic two-dimensional art course, either a design or a drawing class. In such classes, working with various grades of paper, pen and ink, charcoal, and pencil, students learn to draw.

Sculpture courses usually require a few prerequisite courses in two-dimensional problems to provide training with surfaces before also working with depth. Three-dimensional work requires that the art be viewed from all angles, not just one. The media that can be used range far beyond the standard stone, clay, metals, and wood. Again, we can find similarities between art and engineering. Just as sculpture students work with their hands and learn how a material behaves, students of engineering and science discover nature's processes through experiment and trial.

### Why Study Studio Art?

Whereas art history teaches us about the world, studio art focuses on learning about ourselves. You don't have to be a gifted artist—such as the American marine and genre painter, Winslow Homer, or the Russian painter and illustrator, Marc Chagall—to feel successful in an art class. The lessons that each student learns are entirely unique and personal. The interaction between the art student and his or her art work is direct and immediate. Each student works as an individual, totally independent. This environment fosters a self-awareness or, rather, a discovery of one's own character.

Self-knowledge—awareness of one's strengths and weaknesses, however specific—can be quite valuable in life. For example, it is common for engineers to have managerial responsibilities at some point in their careers. A manager plans, coordinates, and directs staff members, so successful managers must have self-confidence, must be able to read people and anticipate their problems and fears, and must be flexible in planning and directing. Such skills are strengthened with each opportunity we have to better understand our own character.

A hypothetical example can best illustrate this process of discovery. Suppose that you are given the assignment of doing a clay bust of a model's head. This is your first experience in working with clay. Initially, you begin by working with the block of clay—punching here, pulling there, and thinking all along that it doesn't seem too difficult. You keep at it, and the piece begins to take shape; a head of sorts begins to emerge. Gradually, after many sessions, you notice that the clay bust does not resemble the model's head. You become more intense, and your efforts become a bit more agitated. Several classes pass, but the similarity between your piece and the subject does not come. Again, your determination increases. At this point, however, no matter what changes you make, nothing helps. You begin to dislike the bust, clay, and sculpture in general.

What lessons can we learn from such an experience? First, there is the surface issue of what it takes to produce art. In addition, there is a deeper issue—insight into how you work when frustration overtakes determination, what evokes self-doubt, what encouragement or reinforcement an encouraging remark can mean. The important point here is that studio art classes can provide a microcosm of many personal characteristics and, for conscientious students, can teach us about ourselves as well as art.

Another valuable lesson to be gained from studio art courses is learning to appreciate the work and contribution of others. There is nothing like standing shoulder to shoulder with someone at a job to appreciate the value of work. It is easy to stand back and criticize the work of another. Too often, however, the critic has neither firsthand experience nor understanding in the labor being judged. The sweat and dust of a studio class can heighten our sensitivity to the work involved in producing art.

## COURSE SELECTION

The instruction and presentation of art history courses generally take an academic approach, similar to the approach in engineering and science courses. The subject matter already exists and usually is presented in lecture and slide form. It is then up to the student to learn the material, understand it, interpret it, and finally, appreciate its value.

Most students are introduced to art history as freshmen or sophomores in a survey course. Survey courses are overviews, often presented chronologically. Here students learn basic tools, which make the first step toward art appreciation possible. In survey courses, you will learn about the history of the artist and you will learn how to compare composition, materials, lighting, technique, color, form, subject matter, and the effect in art over the ages.

One basic tool taught in introductory courses is terminology. Every field has its own language, and to interpret artistic works knowingly, we need a working vocabulary. Students also learn about various techniques used by an artist in creating a particular work, why the technique was significant at the time, whether that technique started a movement or represented a perfection of an already accepted style, and whether the technique provides insight into the development of the piece.

In addition, students can develop an appreciation for the subject matter by looking at what it meant to the society of the period, to the artist, and to the development of art. Students are also introduced to the concepts of form and composition, which enables them to develop the ability to see simple forms in complex designs. Obviously, the ability to visualize three-dimensional design problems in two dimensions is a useful lesson for any engineer or scientist.

The instruction and presentation of studio art courses is quite different from those of most other courses. More than the mind is at work here. In studio work, the course material does not already exist. It is a lesson in discovery—not only of materials and forms, but also of yourself. In other courses, creative acts often depend on the level of freedom and direction the instructor can give; the character and skill of the instructor often determine the quality of the course. But in studio art classes, each student is his or her own taskmaster. The art professor offers basic instruction in technique, but self-reliant students must discipline themselves, initiate the work, use the provided tools and techniques for the discovery of their talents, and learn from their mistakes.

An analogy was drawn earlier between laboratory courses and studio art, both of which require creativity. In lab courses in undergraduate science and engineering studies, the procedures are already outlined and the results are known. Real professional laboratory research, however, is much more like studio art classes, where the student is allowed and encouraged to question and to experiment. Discovery is in the air because the outcome is not already known—something new is being created.

Just as prerequisites are needed before higher level courses in engineering and science make sense, courses in design and drawing are required as prerequisites to more advanced studio classes. Understandably, in both engineering or science and art, the basics must precede the complex. In art history, however, the more specialized or historically focused courses may precede the survey courses. Nonetheless, because the survey courses furnish a broad perspective of art, it is wise to begin with them. In addition, these courses are taught with the assumption that the students probably have had no previous education in the subject. Higher-level courses could prove more demanding.

## CONCLUSIONS

The history and studio creation of fine art probably seem remote to science and technology. Of all the general education subject areas considered in this book, with the possible exception of the performing arts, this one probably seems the most dispensable to the beginning science or engineering student. You almost certainly have had little experience of painting and sculpture, other than an occasional museum visit with your parents. How could learning about Vermeer's Dutch interiors or creating interesting shapes with welded steel possibly be of use to you?

To begin with, education does not have to be directly useful to be valuable. You can derive great personal pleasure from a knowledge of the history of art and from your own artistic attempts. Developing an eye for color, texture, and form will heighten your awareness and enjoyment of a well-crafted piece of furniture, a harmoniously laid-out public park, or a beautifully designed bridge. As a professional who will be called on to analyze and creatively interpret or solve problems in science and technology, what better means can you find to learn these skills than through fine art? Studying how others have created and attempting, yourself, to create a vibrant, expressive work of art from the formlessness of oils, watercolors, bits of fabric, or stone will help expand your imagination, sharpen your analytic capacity, and increase your ability to translate an idea into a physical object of beauty, meaning, and even utility. Are these not the talents you hope to develop?

## EXERCISES

**13.1.** What are the primary colors in painting? What are the primary colors in light? Are they the same or different? Why? What are the secondary colors of each?

**13.2.** Who is considered one of the greatest engineers as well as one of the greatest artists in history? What were three major contributions by this person, and why were these contributions significant?

**13.3.** Name an artist who was trained as an engineer. Discuss how this artist's work reflects engineering principles.

**13.4.** Go to a local museum, and identify an artwork that *you* like. Find out who the artist is and any information describing the work. Share your findings with the class.

**13.5.** Describe whatever experience you have had with art. Which periods of painting do you like best? Try to explain why. What benefits can you think of that knowledge about and experience of art brings to you?

**13.6.** Obtain a book of photographs from the library showing examples from the history of art. Find a picture of a work that is indicative of a culture. What does it tell you about the concerns and forms of expression of the culture?

**13.7.** What are the principal characteristics of the Impressionist movement? Can you think of any ways it is related to the development of science and technology?

**13.8.** Identify a work of art that is also a political statement. What is its message? How does its subject matter convey the message? Is the artistic technique related to the message, or not?

**13.9.** Identify a work of art that celebrates technology. How does it do this? How can it be categorized?

**13.10.** Identify a work of art that criticizes technology. How does it do this? How can it be categorized?

**13.11.** Describe how the work of Leonardo da Vinci and Michelangelo were influenced by their knowledge of the science of their day.

**13.12.** What qualities do artists have that cause them to be considered Masters?

**13.13.** Discuss any similarities you can think of between the studio artist and the engineer in addition to those mentioned in this chapter.

**13.14.** How could taking a drawing or sculpture studio art class help you as an engineering student? In what other ways would you benefit?

**13.15.** Describe a work of art with which you are familiar that tells something about another country or culture. What can we learn from it?

**13.16.** In your undergraduate course catalog, identify courses in the fine arts that would meet both the objectives discussed in this chapter and the general education requirements that you must fulfill for your degree.

**14**

# Psychology and Human Behavior
# for the Professions

*David Bardach*

## INTRODUCTION

We will begin this chapter with a short quiz consisting of four true-false questions:

1. Over 50 percent of engineers enter management positions within five years of their last degree.
2. Intelligence and the need for self-actualization are the primary personality traits that reflect management talent.
3. The following describes the personality of the "average" engineer: constricted interests, apparent in a relative indifference to human relations, to psychology and the social sciences, to public affairs and social amelioration, to the fine arts and cultural subjects.
4. In measuring job satisfaction, studies have shown that salary is the most important factor.

Given the emphasis on theoretical subjects in engineering and science curricula, it is probably surprising to find that question 1 is true. The statistics given in the question are the result of a study conducted at RPI (Steger, 1985). If the 50 percent figure is accurate, it seems reasonable that engineering programs should provide courses to prepare engineering students for their role as managers. Unfortunately, they do not.

Evidently, it is assumed that because engineers and scientists are highly intelligent, their intelligence will be sufficient to enable them to fulfill their role as managers. We might expect, then, that the response to question 2 would be true. Unfortunately, however, question 2 is false, at least when we note the words "the primary personality traits." A study by Ghiselli (see Korman, 1977) reported that both supervisory ability (the ability to direct others) and the need for occupational achievement ranked higher as important personality traits. Intelligence and the need for self-actualization ranked third, with a rating of 64 on a scale from 0 to 100; supervisory ability and the need for occupational achievement had scores of 100 and 76, respectively.

If supervisory ability and the need for occupational achievement are the two most important personality traits for managers, we would hope that question 3 would be false. The personality description in question 3 appears to describe someone who would rather deal with mechanical-technical matters than with people. In fact, personality studies have shown question 3 to be true; that is, engineers are not people oriented. The implication of this, in combination with question 2, is that engineers, and probably scientists, are at a disadvantage when it comes to having a natural inclination for managerial positions. This is reinforced by the comment of Lawrence Beck, president of Chemical Waste Management, Inc.: "Our personnel department tells me, and my personal observation confirms, that the liberal arts graduates who come to us with the skills we need generally move up faster in our organization than those educated in more specialized areas" (Rutherford, 1985).

Finally, question 4 is false, which makes matters worse for the engineer or scientist as a manager. If question 4 were true, the engineer as a manager might be able to use employee salaries as a way of overcoming his or her "personality handicap." However, the factors that lead to employee dissatisfaction are sensitive to the manager's personality traits. A 1968 study (Herzberg, 1968) showed that the three factors that most influenced on-the-job *dissatisfaction* were company policy and administration, supervision, and relationship with supervisor. The second most important factor influencing on-the-job *satisfaction* was recognition. All four of these factors involve sensitivity to the personality of company management. Thus, if the manager is an engineer with the "typical" engineering personality, we would have to assume that the probability of employees being dissatisfied is relatively high, given the correct responses to the four true-false questions (i.e., true, false, true, false).

The point of the foregoing quiz and discussion is that employment in engineering and science is not just technical work; management responsibilities will very likely fall on the shoulders of engineers and scientists, probably very early in their careers. Since the technical content of courses in engineering and science does not prepare students for a managerial role, astute students will seek out general education courses that will prepare them for that future role. Courses in the behavioral sciences, such as psychology, can be of tremendous benefit in helping the student of engineering or science become a more effective manager.

## PSYCHOLOGY: SCOPE AND IMPLICATIONS

What do you think of when you think of psychology? Sigmund Freud! B.F. Skinner's conditioning experiments with rats! Opposing psychologists testifying about the mental health of a defendant in a major murder trial! If these accurately reflect the science of psychology, how can a study of psychology possibly benefit a professional engineer or scientist? Perhaps a more conventional definition of psychology might be enlightening.

Simply stated, psychology is the science of mental processes and behavior, including behavioral characteristics of an individual or group. To some, this definition might seem too broad, while others might not find it broad enough. The purpose here is not to completely delineate the field of psychology but to show how a study of a few aspects of psychology and human behavior can be of value to an engineer or scientist. A study of psychology can include a wide range of topics—such as memory and perception, the biological-physiological aspects of behavior, intelligence, personality, and psychological processes of motivation and learning—many of which have important implications for engineers and scientists.

A study of psychology has obvious implications for the individual in social situations, but it also has implications for the engineer or scientist in organizational situations. For instance, a study of learning and motivational psychology could assist in exploring the types of environments most conducive to learning as well as the most effective methods of self-motivation. Industrial engineers involved in product design use concepts of child psychology when developing children's products that require motor skills acquired by a particular age. Engineers who are involved in package design for these children's products must understand the concepts of human perception, which is a central theme in psychology. The analysis of interpersonal attraction and group behavior, as treated by social psychology, aids engineers and scientists who work in groups. Industrial and organizational psychology is used by management to examine job satisfaction of professionals. Courses in psychology often deal with means of enhancing creative ability, which is commonly viewed as one of the most important determinants to success. Given that engineers and scientists are continually generating new ideas, new products, and problem solutions, a study of creative ability has important professional implications.

Personality is a widely studied topic in the field of psychology. As indicated in the introduction to this chapter, the engineer has a distinct personality. In some respects, this personality may serve as a constraint on the ability of the engineer to solve problems, especially important social problems. Often, engineers are practical, analytical, nonemotional, and intelligent. They would rather deal with things than with people. Furthermore, they are intolerant of ambiguity—but the social aspects of engineering problems are laden with ambiguities. Because of this "engineering personality," engineers rarely step back and look at themselves or at society from a humanistic point of view. However, given the importance of personality to managerial effectiveness, a study of personality and socialization would obviously be of great value to engineers and scientists.

Conflict analysis is another topic in psychology that engineers and scientists should study. Although engineers create products that may be superb engineering masterpieces, the products are worthless unless there is a need for them—and some of them may even be detrimental to society. In developing products to satisfy human needs, conflicts can arise within the engineer himself, within the engineering group, and with management. These are often value or ethical conflicts. To develop the product, the engineer must be able to overcome these conflicts, and doing so requires an understanding of where and why they arise. There are numerous examples of such conflicts:

- Should a fire protection engineer accept employment with a firm that produces military weapon systems when the engineer is personally opposed to military weapons? Even though the fire protection engineer may only be designing systems to reduce the likelihood of fires within the plant, employment with such a firm may create a conflict of conscience.
- In the design of the Pinto, the car was redesigned to transfer the force of impact from the windshield to other parts of the system. There were conflicts within the design group over the best way to do this.
- Whistle-blowing (discussed in Chapter 4) is an example of a conflict between an employee and management. The procedures used in solving such a problem have implications for the career of the individual engineer or scientist, for the reputation of the firm, and for society when social values such as public health and safety are involved.

These are but a few examples of the importance of psychology to engineering and science. Although it is not possible to study all areas of psychology within the confines of an undergraduate education, selected courses in psychology can certainly supplement the technical component of an engineering or science program.


## SELF AND PSYCHOLOGY

One objective of this book is to help the reader develop a better understanding of his or her personal value system; this self-awareness is necessary for anyone who will be making value decisions as an engineer or scientist. The self should be investigated first; an understanding of your own values, your thoughts, and your actions is the first stage in psychology. A good starting point would be the question, "Why am I in engineering or science?" Next, you should analyze your behavior so that you can describe yourself with respect to psychological theories or typologies. Once you know something about yourself, you can prioritize your skills and then deal with motivating yourself to employ these skills. Finally, you should consider the issue of the creativity you need to meet your social responsibilities. Enhancing your creative talents will help you discover alternatives for meeting consumers' needs, be more efficient in your work, and recognize more easily the value issues involved in your work.

### Engineering and You

In evaluating yourself, you may begin by asking why you are in engineering or science. Did you choose a technical career path because of the job market or because you enjoy technical work? Is this the career path you really want, or are you just taking this path because jobs are readily available and it pays well? When you were deciding on a major field of study, did this decision create a value conflict within yourself? Introductory psychology courses help you sort out such value decisions by providing an explanation of your personality and, thus, your personal value system.

### Personality Analysis and Description

Knowing yourself—especially knowing the special qualities you possess as an individual—is an essential human attribute. Your personal value decisions depend on your personal psychological makeup. You can describe yourself by summing your behavior characteristics into a holistic personality type that can be compared to other types. Psychologists have developed several different typologies to classify and categorize behavior according to similarities and differences of certain traits, much as the chemical elements are classified by families according to certain characteristics. One such typology is the Myers-Briggs Type Indicator, which places an individual in one of sixteen categories based on four personality traits. There are a number of such personality tests; although some of them are considered to be "pop psychology," a properly validated test can provide useful information. The methods attempt to identify basic personality characteristics from which patterns of behavior can be inferred. What could knowledge of such a test yield? In general, such tests attempt to identify strengths and weaknesses in an individual's approach to problem solving and decision making. Such knowledge can have the following results:

- It can enhance your ability to use your existing problem-solving strengths.
- It can permit you to identify types of problems for which your current problem-solving approach is not well suited.
- It can enable you to develop new problem-solving strategies to solve problems that are not amenable to solutions based on your existing problem-solving strategy.
- It can enable you to identify problem-solving strategies being used by others so that intragroup communication is more efficient and effective and so that decision conflicts are minimized.

It should be added that such knowledge about problem-solving strategies is especially important in decision problems that involve social values.

The presumed personality characteristics of engineers and scientists suggest that they tend to view problem solving in a specific way. They want a rational solution, and they try to mold a problem into one without any ambiguities. Since they prefer well-structured solutions, they tend to minimize the importance of value issues. This narrow problem-solving viewpoint can limit their effectiveness. It is certainly a factor in their approach to management. By recognizing that many problems faced by managers are not well structured and involve value issues and conflicts, engineers and scientists might be more willing to recognize the importance of adopting new types of problem-solving strategies for use in such situations. A study of perception and personality thus has important implications for engineers and scientists.

### Prioritizing

Psychological typologies also identify personality strengths and weaknesses. As engineers, we learn to prioritize technical matters in terms of our approach to problems and research, but we do not learn to prioritize the values associated with engineering. This is where a knowledge of psychology can help. By studying psychology, you can learn about yourself so that you can call on certain personality traits when needed. Psychology can help you know how much of which value or personality characteristic to use when you are faced with a particular type of problem. Suppose, for example, that Tom, a chemical engineer, possesses the following attributes: friendliness, diligence (he will work on a problem until he solves it), and a good sense of economics. As a plant engineer, Tom is ready to scale up his pilot plant to commercial production. He goes to the plant to meet with the contractors and union laborers, who have been at the site for several months. To work with these people, Tom must prioritize his skills. His most valuable asset in this situation is his friendliness. At this point, he does not need his economic skills, and his diligence will be needed later when problems arise with the operation. Now, however, it is most important that he be friendly and cooperative, facilitating the teamwork necessary to proceed through the start-up stage. If Tom fails to prioritize his skills and instead tries to employ all three skills equally, he will have devoted an excessive amount of time to a minor aspect of the start-up.

### Motivation

Another dimension of the psychological self is motivation. Do you need incentives and rewards to perform certain functions? When you are assigned a homework set, what is your motivation for completing it? Knowledge? Grade? Routine? This concept also relates to the motivation for completing projects on the job. If you were a nuclear engineer, what would be your motivation for completing the plans for a new nuclear reactor? Responsibility to your employer? Enjoyment of the project? Means of income? A study of motivation is beneficial because people who understand why they are doing what they are doing are usually happier and more efficient because they have actively made choices. Topics taught in psychology that relate to motivation include learning, cognitive development, memory, and thinking.

### Creativity

The final aspect of self as related to the engineering career is creativity. During much of your education, you have learned that there is a right way and a wrong way to solve problems. As you progress through your engineering education, problems turn into projects. There may be several ways to complete a project successfully, and all might be equally satisfactory in terms of the technical issues of engineering; however, when you take human behavior and social values into consideration, one solution may prove to be the best. Creative solutions to problems or projects combine the technical aspects of engineering with the aspects people consider important. Engineers can use concepts from psychology to understand the factors that stimulate and inhibit creativity. Psychology topics such as emotions, thinking, personality, and learning would help engineers and scientists enhance their creative talents.

### Attitude and Individual Behavior

In a study of psychology as it applies to the individual, four topics are especially important. Individual behavior is a function of one's attitudes, learning ability, perception, and personality. Without trying to define these terms in psychological terms, we will demonstrate their importance using an array of diverse examples.

It is widely recognized that attitude is a partial determinant of job performance. The phrase "he has a bad attitude" is used to refer to an individual who does not work well within a team; such an individual may limit the effectiveness of the group. especially when he or she is a group leader. A number of courses in psychology programs discuss attitude as a behavioral determinant, and courses on attitude modification would certainly be of value to someone who planned to be a manager. Attitude is also role-dependent. Studies have shown that as an individual moves from a position with technical responsibilities to a position with managerial responsibilities, his or her attitude changes. In one's personal life, attitudes toward child rearing change when one becomes a parent—that is, when one changes roles. Attitudes can also serve as creativity inhibitors. Bailey (1978) lists the following as attitudes that stifle creative ability: conformity, unquestioning, disorderliness, conservatism, pessimism, timidity, and making excuses to stop work. Other attitudes—such as self-confidence, humility, honesty, questioning and confident doubting, openness, and determination—serve as creativity stimulators. Knowledge of topics in psychology can lead to modifications in behavior that can enhance creative ability.

The meaning and importance of learning as an element of individual behavior is probably evident, especially to a student in engineering or science. An initial topic in learning theory in an introductory course in basic psychology is learning acquisition—specifically, classical and operant conditioning. The classic example of material studied in such a course is Pavlov's experiments with dogs, which led to the conclusion that individuals learn faster and better when they are given positive reinforcements. One implication of such material is that a manager might improve productivity related to learning by providing reinforcement. Another topic in learning theory that could be important to the engineer or scientist as a manager is learning intervention strategies. Knowing about the extinction of undesirable behavior through negative reinforcement would be important to a manager who wished to change a certain behavioral characteristic of an employee. For example, a manager may wish to change the behavior of an employee who is consistently late for work or one who talks too much. Extinction and punishment are two topics discussed in a basic pyschology course that deals with reducing or eliminating undesirable behavior. The implications of such material with respect to child rearing should be evident; thus, the material has personal as well as professional benefits.

Perception—another topic taught in basic psychology courses—is also important professionally in a number of ways. Senger (1971) showed that managers tend to evaluate the work performance of their employees who have values similar to their own as more effective than the performance of employees who have values dissimilar from their own. This is, in part, a problem in perception. Perception is usually taught in relation to sensory stimuli; but it is a broader concept. It represents the way individuals respond to various stimuli, not just physical stimuli. Engineers and scientists who design workstations must understand the effects of the way workers will respond to the workstation environment. Managers may make wrong decisions because they have stereotyped their employees according to perceived behavior similarities with other employees. Individuals characterize themselves according to the way they perceive their own conduct in comparison to that of others; this perception, or self-concept, will affect their own behavior, personal and professional. If individuals perceive themselves as less creative, they may not apply for positions that require a creative attitude. If they perceive themselves as introverted, they may shy away from management positions that require sales activities. Similarly, a self-perception of introversion may reduce one's ability to respond to social situations. A study of psychology can introduce topics related to perceptual difficulties, and such knowledge can be useful for improving behavior.

Personality—the fourth component of human behavior considered in basic psychology courses—is the pattern of collective character, the behavioral, temperamental, emotional, and mental traits of an individual. As suggested earlier, engineers have a distinctive personality. As indicated by Florman (1976), engineers are perceived as practical, analytical, and nonemotional; their interests center on mechanical-technical matters and on athletic and outdoor activities. Most important, engineers would rather deal with things than with human beings. Other studies, which provide a contrast, indicate that executives score higher in areas such as economic, political, and religious values and interests but lower on theoretical values. Personality traits influence one's creative ability. For example, although engineers typically dislike ambiguity, creative idea-generation techniques, such as brainstorming, require ideas that run counter to immediate practicality. This might limit the creative ability of an engineer. On the other hand, creativity also requires determination, and engineers are usually a determined lot. Thus, some personality traits might enhance the engineer's creative ability.

Role-taking behavior is also affected by personality traits, and role conflicts can create stress. A study of basic psychology can lead to an understanding of the effect of role-taking on personality. A woman in engineering or science may find it necessary to take on the possibly conflicting roles of both mother and professional. A role conflict can occur when an engineer or scientist who takes on management responsibilities lacks the personality traits to handle the position. A young man who finds out that his brother has a fake ID may find his position stressful because of his desire to be both a loyal brother and an honest son. Should he tell his parents?

The leadership role is extremely important in engineering and science. Three elements of a leader were identified in Chapter 6: pathfinding, decision making, and implementation. Engineers and scientists usually make good decision makers because of such personality characteristics as rationality and dislike for ambiguity. Pathfinders must generate ideas and must have a sense for the aesthetic—traits that do not fit the personality of the typical engineer or scientist. Implementers must enjoy working with other people. Again, engineers and scientists do not rate high on this personality trait. Thus, an engineer or scientist who wishes to be a leader must play several roles while avoiding internal role conflicts. A study of psychology can help the engineer or scientist overcome these personality constraints and become a better leader.

## THE GROUP

The second area in which psychological relations are important is the group. For centuries, people of the world have entered and maintained relationships through implicit and informal bonds. This is just a fancy way of saying that instead of formal, rule-based relationships, the roles of community members were set by tradition and culture. This type of relationship, called *gemeinschaft,* was common in rural societies. It is becoming increasingly rare to find such societies. We live in a world based on formal and explicit bonds—a society in which people come together through formal institutions, such as schools, churches, or places of employment. This type of relationship, called *gesellschaft,* is the predominant bond in our society.

Recognizing these formal and explicit bonds, engineers must also recognize that no one functions entirely alone. Engineers and scientists must depend on other engineers and scientists to complete their assignments. Consequently, they must maintain a positive attitude toward and continued interaction with other group members if they are to maximize their abilities. Considering group relationships from a value standpoint, group *harmony* is important if group *efficiency* is to be maximized. *Knowledge* and *efficiency* will be enhanced when role conflicts in the group are avoided. Problems within a group decrease both interpersonal *trust* and on-the-job *pleasure* and can reduce the feeling of *loyalty* that an employee should have for the firm and client.

### Attitude Toward the Group

As engineers and scientists, we should realize that we do not work in isolation; we work in organizations. We perform our work in the context of an organization that sets standards and rules for us to follow. Instead of viewing the organization as a limiting factor to our productivity, we must consider the organization a means to guide and enhance our productivity. For example, in the organization called the high school math classroom, you may have felt that the teacher (manager) forced you to do work when you did not want to. You may have felt that you were studying unimportant topics. If so, what did you do about it? Probably, you complained to your classmates. But try to view the same situation in a different way. The teacher knew more about math than you did and, utilizing his or her personal experience, was able to select the appropriate subjects to study. Furthermore, if the work load was too great, you could have approached the teacher to try to come to an agreement on a lesser amount.

This situation may seem a bit far-fetched, but it illustrates an important point. Your attitude toward or perception of a group can make a difference in your behavior and your mental health. In addition, different viewpoints challenge your technical skills as well as your professional judgment.

Learning about the individual (yourself) in an organizational context allows for prediction of behavior, motivation, and quality of life. If you like a class, you will usually do its required homework before doing work for other classes. Similarly, if you are happy with your work role, you are likely to perform at higher standards.

### Interaction Within the Group

Working effectively within an organization requires working with other people to accomplish a common goal. In all engineering and science disciplines, we work with other professionals—for example, as a design team or in research and development. A knowledge of psychology can improve your ability to interact with others, particularly with those who have dissenting views. If you know the thought processes leading to the decisions recommended by other group members, you can at least appreciate their behavior and problem-solving strategy. Furthermore, an understanding from a psychological viewpoint of why people have different views about what is right and wrong will help your group function better. For instance, two civil engineers are arguing over a design for a bridge with a certain maximum load. One of the engineers, who is more practical and business oriented, proposes a design that meets all safety and design standards for the maximum load as a limit to minimize cost. The other engineer, who is guided by her principles and concern for others, proposes a design that increases the maximum load by a certain percentage to maximize safety. The two engineers continue to argue. Which bridge is better? It depends. Both bridge designs have merit, but neither engineer can understand why the other engineer would want to design the bridge with such constraints. A knowledge of psychology could lead these two engineers to a discussion and subsequent appreciation of one another's designs. As noted earlier, the Myers-Briggs Type Indicator, a tool that categorizes individuals, can help individuals gain a perspective on why others do not solve problems with the same strategies they use.

Obviously, communication is an integral part of teamwork. Whether written or oral expression is used, communication implies an exchange of information or knowledge with your partners, management, and the general public. No communication implies no knowledge transfer, which implies no creation, which, in turn, implies no new engineering products. To achieve successful communication, you must be capable of conveying your ideas to others in such a way that they can understand them. This concept is probably not new to you; however, it is easier said than done. For simplicity, we can divide individuals into two groups: introverts, who concern themselves with the inner world of concepts and ideas, and extroverts, who concern themselves with the outer world of people and things. Surely you have been in groups where one person constantly expresses his or her ideas while another person sits quietly, internalizing his or her ideas. The quiet person (the introvert) may have as much technical knowledge as the louder person (the extrovert), yet no one is aware of that knowledge because he or she does not speak out. Some people cannot express themselves in group situations, but their input may be critical to your engineering team. An understanding of psychology can help you to overcome the dominating extrovert and improve the communication abilities of the passive introvert.

The usefulness of social psychology to your engineering group depends on the context of the situation. You may have a group of friends with whom you go out, study, and work on projects. Your role in the group, as well as the group interaction, depends on what the group is doing. You will have a more casual relationship at a party and a more formal relationship when presenting your project. This also occurs in real-world engineering, where your friends may be your employees, your partners, or your managers. A knowledge of psychology will help you analyze and determine the appropriate behavior for each circumstance.

## MANAGEMENT

The third and final area of psychological relations is management, and the branch of psychology that is most directly related to management is industrial and organizational psychology. Four components of industrial and organizational psychology apply to management in engineering and science: working with people above and below you (i.e., the hierarchy dilemma), managing a business, getting people to work together in a group, and coping with stress. These are discussed briefly to illustrate a few select points.

### The Hierarchy Dilemma

Although some groups include only members from the same level, in management you often interact with people in positions above and below your position. A study of psychological theories of leadership and motivation would benefit managers by making them better able to relate to employees. A common problem for many managers is how to manage a group of professionals who are experts in their technical specialties. As employees, the engineers or scientists are technically trained and possess the knowledge and skills that are necessary to operate independently on a technical level. Managers must use the engineers' resources without offending them. A similar situation exists for high school principals who have to manage a group of teachers who are trained educators in their various subjects.

On the other end of the spectrum, managers must report to higher-level managers. Relationships with high-level management are often difficult for two reasons. First, high-level managers are often under strict time limitations, so lower-level managers must present their information and ideas quickly and efficiently. Second, high-level managers who have a technical background possess a mixed personality type; part of their personality derives from the engineering personality and part from their experience as a manager. This poses a problem for some managers. On a personal level, it can contribute to stress. On a professional level, it can reduce job satisfaction and productivity. Engineers or scientists who understand the problems will more likely be more effective managers.

### Creating Cooperation

A primary responsibility of a manager is to facilitate group participation. But how do you develop a cohesive group? How do you assist the decision-making process without being directly involved? An understanding of group dynamics models will enable a manager to select the appropriate model for a situation or company. In addition, managers are responsible for ensuring the job satisfaction of their employees. Employees should not only be proud of their work, they should also be happy, because happiness leads to greater productivity, greater effectiveness, and a better quality of life. A study of industrial and organizational psychology will provide future managers with methods to increase their employees' happiness.

### Managing a Business

Whether you become a manager within a company or the manager of your own company, running a business requires certain people skills. Often, engineers are technically competent but not socially competent. Hence, it would benefit the engineering manager to take an organizational psychology course to learn such skills as employee motivation, communication, selection, training, and placement. For example, most engineers with engineering degrees are not qualified to hire another engineer—not because they do not know talent but because they are unfamiliar with such matters as legal nondiscrimination requirements and personnel selection criteria.

### Alleviating Stress

All these management pressures can lead to stress. Since much of a manager's responsibilities relate to people matters, and since engineers are not people oriented, stress is more evident in managers who have risen from the ranks of technical engineers. Psychology courses on controlling stress and tension are available, and a student who takes such courses in college may be better prepared for management responsibilities.

## HUMAN FACTORS ENGINEERING

Using engineering technology, we produce equipment that is designed for human use. It is often necessary for engineers or scientists to cooperate with psychologists in such design work. The equipment design must consider the users' capacity to use it, which involves the types of motion required for use as well as the communication of instructions to users. Engineers are constantly concerned with improving product design so that products are easier to use and safer. A field of applied psychology that deals with the design of products for human use is called human factors engineering.

Besides recognizing that human factors engineering combines the talents of engineers and psychologists, it is important to recognize the value issues that are involved. One purpose of human factors engineering is to design products that are easier to use. Along with the efficiency value of the product, however, the product must be safe. It should be obvious that public safety is a social value that is important to both engineers and psychologists. Public health can also be enhanced by reducing user stress associated with machine use. Work efficiency, which is important to those in project management, is also an important element in human factors engineering. Thus, discussions of value issues that arise out of a study of human factors engineering are important to an understanding of specific social responsibilities in managing the work of engineers and scientists.

In our brief discussion of human factors engineering, we will review four problem areas: communication, information processing, fatigue, and equality of the sexes.

### Communication

As discussed earlier, there are often breaks in communication between people. Psychologists determine how to improve the communication process and make it more efficient. For example, in a fast-food restaurant, the only way Sue, the cook, knows when the store gets busy is for Jane, the cashier, to say, "Sue, we are busy!" The communication process between the cook, the waiters and waitresses, and the cashier would be much more efficient if Sue could determine for herself how busy the restaurant is. Although the design of a fast-food restaurant may seem rather routine, a civil engineer engaged in structural engineering could facilitate the communication process by installing a window so that the cook could see the level of business in the restaurant. This engineering design would be more efficient for the restaurant employees and, therefore, for the public.

### Information Processing

Different people process different information cues at different rates. By studying human behavior, psychologists examine how quickly people process different information cues, such as auditory and tactile cues. Engineers can take advantage of psychological studies by placing critical controls in such a location that human error does not result in catastrophe. For example, in an aerospace engineer's design for an airplane control panel, the landing gear control should not be next to the eject button. Again, public safety is an important value issue that must be considered by design engineers.

### Fatigue

Performing the same task continuously for several hours causes human fatigue. Psychologists study the effects of fatigue on the job and how to reduce it. In today's world of computers and data processing, computer monitors are commonplace, and many people sit in front of these monitors for much of their eight-hour work shift. Using psychologists' findings, electrical or computer engineers could design monitors that minimize fatigue by using optimum intensity and color levels. Studies of fatigue as an action inhibitor could also be used by industrial engineers to design assembly lines with optimum work space and work schedules.

### Equality of the Sexes

A final example illustrating psychology's influence on product design relates to gender. For many years, women have been the target of job discrimination, and psychologists have sought to determine the cause of such discrimination. For many years, women were never telephone repair people, not because they did not know how to fix telephone lines but because not all women were capable of lifting the ladder to put it on the truck. Mechanical engineers redesigned the equipment so that strength was no longer a factor. They redesigned the truck so that its middle would act as a fulcrum at the middle of the ladder, thus requiring a minimal amount of strength to lift the ladder.

The foregoing examples are but a few cases in which engineers have changed products so that consumers could use them more efficiently. Engineers have a deeply rooted drive to produce tangible and useful results. Furthermore, engineers consider their work in creating useful products very important. An underlying principle in these examples is that no product is a good product unless people want it. A knowledge of human behavior allows engineers to determine need and demand so that they can create new and useful products. But engineers and scientists must continually remember that consumers want and expect products that are safe as well as efficient.

## COURSE SELECTION

A basic psychology course can provide a good overview of many of the topics discussed in this chapter, including learning and creativity, problem solving, perception, behavior and development, motivation, and personality. One problem with many of these introductory courses is that the connection between theory or experiments with animals and human behavior is not evident. Although this lessens the value of these courses, the material covered is a prerequisite for more advanced courses in psychology.

Beyond a basic psychology survey course, there are other introductory courses that center on a single topic, such as learning, personality, or behavior. Such courses usually discuss the importance of the subject matter to individuals in their personal life, but they rarely identify professional applications of the material. For example, a course on personality would very likely discuss the major theories of personality, the methods used to validate the theories, and the implications to behavior. If the course does not discuss material that could be applied in either professional group or management situations, the student should question the instructor about practical application of the material to the situations discussed in this chapter.

A number of courses taught in psychology programs deal with value issues. A course in social psychology might identify factors that influence individual and interpersonal behavior. A course on the psychology of human sexuality would discuss the responsibilities in personal relationships; such a course might also deal with political and social issues that currently affect sexual relations, including such values as loyalty, truth and honesty, and responsibility. A course in clinical psychology should discuss the relationship between the psychologist and patient, which might be extrapolated to the relationship between the engineer or scientist and the client. Such values as confidentiality, honesty, and loyalty would be involved. A course in the cultural context of psychological development might discuss the effect on the values of a culture of the way people develop psychological competencies.

A wide variety of psychology courses might address issues related to work within an organization or group. A course on the psychological foundations of personnel selection and training would certainly be applicable to the tasks of an engineer or scientist in a management position. A course on thinking and problem solving would enable a manager or group leader to understand the alternative prob-lem-solving strategies used by others in the group or organization. A course on the psychology of leadership might help engineers or scientists who have the personal-ity characteristics described in other chapters of this book to supplement these characteristics so that they can improve their leadership skills. A course on thinking and learning might help develop creative problem-solving skills, which are impor-tant in any organization.

Courses that discuss psychology and human factors engineering can be found within psychology programs and in other programs. Programs in industrial tech-nology, business management, and physical education often include courses that would be appropriate for engineers and scientists. Courses in industrial safety, the application of technology to societal problems, and industrial design could discuss issues related to engineers and scientists as managers and to the social responsibili-ties of those in management. A physical education course in human movement might be of value to an engineer or scientist planning on a career involving design for the handicapped. Several courses in business management might discuss topics related to organizational behavior, personnel management, and motivation within a work environment. These courses would be of value to engineers and scientists and would complement material discussed in psychology courses.

## EXERCISES

**14.1.** Choose two areas of psychology discussed in this chapter and explain how knowledge in those areas would have helped you in a job you had during high school or a summer job.

**14.2.** Think back to your high school science labs—chemistry, physics, and biol-ogy—and think of your lab partners. If you could change one thing with respect to responsibilities in the lab, what would it be? If you could change one thing about your partner's attitude toward the lab and/or the group, what would it be? Finally, if you could change one thing about your atti-tude toward the lab and/or the group, what would it be?

**14.3.** *Management* is a frequently used word in a technological society. What are the characteristics of the perfect manager with respect to the company, the employees, and himself or herself? Specifically address this from a value standpoint.

**14.4.** In your course catalog, identify courses that would apply to each of the topics discussed in this chapter.

**15**

# Values and Professional Ethics in Business and Economics

*Michael E. Bohse*

### INTRODUCTION: WHY BUSINESS AND ECONOMICS?

For a number of reasons, it is usually not difficult to interest engineering and science students in courses on economics and business. First, most students recognize that professional practice is a business, and they believe that courses in economics and business will apply to the technical aspects of their careers. Second, some students plan on pursuing an **MBA** degree after receiving their baccalaureate degree in engineering or science, and they believe that the courses will be beneficial in gaining admission to an **MBA** program. Third, courses in economics and business are viewed as more technical than courses in the arts and humanities. Therefore, students in engineering and science find such courses more comfortable (i.e., more like their own technical courses), more challenging, and more work. Such reasons are not unjustified, since as Steger (1985) reported, over 50 percent of engineering graduates serve in management positions within five years of their last degree.

The study of economics and business is a good idea for other reasons, however. First, advances in technology represent business opportunities, and courses in subjects such as marketing can show how to maximize profits from new technologies developed by a firm. Second, engineering and science practice involves significant amounts of teamwork, whether as members of a research and development team, a project design group, a planning committee, or a policy committee. Courses in group dynamics would be an obvious advantage in such efforts. Third, courses in organizational structure and behavior are very useful both in solving in-house communication problems and in enhancing employee motivation. These are just a few examples where a background, even a minimal exposure, in economics and business can be important to the practicing engineer or scientist; other examples will be illustrated throughout this chapter.

In addition, a study of business and economics provides personal growth opportunities to the individual. Some of the possible benefits include the development of community leadership skills, self-confidence, and independence, all of which are important both in the business world and in interpersonal relations.

## THE IMPACT OF TECHNOLOGY ON THE ECONOMY

We all benefit from the implementation of technology. Technological advances produce economic as well as value benefits. The cars we drive provide freedom and pleasure. Electronic devices such as stereos and televisions also provide pleasure. Labor-saving devices such as dishwashers and clothes washers reduce boredom and increase our freedom for other activities. These value benefits are the result of manufacturing and distribution technology that has reduced the cost of production of these items to levels that most of us can afford. Previous generations would have considered such things luxury items.

The hand-held electronic calculator is one example of technology that is very important to students in engineering and science. Not too many years ago, the first of these now-ubiquitous devices was capable of only simple arithmetic computations and cost hundreds of dollars. Since then, computer scientists and electrical engineers have refined the technology of the microprocessor, the heart of these devices, to the point that a typical unit can perform the same functions that once would have required a room-sized computer. With the additional help of industrial and manufacturing engineers, the production techniques for these devices are now sufficiently economical to provide sophisticated and reliable models for a small fraction of the cost of their forerunners.

Another product of technology often taken for granted is the automobile. It is quite remarkable that this complex piece of machinery, assembled from thousands of parts, can be manufactured and sold at a price within the reach of most families. Many cars feature such amenities as air conditioning, which wasn't even available in our grandparents' houses, much less in their cars (if they had one). For this feat, we can thank all the automotive, mechanical, and industrial engineers who have been involved in automobile design, manufacturing, and distribution over the years.

Improvements in technology and manufacturing have allowed the productivity of our work force to increase substantially. In 1970, the average output per person-hour in industry was almost twice what it was in 1950 and more than five times what it was in 1900 (Fowler et al., 1955; Poulson, 1981). Many of these gains are attributable to such technologies as interchangeable parts and assembly-line production techniques, which were the cornerstone of the Industrial Revolution of the 1800s. Similarly, the gross national product, a measure of the value of the goods and services produced in this country, has reached levels inconceivable in our less technologically oriented past. In 1980, for example, the GNP was approximately $1.4 trillion (1972 dollars), ten times what it was in 1900, even after discounting for inflation (Weiss, 1981).

Advances in technology have also been responsible for changes in American culture. Some of these improvements are not quite so obvious as the examples already cited. Consider the interstate highway system (discussed in Chapter 3). In addition to changing our lifestyles, this system made possible one of the best distribution systems in the world. Manufactured goods such as furniture and perishable foodstuffs can be transported across the country, generally by truck, in a matter of a few days. Besides increasing the variety of products available, the interstate highway system has reduced the costs of perishable cargo to the consumer.

Today, gains continue to be made. The advent of automated control techniques (robotics), now under intense study by mechanical, electrical, and other engineers, is viewed as the next stage in increasing productivity by letting machines handle dangerous or monotonous tasks efficiently and without complaint. Another gain, on a global scale, is the effort under way by industrial engineers to use manufacturing technology to allow the use of unskilled labor in underdeveloped countries that are trying to increase their manufacturing capabilities.

## THE VICTIMS OF TECHNOLOGY

The economic and value effects of technology are not always clearly positive, such as improved products with lower costs and improved safety. The same technology that has benefited most of us has also hurt people. During our Industrial Revolution, while productivity and production were growing so furiously, a complete reorganization of our economy was begun. Those who owned or ran small manufacturing facilities and were not able to adopt mass-production techniques were often put out of business by competition from larger firms, which could charge lower prices. To a large extent, that era saw the end of the small manufacturing firm and, to an even greater extent, the craftsman. Some have considered this change in our culture an example of the detrimental effects of technology; some argue that it has been partly responsible for a change in the source of our values.

Much of our economy is now centered in large corporations, many of which maintain activities throughout the world. General Motors, for example, is so large that the value of one year of its sales is greater than the gross national product of all but a few dozen of the nations of the world. Today, a similar reorganization may be taking place in the farming industry; our newspapers report that the small farmer is being replaced by large corporations. For the most part, the media portray the negative side of this social restructuring. However, businesspeople often argue that it will reduce the cost of food and increase the reliability of our food distribution system.

As another example, we can look to electronic calculators once again. As these machines became standard equipment for engineering and science students, the slide rule used by past generations of engineering and science students became obsolete; companies that produced slide rules were forced to either reorient their business or go the way of the dinosaur.

Today, our large manufacturing firms have their own set of economic technological problems. First, gains in robotics are reducing the need for assembly-line workers while increasing the need for more skilled technicians to control and maintain equipment. This causes a shift in the employment market, and its possible effects are receiving much debate. Many workers resent the technology because they feel that it threatens their jobs (as discussed in detail in Chapter 3). Manufacturers defend the new technology as a means of cutting costs and increasing quality. This is a classic example of a value conflict in which engineers and scientists play a significant role.

A second and perhaps more severe problem is the rise of technology in foreign countries, often in developing regions. Because labor in these countries is generally less expensive than it is in the United States, increasing numbers of manufacturers have found it more economical to produce their products in a foreign country and import them to this country. The results have been closings of American plants, a loss of American jobs, a need for more government aid to hard-hit areas, and a tendency toward a negative trade balance with these other countries. The electronics industry is a case in point. It was once dominated by U.S. manufacturers, but now most televisions, stereos, and other electronic goods are made abroad. A similar process is under way in the automotive industry, which faces fierce competition from several other countries, most notably Japan.

## VALUES, TECHNOLOGY, AND ECONOMICS AND BUSINESS

Chapter 2 identified a number of values that are important in our society, and we can discover many of these values in the interplay of technology and economics. For example, our calculators can increase our *knowledge* by allowing us to concentrate on the underlying principles of a problem without being bogged down in the arithmetic computations. Our cars give us both *mobility* and *freedom* to go where we want to go, when we want to go. Robotics can increase both the *pleasure* and *safety* of employees by relieving them of boring and dangerous tasks. Television sets and stereos entertain us, thus increasing our *happiness.* A feeling of *security* and *safety* can be provided by an electronic burglar alarm. Advances in medical technology improve *public health* and can even prolong the *life* of the average person.

It is obviously important for engineers and scientists to be aware of the possible economic impacts of their actions and the values that are brought into conflict. When a new technology is emerging, these impacts are rarely clear and often are completely unforeseen. Therefore, we must be at least cognizant of the fact that there are interrelationships between technology and the economy and that nothing good comes without change. To achieve this awareness, engineers and scientists must clearly understand the relationship between technology and economics and business.

## ECONOMIC DECISION MAKING AND INTANGIBLE VALUES

Just as engineers and scientists influence the economy, so do economic considerations influence the activities of scientists and engineers. We all make decisions based on economic considerations, in our personal lives and in our professional careers. These economic decisions can be traced back to value decisions. When we decide to spend part of a paycheck on a new stereo component or new clothing instead of putting it into a savings account, we have made both an economic and a value decision. In this case, we weighed the pleasure and happiness that would result from the purchase against the possible pleasure that could result from a future, as yet unknown purchase and the security of knowing that the money is in the bank ready for a future need.

A common decision faced by many college students is whether to get a job immediately after graduation or to forgo several years of income to attend graduate school, hoping for rewards further in the future. These potential rewards may be either higher future income or the increase in knowledge, prestige, and job responsibilities and satisfaction that go with an advanced degree. This is both an economic and a value decision. The value conflict here involves weighing the short-term pleasure and security of a steady income against the possibility of greater pleasure, knowledge, and respect in the future.

When the decision elements are completely quantifiable, the process of economic decision making requires weighing the costs against the potential benefits of the action in question. (The concept of benefit-cost decision making was discussed in Chapter 2.) Decision making can also involve a weighing of values, which may not be quantifiable; this was also discussed in Chapter 2 and was shown to be a similar but more involved process. The process is the same whether the decision involves making a consumer purchase in one's private life or creating an engineering design as a professional. To be successful, it is important that engineers and scientists understand the economic and business aspects of the projects with which they are involved so that they can make the best decisions. A good working knowledge of these disciplines is essential to this understanding.

One of the fundamental goals of the design process is to produce the best possible product for the least possible expense. Because cost is crucial, "overdesigning" is not desirable; that is, a product should be only as good as it has to be. An overdesigned product will probably not be able to compete against lower-cost items that can fill the same needs. Most of us recognize the advantage of using a cheaper material or process when the result will be the same as that achieved with a more expensive material or process. For example, there is no reason to use an expensive, high-strength steel alloy to produce an automotive component when cheaper steels are available that meet the requirements of a safe and appealing product. Where public monies are involved, overdesign represents a waste of public resources; the value implications of overdesign are thus obvious.

Similarly, underdesign has undesirable consequences, in that an improperly designed product may represent a public safety hazard. If the aforementioned automotive component is made of an inexpensive but inadequate material that does not meet the functional requirements, failures may occur, resulting in inconvenience, injury, and even death. Although it is difficult to place a dollar value on public safety, the balancing of monetary benefits and cost must not be done without considering nonquantifiable goals and social values, such as public safety.

As indicated earlier, decision making related to new techniques and expansion of existing industries is not entirely a problem in economic analysis; it is often necessary to incorporate value considerations. A study of economics is important for evaluating these intangible values and for finding the means to balance the various conflicting factors. For example, consider the task of designing a factory. It would obviously be easier and cheaper to design and build a factory without considering pollution control and safety equipment. The American culture, however, values clean air and worker safety. Although these are difficult values to quantify, they represent benefits that have acceptable costs associated with them. To ensure a minimum performance level in these areas, regulations and laws have been adopted that require manufacturer compliance. Two of these laws are the Clean Air Act of 1975, which limits the amount of pollutants allowed to be emitted from factories and other businesses, and the Occupational Safety and Health Act of 1970, which sets minimum working conditions for various types of potentially harmful or dangerous work.

A similar example is the development of environmentally sensitive lands such as forests and wetlands. These areas have value in and of themselves, such as beauty and the preservation of wildlife. Development, unless it is done properly, can reduce the attractiveness of these lands from both an economic and a value standpoint. Because our society places social value on the aesthetic quality of these lands, local ordinances have been written to ensure that the quality of the lands is not degraded; in many localities, environmental impact statements are required before development can proceed in or near these lands.

Engineers and scientists are often accused of failing to show a sensitivity to value issues. To change that view, engineers and scientists, in attempting to produce economically attractive designs, need to consider *all* of the costs and *all* of the benefits. Thus, they must give adequate consideration to value issues associated with any design. For example, adequate lighting should be included in the design of a complex of buildings to provide a sense of security and safety to those in the area. Plans should be provided for proper waste disposal at a chemical plant, again to enhance public health for both present and future generations. Landscaping and environmental integration should be included in the design of any building or factory to increase its aesthetic appeal and minimize its impact on the environment. In many cases, the monetary costs associated with the value issues increase the total worth of a project; this leads to a greater benefit-cost ratio even after considering the additional effort and resources required to incorporate the planning and design for the value issues. Urban flood control reservoirs provide a good example of this. The increase in the value of property located near the reservoir is greater than the increase in the cost of the project due to the reservoir. Thus, the flood control reservoir reduces the fear of flooding, increases the aesthetic appeal of the neighborhood, improves the feeling of community togetherness, and provides a habitat for urban wildlife. These value enhancements are in addition to the monetary benefits of the flood control.

The 55-mile-per-hour speed limit provides another example of economics versus values. Originally, the 55-mph law was passed as an energy-saving measure during the Arab oil embargo of 1973. However, it also reduced traffic fatalities. Although there were both economic benefits (i.e., savings in personal income spent on gas) and value benefits (i.e., improved highway safety), there were also economic and value costs. Economic costs included the cost of educating the public and the cost of changing road signs. Value costs included increased travel time. A recent study (Transportation Research Board, 1984) indicated that about 350,000 additional hours, or about forty years, of driving time were spent for each life and serious injury saved because of the 55-mph law. The researchers concluded "that the effect of the 55 mph speed is to gain approximately one year of life for the expenditure of one year of driving time." However, they also declined to put a dollar value on the lives lost. In this case, the value issue (i.e., life) could be quantified, but a criterion that could be used to balance the value criterion and the economic criterion could not be agreed upon.

## THE ENGINEER OR SCIENTIST AS A BUSINESSPERSON

Although engineers and scientists may not consider themselves as such, they are, in a very real sense, businesspeople. For this reason, it is helpful for them to understand how to start, operate, and maintain a business. This understanding provides the engineer or scientist with the "big picture" of the company and a recognition of the possible conflicts between the business aspects of a project and the technological elements. Because they are part of a business, engineers or scientists will always be constrained in their technical activities by the business aspects.

As people with technical knowledge, engineers and scientists are frequently required to present findings to their superiors and/or clients, who are generally highly business oriented. Along the same lines, engineers and scientists often must solicit work from new clients by presenting proposals and discussing options. To succeed at either of these tasks, engineers and scientists must first be able to communicate in a language that the businessperson will understand. Second, they must demonstrate an understanding of and a consideration for the business aspects of a project that they know will be of concern to the client. Whereas no one would expect a businessperson in an automotive company to design an automobile, automotive engineers are required to assume a dual role in their normal range of activities;

that is, they must be conversant with both the technical and the business aspects of a project.

Consider, for example, the engineer who makes a presentation of a design study for a toaster to his or her superior. That engineer must be able to justify every penny of the anticipated production cost in terms of the materials chosen, the processes to be employed in making the toaster, and the desired performance, reliability, safety, and so on. Although any technically well-trained engineer may be able to design a satisfactory toaster, it takes one with enough business knowledge and communication skill to convince others of the quality of the design. The inability to communicate is often a primary reason for having good ideas rejected.

This dual role is not unlike that of a salesperson. A successful engineer or scientist must combine a technical understanding and talent with the ability to convince a perhaps skeptical customer that his or her product or service is the best alternative. It is therefore useful for engineers and scientists to understand the product side of business—that is, marketing and advertising. In any aspect of science or engineering, be it design or consulting, one must be aware of the needs of the customer. No matter how technologically advanced or high quality a product is, if no one needs or wants it, it will not sell.

Those who work for large firms involved in manufacturing must always work with the marketing department in their design work. Long before a product is produced, marketing people conduct detailed studies to establish the need for such a product, the performance that will be necessary, the desired appearance, and even the desired price range. If designers do not work within these requirements, they may end up with a product that is inadequate for the market, one that is superior to the market's needs but too expensive, or perhaps one that is just too ugly for people to buy. In each case, time, effort, and money have been wasted. Obviously, an engineer or scientist who cannot make adequate cost projections may find his or her productivity rating low; this may translate into poor job performance ratings, few salary increases, and no job advancement.

For engineers and scientists in smaller firms without marketing departments, or for those involved in small consulting firms, a knowledge of marketing is even more crucial, as these individuals are more directly responsible for their end products. Somehow they must be able to gauge the wants of their current and potential customers, or their business will not succeed.

## THE ENGINEER OR SCIENTIST AS A MANAGER

Although most engineers and scientists begin their careers in some form of technical position—in design, research, or development—a large percentage gradually make the transition to management positions. As mentioned in Chapter 14, one study indicated that over 50 percent of engineers were in management positions within five years of their last degree. Having worked in a technical area of a firm or industry gives these scientists and engineers a unique understanding of what goes on, making them well prepared for that aspect of management. Unfortunately, however, they are not always completely prepared for the move from worker to "boss." The qualities of a good manager are not necessarily the same as the qualities possessed by the better technical people. Also, managerial issues are often not introduced in engineering and science curricula.

Above all, a manager must be a leader—creative, confident, and respected. A manager must be able to maintain control over a group of people without letting personal feelings interfere. He or she must be able to handle problems that suddenly come up and make reasonable decisions, often on short notice. He or she must be objective and fair. In these requirements, we see many of the values that have been discussed in other chapters, as values are common to many fields of study. Like a good engineer or scientist, a good manager is one who sees his or her role as more than the sometimes narrowly defined stereotype of it. Although management courses provide the basic tools of the trade, they are not the whole of a manager's education. Most business and management programs, therefore, require a considerable amount of liberal arts study, much more than that received by the typical engineer or scientist. It is this broad background that provides a solid basis for a good manager; its lack can be a serious detriment for the engineer or scientist turned manager.

Many parallels can be drawn between technologists and managers, and there is no inherent reason why an engineer or scientist cannot adjust to a management position. Both are confronted with problems for which they must examine the alternatives and choose the best solution. Simple "book knowledge" is not enough; a certain wisdom, creativity, and confidence, among other things, are necessary to meet the challenge. Just as an engineer or scientist may be faced with the problem of reducing the exhaust pollutants from an automobile engine, a manager may be confronted with the task of restructuring an inefficient department. Obviously, the natures of the problems are considerably different, but the approach is the same: studies are conducted to determine the possible solutions, and critical evaluations are made of each alternative to narrow down the possibilities to just one. Like technological fields, management is a dynamic area; methods, applications, and practices are constantly under study in an attempt to find better, more efficient ways of doing things.

Probably the typical engineer's or scientist's major shortcoming as a manager is in dealing with people from a leadership position. It is often said that technologists would rather work with circuit boards, car engines, or whatever the technical details of the job are than with people. For example, when a technologist is faced with a decision on how to modify an engine, his or her choices are generally based on functional requirements and costs of the components used. Although the same concept could be applied to a manager's problem, the manager may also be faced with the possibility of laying off or transferring employees. This personal aspect complicates the decision process, since the choices made involve value decisions that will affect people directly. Critical decision making and dealing with people are two basic areas covered in management courses. Some routine tasks of management that are unfamiliar to the typical engineer or scientist but are dealt with in these courses include recruiting personnel, evaluating employees, handling problem employees, motivating employees, and improving job satisfaction among employees.

Although taking a few courses in management cannot make a person an instant manager, it can instill in the individual a general feeling for the requirements and responsibilities of a manager and his or her role as a leader. In addition, it can help a nonmanagerial engineer or scientist understand the position of those in charge and deal effectively with co-workers, both those "above" and those "below" him or her.

## ENGINEERS AND SCIENTISTS AS THEIR OWN MANAGERS

The lives of engineers and scientists are not limited to their professional careers, nor is the usefulness of a knowledge of economics and business limited to their professional lives. Engineers and scientists are also members of families, communities, and society as a whole. Whether or not they have the ability to manage large groups of people in business settings, it is even more important that they be able to manage their personal lives.

We all have social interactions with other people on a regular basis, and it is important that we be able to communicate our thoughts and ideas with confidence and leadership in dealings with family, friends, or neighbors. When we have suggestions or criticism, we should present them in a logical and well-thought-out manner, showing a concern for the problem. When we have differences of opinion, we should be able to discuss our positions rationally without forcing our views on anyone, while at the same time listening with understanding to opposing views.

A second managerial aspect of everyone's life is decision making. We face a variety of decisions virtually every day. Should I buy a new car or keep the old one for a few more years? Should I go to the beach on vacation this summer or get a job and save money? What should I major in in college, and where should I go? These are just a few of the vast number of decisions we face in our lifetimes. Although a knowledge of management and economics does not provide a simple yes-no decision criterion like the flip of a coin, it does lead to more rational and efficient decisions. It allows for a more complete analysis of decisions in terms of alternatives, costs, and benefits. It encourages decisions in which monetary benefits and costs are better balanced with nonquantifiable goals. For example, it demonstrates the value of delaying purchases so that resources will be available for future plans, such as when a young couple postpones current spending to save money to buy a home in the future.

As another example, consider our lives as consumers. From the time we are very young, we are confronted with a flood of advertising for products ranging from luxury automobiles to mouthwash, from fast food to high-tech stereo and television equipment. Somehow we have to decide what we really want, need, and can afford. Understanding how advertising and marketing work can help with these decisions, allowing us to see beyond the empty promises and gimmicks of advertising.

Other examples of the importance of economics and business in our personal lives abound. Just keeping track of personal finances requires a basic knowledge of accounting principles. For some people, personal finances may be as simple as balancing a checkbook and keeping track of a savings account balance. For many of us, however, it includes understanding loans and interest rates, credit card agreements, and so on, since we can't always afford the things we think we need. And in the case of large loans, such as mortgages or car loans, it is essential that we realize what our responsibilities will be and the consequences of not meeting them. Too often, people get in over their heads because they fail to understand the fine print beyond the bold advertising claims of "low monthly payments." Knowing about economics and business is also useful to those who are interested in investing money; there are now investment opportunities for almost anyone, not just the wealthy. On the negative side, dealing with the complexities of the American tax system is a nightmarish task that everyone must endure.

After graduating from college and joining the ranks of employed professionals, we move toward integrating ourselves into the community in which we choose to live. This may include participation in religious activities, community government, volunteer work, and activities in nonprofit organizations, such as boys' and girls' clubs. In many cases, we will participate in the financial aspects of such activities, such as budgeting and fundraising. Thus, a knowledge of economics and organizational management can be useful in our service to the community.

Beyond our own concerns and those of our community, we are all members of a common society. Therefore, it would be beneficial for us to comprehend at least the basics of how our society runs. One benefit of such an understanding would come from the satisfaction of being knowledgeable people who are aware of the system in which we play a part. In terms of economics, this obviously involves a complex process with numerous inputs and outputs. We all know that taxes play a role in the economy, and we've heard of inflation, unemployment and high interest rates, but how many of us really understand the relationships among these four socioeconomic factors? A study of economics can teach the basics of how the economy works and can even demonstrate possible solutions to the problems our society faces. It is a basic premise of economics that no matter how big a problem may appear, there are always ways to reduce or eliminate it. A study of economics can illustrate the necessity for public government and taxes and can help us better understand the news we read in the paper and see on television each day. It also can make us better citizens when we use the knowledge we have gained to make informed choices at the election booth.

Furthermore, a study of economics can expose us to economic systems other than our own as a means of exploring another culture, time, or approach to society. Because the economic system of any society is ingrained and therefore inseparable from other factors of the culture, economics can provide a "window" through which to view a culture. For example, finding out more about communism and Marxist philosophy might help us understand the society of the Soviet Union and other communist countries. We can explore the beginnings of our own free market economy through the works of Adam Smith. Studying the theories of John Maynard Keynes can give us a perspective on our modern economy and on the reasoning behind the increasing role of government in controlling the economy, which, as noted in Chapter 4, was one of the factors that affected the development of technology.

## COURSE SELECTION

Throughout this chapter, we have attempted to illustrate the usefulness of economics and business to engineers and scientists as professionals, as individuals, and as members of society. Obviously, the intent has been to stimulate some interest in economics and business as areas of study. Within the usual framework of the GERs, it is not possible to get a detailed knowledge of everything in these fields, but taking a few courses can at least develop your interest and confidence in the subject.

In economics, there are often single-semester courses designed specifically for nonmajors to provide them with an orientation to economic life and activity. Such courses are generally designed to be self-contained and are taught on a conceptual level; they usually deal with modern economic and social topics, such as unemployment, in terms of their nature, their causes, and their policy implementations. Engineering and science students should also consider taking an introductory economics series for business majors, generally two semesters. These courses are taught at a more analytical level than the single-semester courses and are intended as building blocks for those who are interested in continuing the study of economics. The courses cover topics ranging from growth and inflation to wage and price controls, distribution of income, and poverty. Either of these options would give students a grasp of the role of economics in their lives and in their culture, knowledge that every member of our society should have. In addition, these courses introduce the concepts of economic decision making, cost-benefit analysis, and nonquantifiable goals.

Although such courses are likely to be the full extent of most students' ventures into economics, further opportunities are available. To continue with the general study of economics, students could take a higher-level course sequence. Such courses go into much greater detail than the introductory courses and explore more closely the relationships between various economic factors, often using economic models to demonstrate the interactions between them. These courses are sometimes available in special, highly analytical versions that may appeal to engineering and science students. The depth provided in these courses strengthens the knowledge obtained in earlier courses.

Besides general economics courses, numerous courses that discuss specific economic issues can be both valuable and interesting. These courses cover such issues as environmental economics—which considers the economic problems associated with the environment, exploring the conflicts between the values of public health and a clean environment versus the costs, loss of freedom, and industrial controls necessary to achieve them—and economics of natural resources—which explores the problems of preserving our limited resources while trying to maintain growth. Other courses on current issues in economic policy are similar to the introductory courses but have a narrower focus on the policy aspect of problems and on the difficulties of finding satisfactory solutions to them. A course on the development of economic ideas would provide a historical perspective on economics, giving a glimpse of past cultures, cultures of other nations, and even the development of our own economic system. Finally, a course on the economics of American industries would explore the organizational theory and public policies of various industries, which can be useful to any engineer or scientist who is planning to enter industry.

Numerous courses are available in the sphere of business and management. Course selections can be made on the basis of specific interests and career objectives. Some beneficial courses would be accounting, which is useful for almost anyone for keeping track of personal finances, and cost accounting, which explores the costing aspects of production and would be useful for designers since it considers the challenge of finding the best compromise between product performance and cost.

A very important course is personnel management, which teaches the basics of managing a group of people, including leadership, fairness, and efficient decision making. Every engineering and science student should consider taking such a course, whether or not they plan to enter management. Another important course is organizational theory, which covers the structure of a business, stressing the role and responsibilities of the management process. Another possible selection is promotion management (marketing), which covers the concepts of tailoring a product for and selling it to a particular group of consumers according to their needs and wants; as noted earlier, this same process is required of engineers and scientists.

Other courses worthy of consideration include traffic and physical distribution management, which covers product flow through manufacturing and distribution; this would be a useful course for those entering manufacturing fields. Also, a course on labor relations would examine the relationship between management and labor in terms of disputes and conflicting goals—a good course for those who intend to enter management. Anyone who intends to start up a business should consider a course in business law, which covers the legal aspects of running a business. Obviously, most students will be able to cover only a few of these courses during their studies.

## CONCLUSIONS

Economics is an integral part of our society and of our lives. Even as students, we face economic choices daily; the number and complexity of these decisions will only increase when we enter the working world and begin to raise a family. As consumers, we need to understand the economic system in which we consume, which will enable us to make the most of our limited resources. And as members of society in general, we should have a grasp of the economic problems of our day and a realization that these problems have solutions; in casting our ballots in local, state, and federal elections, we can influence the methods used to solve these problems.

As engineers and scientists, we have a special perspective on economics; our efforts in technology and research can have profound effects on the economy, both good and bad. It is often said that progress is never painless, and the implementation of technology through the ages had proved this to be true. Therefore, we must consider the possible economic repercussions of our actions and try to balance the values that are in conflict; we cannot proceed without a social conscience. Although such technological developments as robotics are considered long-term benefits to our economy and to us as consumers, some of these changes in our society will be painful to some people in the short term. Other technologies, such as nuclear power, may have hidden costs, such as environmental damage and public health hazards. Thus, value issues are certainly as important as economic issues, and an understanding of the basic interrelationships between various economic and value forces is essential.

The personal lives of engineers and scientists are also influenced by business and management. In whatever we do, we must be able to manage ourselves and our lives and interact with others. We have an income to manage and bills to pay, and we may be involved in community or volunteer work.

For the most part, we work in businesses. Therefore, successful engineers and scientists need to have good business sense and the ability to play the roles of businessperson and salesperson as well as their primary roles. We need to be able to communicate our ideas and suggestions with confidence and make rational and well-thought-out decisions. Often, we will find ourselves in leadership roles—as technical project or program managers or even in permanent management positions—and we need to be able to handle the responsibilities of these positions. Management courses can help prepare us for these situations by stressing the values represented by a good manager: creativity, leadership, confidence, objectivity, understanding, and respect.

Finally, we must remember that economics and business are not isolated. As noted earlier, the making of a good manager requires a broad background, not just four years of economics and management courses. A study of either of these topics can provide students with some of the tools they will need to handle their exposure to these fields, but without the broader base and understanding of human values, these tools are useless. Therefore, students shouldn't take economics and business

courses to the exclusion of the other subject areas described in this book just because they appear to be the most practical.

In fact, many of the other subject areas covered in this book are related to economics and business, either directly or in terms of the values inherent in them. Sociology courses, for example, involve many issues that are both economic and social, such as unemployment and welfare. This is understandable given the highly involved relationship between society and economics. In economics courses, we often study the economic aspects of social problems; in sociology courses, we look at the social aspects of economic problems. In psychology, we study human behavior, an understanding of which is critical to the manager, who must deal regularly with all types of people. A study of government and politics is not complete without an exploration of economic systems. Likewise, history courses always consider the economics of the age and culture under study. History can also be presented in terms of leadership, a crucial value in both history and management. Philosophy has an important role in the establishment of economic systems, such as capitalism and communism. The arts, too, are related to business and economics, by way of the creative element. Just as creativity is an important value for the performing artist and the painter or sculptor, it is important to managers, in that a good manager should always consider new ways of doing things that may be more efficient or pleasurable and, hence, superior. Similarly, product designers and marketing people need to be creative in putting together a desirable product and presenting it effectively to the potential market.

## EXERCISES

**15.1.** Most engineering and science students are anxious to get their diplomas and quickly enter the work force. A relatively small percentage stay in college for an advanced degree, although many return to school after a few years of work or take classes part-time while working. Explain the values that affect a student's decision about getting an advanced degree. Is there too much emphasis on the short-term monetary concerns?

**15.2.** Choose an economic philosopher from the past (e.g., Marx, Malthus, Veblen) and find out a little about his ideas. How do these ideas and values compare or contrast with those of the society in which the person lived? What possible benefits could be achieved by studying these philosophers?

**15.3.** Economics is an integral part of society. In your course catalog, identify economics courses that concentrate on social aspects and problems and sociology courses that include economic considerations. In what different ways would these types of courses be beneficial to an engineering or science student?

**15.4.** Communication skills are essential to all professionals in their careers, yet engineering and science students rarely receive any formal education in this area. In your course catalog, identify several courses (either in the business/management department or in any other department) that would be useful in improving communication skills.

**15.5.** As noted in this chapter, economic decisions are a part of our daily life. Describe an economic decision you have made recently, and explain the values you considered in making your final choice.

**15.6.** As mentioned in this chapter, engineers and scientists are always constrained by the economics of the situation. Frequently, we hear news reports of companies being sued for knowingly cutting corners in design and/or construction to save money. Examine the inherent value conflicts between engineers/scientists and managers in charge of a project. Would these conflicts be relieved somewhat if the managers had a better background in engineering and science?

**15.7.** Claiming that there's no room for loyalty in business, a manager argued that completing job assignments is an act of loyalty to oneself, not the firm. Also, if a firm doesn't lay off an employee in hard times, it is not because of loyalty to the employee but because of loyalty to itself. It wishes to maintain that person as an employee because he or she has a good record and the firm can expect continued good effort in the future. Can an engineering firm afford to show loyalty to an employee? Would an employee be disloyal to the firm if he or she sought employment elsewhere? Explain your answers from both an economic and a value standpoint.

**15.8.** Some engineers and scientists are required by state law to be members of unions. Discuss the value conflicts created by such a requirement. Identify economics courses that discuss unions, and evaluate their usefulness to a study of a situation where such state laws exist.

**15.9.** Consumer product safety is both a value issue and an economic issue. Discuss the economic and value considerations involved. Identify courses that discuss the issue, and evaluate the value of these courses to students in your major.

**15.10.** Review your undergraduate course catalog and identify courses in business and economics that might discuss each of the following topics: (a) social values; (b) public policy; (c) technology; (d) organization structure and behavior within an organization. Discuss how these courses might benefit someone in your major.

**15.11.** Attending college is certainly a business decision as well as a value decision. Identify the business and values associated with attending college. At what point does the cost (tuition, room and board, etc.) outweigh the value issues?

**15.12.** Spending spring break at a beach or ski resort involves economic and value issues. Discuss both the issues involved and the method you believe most students use in making such a decision.

**15.13.** There are certainly economic benefits involved in kickbacks (discussed in Chapter 4). However, there are also both economic and value disincentives involved. Discuss the economic/value conflict associated with kickback schemes. Also, discuss why some individuals choose to participate while others reject proposals for kickbacks.

**15.14.** Businesspeople have been accused of being insensitive to the public's concern for the environment. Taking a neutral position, identify the issues and discuss the values involved. What position should engineers and scientists take? Why? Does it violate the *freedom* of business if restrictions are imposed on business for controlling environmental damage?

15.15. Robotics is a new technology that some believe to be a blessing and others believe to be a curse. Discuss the problem from both an economics and a value standpoint. What criteria should be used in deciding whether or not to automate a specific industrial plant?

15.16. Outline a three-course sequence of courses in economics and business that would serve to develop your awareness of the social responsibilities of engineers and scientists.

15.17. Identify parts of the NSPE Code of Ethics (see Chapter 4) that might have negative economic consequences for an engineering firm. Discuss your reasons.

**16**

# The Professional's Role
# in Politics and Public Policy

*James M. Wallace*
*Richard H. McCuen*

## INTRODUCTION

The greatest scientist of our century, Albert Einstein, once said that politics is more difficult than physics. How can human political relations be considered more complex than the mysteries of elementary particles or the secrets of the cosmos? It is certainly more difficult to find patterns in politics because of the enormous number of factors that influence political opinion, policy, and action; psychological, historical, economic, and legal factors, among others, all enter political equations. In earlier chapters of this book, we have sought to demonstrate that the activities of engineers and scientists—the creation of technology and new scientific knowledge— are never done in social isolation. The context of these activities is the political, economic, and cultural matrix of human life. Inevitably, these technical and scientific activities will have social consequences, for good or ill, which will depend, to a great extent, on the political choices exercised by the society in implementing the fruits of technology and science. It simply will not do for those of us involved at the heart of the creation of technology and science to be ignorant of these political processes. At the very least, it is our responsibility as good citizens to be aware of these policies and to participate in shaping them for the public welfare. Furthermore, as responsible professionals with specialized knowledge, we have an added responsibility to work intelligently within the political system to help steer a course beneficial to humankind. But besides these lofty motives, it is simply interesting to know something about the political events, processes, and personalities of our time and to see how they relate to the ways in which past societies have organized themselves through politics.

## POLITICAL SCIENCE

In the latter part of the nineteenth century, a new academic discipline developed, drawing on forms of inquiry that date back to the Greek philosophers Socrates, Plato, and Aristotle but also utilizing methods taken from the physical sciences. Thus was political science born. We often think of political science as involving only the study of government. This is one of its big concerns, of course, but it certainly is not limited to it. More generally, political science is the study of the forms, institutions, and processes involved in the governance of groups as diverse as the Congress of the United States, a voting rights group, or a sailing club. Dahl (1976) defines a political system as "any persistent pattern of human relationships that involves, to a significant extent, control, influence, power, or authority." In our everyday language, we often speak of company politics, university politics, or even club politics in the same way that we speak of national politics. If you have been a member of a high school club, you are certainly aware of some or all aspects of this definition.

The academic study of political science is usually subdivided into the study of (1) political thought or philosophy, usually from a historical standpoint; (2) the structure and operation of governments; (3) public administration; (4) constitutional law; and (5) international relations, including politics, law, and organization. Most universities offer courses in most if not all of these subject areas in departments of political science or government and politics. In an introduction to political science you might write essays on readings from such diverse sources as Plato's *Republic,* Dante's *On World Government,* Machiavelli's *The Prince,* Rousseau's *The Social Contract, The Federalist Papers* of Hamilton et al., and *The Communist Manifesto* of Marx and Engels. You will discuss how resources and goods are distributed, the kind of government a society chooses and why, the relationships between citizens and rulers, how power is divided in a society, and how it is exercised. In a course on international relations, you might concentrate on the history of arms control attempts in the nuclear age.

Like any science, political science attempts to develop abstract concepts and theories of general applicability and to test them against the concrete facts of political experience. For example, it might be hypothesized that 18-year-olds voting in an American presidential election for the first time will usually vote as their parents vote. This is a theory that can easily be tested with a high degree of accuracy using exit polls, and it would be of great interest to politicians. If true, it also would clearly dampen radical shifts in the nation's political direction.

### Orientations of Political Analysis

Dahl (1976) describes four overlapping types of orientation used in doing political analysis: empirical, normative, policy, and semantic. Any course in government or political science will call on all four orientations at various times.

*Empirical orientation.* This analytical approach is most closely related to the methods used in the physical sciences. It involves attempting to discover the laws that govern the relationships among events, policies, and people from the concrete facts of experience and then testing these laws against further facts. The hypothesis about the voting patterns of 18-year-olds has this orientation. As in a scientific experiment, one set of data is inadequate. The thesis must be tested against the facts in many elections before it can have anything like the status of a law. It is likely that the political scientist may find that many other factors influence how 18-year-olds vote. For example, besides their parents' preferences, their vote almost certainly will be affected by whether or not the country is at war and whether or not there is a national draft.

*Normative orientation.* This form of analysis is at the heart of ethics and political philosophy, which was discussed in Chapter 9. It attempts to ask such questions as "How do we know what is a good or bad political decision?" or "What is the *best* public policy we should pursue for some problem?" The answers to such questions rest, to a large extent, on our beliefs about the nature of things, not simply on our experience of them. For example, if you think that laws prohibiting abortion should be enacted, this derives from a belief about the status of a fetus in the hierarchy of nature. On the other hand, if you think that the law should protect a woman's right to choose, this is grounded in a belief about the primacy of women's control over their reproductive processes.

*Policy orientation.* This approach attempts to analyze a situation as it currently exists in order to improve it. It is an analysis of alternatives and their consequences. For example, if a chosen political goal is the reduction of environmental pollution by automobiles, a policy analysis would look at the effects of various means to force automakers and users to emit fewer pollutants, such as catalytic converters, on the public health and economy. Such means might be voluntary guidelines, statutory laws, or tax credits to implementers.

*Semantic orientation.* This form of analysis attempts to clarify the meanings of words and concepts in political usage. For example, the words *democracy, freedom, totalitarianism, socialism,* and *equality* are often used by different people in very different ways. If the other three methods of analysis are to have any commonly accepted use, the meanings of terms and concepts must be clarified and shared. You probably have experienced the need for this clarification in your everyday life—for example, when you have had a misunderstanding with a friend who said the same thing you did but understood it differently.

### Uses of Political Science

In their review and appraisal of political science as an academic discipline for the Committee on Science and Public Policy of the National Academy of Sciences and for the Problems in Policy Committee of the Social Science Research Council, Eulau and March (1969) identify four principal uses of the study of politics and government: (1) education for citizenship, (2) preparation for professions, (3) involvement in public policy, and (4) public information.

*Education for citizenship.* Being a politically aware and involved citizen is certainly a worthy aspiration for an intelligent adult. In the United States, our formal education in political ideas, ideologies, norms, and institutions comes primarily in high school civics courses and in the government and politics courses of colleges and universities, as part of our basic liberal education. Democracies depend for their well-being on an informed, participating citizenry. Surely, then, we have an elementary responsibility to acquire a good working knowledge of this area of human thought. When you vote in local, state, and national elections, you will need to know not only the various sides of the issues but also the various players in these issues and what degrees of influence they have.

*Preparation for professions.* Although a more sophisticated knowledge of political theory and practice is no doubt required for those who are training to be public administrators, lawyers, diplomats, or journalists, students who are training to be engineers and scientists will surely be well served by at least some serious understanding of things political. Civil engineers, for example, are often enmeshed in questions of zoning, public safety standards, and environmental law when they construct large-scale projects such as bridges, dams, buildings, and highways. Also, aviation in the United States is a business almost entirely underwritten and regulated by the federal government. The cost of research and development of new commercial and military aircraft is no longer borne by private companies, and route selection, safety procedures, and even pricing are controlled by the Federal Aviation Administration. Therefore, aeronautical engineers who are unaware of the politics and public policy surrounding aviation are endangering their own livelihood. Moreover, the vast majority of scientific research in the United States is carried out in universities and is supported by grants from federal agencies. Therefore, public policy, which determines the direction and level of governmental support of science in this country, directly affects the career prospects of aspiring scientists. Thus, simply from the standpoint of one's own professional self-interest, a working knowledge of political processes is a valuable goal.

*Involvement in public policy.* Those who practice political science are usually not just armchair academicians. They, along with economists, are probably the academics most involved with local, state, and national government as advisors, analysts, and sometimes even politicians. They are often activists as well as theorists. As this book makes abundantly clear, we believe that scientists and engineers should also be active players in the political process in shaping policy, particularly in areas where they have special expertise. We will have more to say later in this chapter about ways in which they can be specifically involved.

*Providing public information.* Political scientists, along with journalists, are undoubtedly the most acute observers of political activity. Without the long-range perspective and contextual interpretation of fast-breaking political news, we would be hard put to make sense of the welter of information around us. By learning some of these skills, you will be much better able to read the daily newspaper perceptively and interpret the meanings of the images flowing across your television screen on the nightly news. You will also be better prepared to give informed opinions on issues about which you have special knowledge in public forums.

## Perspectives of Political Science

Eulau and March (1969) focus attention on seven political science perspectives—power, institutions, processes, functions, ideologies and movements, international relations, and political behavior—that help us understand the nature of political events and relationships.

*Power.* The exercise of power in group relationships has been thought about and analyzed throughout history. In a sense, it is the easiest way of looking at politics. In modern life, however, power is often highly dispersed among people or institutions that are not formally vested with it. These are the people or groups "behind the scenes" who really decide what your school club or the U.S. Senate will do. It is not always evident who they are and what influence they have. Still, the exercise of power, for good or ill, is at the very essence of what we mean by politics.

*Institutions.* Heretofore, you have probably thought of American government and politics as what was formally described and set forth in the Constitution of the United States, now almost 200 years old, which you first studied in your high school civics course. Our national government is supposed to have powers and functions divided among the executive, legislative, and judicial branches, which check and balance each other. If politics were simply the study of how these formal, constitutionally defined institutions are meant to operate, it would be a relatively easy matter. However, the genius of the U.S. Constitution is that it is a relatively simple and general document that has allowed the American federal government to evolve into something altogether unforeseen by its original framers. One of the goals of political science is to attempt to get beneath the surface to the "living" Constitution. The constitution of the Soviet Union is quite similar in many ways to that of the United States; it provides for elections and guarantees the human rights of assembly, free speech, and so forth. However, the practice of government and politics in the Soviet Union is quite different from that in the United States, and this has been a continual source of conflict between the two nations in the last forty years. Constitutions of developing countries, although they often follow the Western model, have allowed for the development of charismatic-autocratic governmental forms; for example, Kenya was for decades under the one-party rule of Jomo Kenyatta. From the perspective of institutions, political science is an attempt to look at how they really function, not just how they were meant to function.

*Processes.* Seen formally, institutions are static entities; however, seen from the point of view of political process, the third perspective noted by Eulau and March (1969), they perform much more dynamically. For example, a federal agency such as the Department of Education is formally part of the executive branch of our national government. In fact, however, in the process of carrying out education policy, it makes policy, administers it, and rules on the full range of educational questions, thus taking on all the functions of the executive, legislative, and judicial branches of the government. This is evident in decisions as diverse as those regarding bilingual education and athletic scholarships for women at universities.

*Functions.* From the point of view of the function of a political institution or activity, one might ask whether the intentions are being fulfilled. For example, reform in the laws regulating political contributions to political parties, instituted in the 1970s, were intended to reduce the influence of particularly wealthy individuals and groups by limiting the amount they could contribute. An unintended consequence was the enormous growth of political action committees (PACs)—highly organized, ideologically coherent groups that have radically reshaped the contours of American politics in the 1980s. Another use of the concept of function is to look at the already cited example of the constitutional separation of powers of the American national government to determine the real functions the three branches play in our national life. For example, under the leadership of Chief Justice Earl Warren in the 1960s, the Supreme Court played an enormously active role in shaping social policy regarding racial and sexual discrimination and the rights of the economically underprivileged. This was a role that previously had been jealously guarded by the president and the Congress.

*Ideologies.* Politics is never merely the pragmatic working out of the objectives of groups and institutions. It always reflects the beliefs and values that are used to justify those objectives. These systems of beliefs and values of individuals and groups are called ideologies. Three examples of political economic ideologies in the modern world are liberal-democratic capitalism, social democracy, and authoritarian communism. One of the age-old tasks of political science has been to examine the origins of ideologies as formulated by persons as diverse as Adam Smith, John Stuart Mill, and Karl Marx and to trace how institutions and policies that were originally based on their ideas have evolved and changed. For example, a rich area of study is the nature of the state in the present-day Soviet Union and its relationship to its citizenry as compared to views of the state articulated by Marx and developed by Lenin. Or one can look at the democratic ideals first formulated in an almost completely agrarian society by Thomas Jefferson in the American Declaration of Independence and elaborated on in his later writings and compare them with the real political roles of groups and individuals in a modern-day America dominated by huge agglomerations of corporate economic power. Right now, the popular ideology of laissez-faire individualism is being used to mask a public policy that, in fact, is shifting power in our society to an alliance of the military establishment and big business. The ideology of nationalism, which gave rise to the modern nation-state, is common to all modern countries, no matter how different their political systems. The meaning and coherence that a national identity gives to its citizens, which resulted in the decolonization of much of the world in the period after World War II, partially explains the unending tensions between the superpowers. Many observers feel that nationalism is an outdated concept in the modern world of nuclear weapons, but its continuing force as an ideology makes it of extreme relevance to international political relations. More than half of American scientists and engineers are employed in an arms race that feeds on national ideologies. Surely, an important value question for us is whether to choose such employment.

*International relations.* The crucial problem in international relations among the nation states that have evolved in the last 300 years is that there is no supreme political authority with legitimate force to ensure harmonious relations. Each nation in the world, no matter how large it is, believes it has the right, limited only by its ability to enforce it, to act in its national self-interest. To keep this system from becoming a totally chaotic and violent clash between nations, a body of law and a number of international, cultural, technical, and social institutions have developed, principally under the auspices of the United Nations. The study of international politics, which long concentrated on power and national self-interest, is now more concerned with the internal conditions within nations that define policy alternatives, goals, behavior patterns, and strategy. Science, which is international by nature, depends greatly on harmonious international relations. Thus, scientists and engineers would do well to learn why they are usually anything but harmonious.

*Political behavior.* Most of us have been fascinated at some point by the personalities of famous and infamous political leaders, from Napoleon to John F. Kennedy. For many decades, political science eschewed the study of political personalities as being too simplistic an approach. Recently, however, professional political scientists have become interested in the motives and behavioral characteristics of political leaders and of those whom they lead. Political biography is a literary genre that is providing rich material to help us understand how far-reaching public policy is affected by the personalities of political leaders. For example, recent studies of Lyndon Johnson give us insight into the causes of his disastrous Vietnam War policy. To take a happier example, studies of the personalities and relationship of Franklin and Eleanor Roosevelt help us understand much of the humanitarian concern of the New Deal era.

The use of public opinion surveys, a highly developed tool of modern political analysis, has provided immense sources of information for understanding the political hopes and aspirations and the ideological set of beliefs of the American public. Such studies of mass political behavior have introduced a more rigorous and quantitative data base into political analysis than had heretofore been available. The statistical analysis of such data draws on well-proven mathematical methods long used in the physical sciences.

## PUBLIC POLICY

One of the four uses of political science suggested by Eulau and March (1969) is its relevance to public policy. Political science can only rarely provide a direct answer to a policy question; rather, in concert with social, behavioral, biological, and physical sciences, it brings its special expertise to policy questions, suggesting an effective means of attacking them. In particular, political analysis will help clarify how the holders of power in the society can be mobilized to bring a new public policy into effect. This analysis will include identification of the most important supporters and opponents, sources of institutional inertia and self-interest, ideologies that shape public opinion, and behavioral idiosyncrasies of the principal political actors involved in the policy change.

A policy is a plan of operation adopted by a club, a business organization, a government, or some other group. For example, a public high school may have a policy on student smoking or a private school may have a standard dress policy. A policy is intended to influence the actions of individuals within a group, such as the students in the two examples cited. A business organization may have a personnel policy that provides guidelines on hiring, firing, and promotions. When a plan of action or guiding principle is established by a government, it is called a public policy. For example, we discuss American foreign policy, the president's farm policy, or a local government's policy on flood control. Policies are developed so that those involved with an organization will know the direction of the organization on a specific issue. Policies are inseparably intertwined with human values. Certainly, company policies should reduce uncertainty among employees, thereby increasing harmony within the group and, if the employees favor the policies, improving job satisfaction and enhancing loyalty to the organization. As indicated in Chapter 6, one of the characteristics of a good leader is one who develops a respected group policy.

Although organizational policy is important to engineers and scientists, especially those who hold management positions, our aim here is to examine the role of engineers and scientists in public policy. Engineers and scientists should be involved in the formation of public policies at all levels of government. Unfortunately, the role of engineers and scientists in public policymaking has been rather small. These professionals who develop and implement military weaponry should exert their influence on public policy, at least on issues related to their knowledge and specialized skills and at a level commensurate with their experience. Similarly, engineers whose expertise lies in the design of public works should seek to influence policies related to them. For example, those with a knowledge of the supply, demand, and quality of water should seek to be involved in the development of policies related to water treatment facilities and hazardous waste cleanup. Tribus (1978) points out that engineers and scientists should be involved in public policy because they have the necessary knowledge and specialized skills, because they develop the technology that affects most important public issues, and because they are respected by the community. Obviously to fulfill our value goal of enhancing the public welfare, we engineers and scientists must become more involved.

### Why Are Engineers and Scientists Uninvolved?

A number of factors are responsible for the relatively minor involvement of engineers and scientists in public policy formulation.

*The technical personality.* As noted earlier, the personality of engineers and scientists is oriented toward things, not people; facts, not feelings; and logic, not emotion. Policy issues usually center on effects on people, but engineers and scientists prefer mechanical-technical or abstract-conceptual matters. Engineers and scientists develop solutions to problems by starting with the underlying physical laws or the facts, whereas problems involving policies deal with the feelings of the people affected by the problems. Quite often, public policies will be adopted that reflect the level of emotion of affected citizens that is generated by the alternative solutions. Engineers and scientists often have difficulty accepting such solutions because the solution is not the most "logical" choice. Unfortunately, after a few such "illogical" decisions, engineers and scientists often develop an aversion to public policy.

*Technical education and experience.* The education and experience of engineers and scientists contribute to their relative lack of participation in public policy formulation. A technical education is highly quantitative, with an emphasis on mathematics, physics, and other quantitative subjects. Very little of the educational programs of engineering and science deals with people-oriented topics. Senior design courses apply the physical laws learned in the preceding three years, and even interdisciplinary projects assigned as part of senior capstone courses emphasize the quantitative aspects of problem solving. Where these interdisciplinary projects have to consider the human aspect of a problem, every attempt is made to find a quantitative criterion. For example, if the project is to solve a traffic problem, the criteria used to assess alternative solutions are usually such factors as travel time, traffic density, or number of accidents. Rarely is any effort made to use a people-oriented criterion such as driver stress in selecting the best alternative.

The professional experience of engineers and scientists usually centers on the same types of problem solving they encounter in educational programs. They are usually hired to solve the technical elements of a problem, leaving the "people" elements to planners and other generalists who have an educational background in the liberal arts. Problems with land development near wetlands provides a case in point. For such problems, an engineer would be hired to assess changes in the flood and erosion potential of development projects near wetlands. The engineer would not be trusted with the assessment of the visual impact of the development on the site. Instead, a resource manager, landscape planner, or forester might be hired, since educational programs in their disciplines involve a greater emphasis on perception, culture, and values, thus preparing them better for the task of assessing visual impacts.

*Setting the public agenda.* A third factor that contributes to the difficulty engineers and scientists have in public policy participation is their tendency to solve problems that are given to them rather than being involved in the decision process that determines what ought to be solved (Tribus, 1978). This is partially the result of the two factors already mentioned—their personality and their education and experience. Problem solving in engineering and science education too often involves only end-of-chapter exercises for which there is but one correct answer. Problems in which multiple solutions are possible are rare. Thus, instead of learning what ought to be solved, students learn how to solve well-defined problems. As noted in Chapter 2, real-world problems, which involve value conflicts, are complex and require a decision-making process that differs from the technical decision-making process that is so familiar to engineers and scientists.

*Professional image.* The fourth factor identified by Tribus (1978) is the image of the profession. Engineers and scientists are viewed as disinterested professionals who are the "savior/servants" of society. They save and serve society by solving the problems presented to them by society. In contrasting engineers and scientists with lawyers, Tribus points out that they are taught to serve rather than to develop power bases from which decisions can be made—a role that lawyers seek. This does not imply that engineers and scientists are not capable of achieving power, only that their personality, education, experience, and professional structure are not geared toward this objective.

### Becoming More Involved

Is public policy formulation of sufficient importance that engineers and scientists should be concerned with it? If it is important, what can be done to overcome the problems we have identified? As discussed in Chapter 4, the value goals of professional societies are stated in their codes of ethics, most of which indicate that public safety, health, and welfare are of paramount importance. For example, the code of ethics of the National Society of Professional Engineers (NSPE) includes the statement: "Engineers, in the fulfillment of their professional duties, shall hold paramount the safety, health and welfare of the public in the performance of their professional duties." The Accreditation Board for Engineering and Technology (ABET) begins its code of ethics with the statement: "Engineers uphold and advance the integrity, honor, and dignity of the engineering profession by using their knowledge and skill for the enhancement of human welfare." Given this emphasis on society in professional value systems, the answer to the question of whether public policy formulation is important to engineers and scientists must be an emphatic yes. Obviously, the ability of engineers and scientists to enhance human welfare is limited when they deal only with technical issues. Involvement in public policy formulation enables them to use their knowledge and skills in enhancing human welfare in the most efficient manner, through both forming policy *and* solving technical issues, not just the latter.

Now to the second question: What can be done to overcome the obstacles to such participation? The first step in overcoming the personality problem is to recognize that although the engineering personality has some good characteristics, other characteristics are detrimental to achieving the value goals of the code of ethics. Having acknowledged a personality limitation, a student of engineering or science can work toward overcoming the limitation. Courses in psychology deal with personality, human behavior, and social influence, and a study of the Myers-Briggs index discussed in Chapter 14 would be one way to place one's personality in context. Courses in sociology that deal with socialization can also help the student understand the relationship between personality and society.

Professional experience was also listed as a possible factor in the low participation by engineers and scientists in public policy issues. To overcome this limitation, they should seek out multidisciplinary projects that include preliminary evaluation of a technical problem as well as its solution. The technical elements of a project should not be undertaken unless the engineers or scientists in charge have agreed that the policy under which the solution is sought is reasonable.

Professional societies can also make major contributions. The effort they expend on public policy issues should be increased, without, of course, decreasing the effort spent on advancing the state of the art of technical issues. On college campuses, student chapters of the professional societies should increase their involvement in policy issues. This might involve minor changes, such as increasing the number of speakers who discuss policy issues, as well as greater participation of engineering and science students in campus policymaking activities, such as student government and campus committees that include student representatives. Student chapters of professional societies could also sponsor field trips to meetings at which public officials are debating and acting on policy questions, especially policy questions for which the special knowledge and skills of engineers and scientists would be useful. In other words, field trips should not be limited to project sites, where technical issues are the only concern.

Educational programs in engineering and science were also identified as an important reason for the low profile of engineers and scientists in public policy issues. Changes can be made in both the technical and general education requirements of engineering and science curricula to improve the students' awareness. Public policy issues could be introduced in technical courses to illustrate how technical issues affect society and how social values may be a limiting factor in technical solutions. For example, when discussing safety factors and building codes, the value and policy aspects should be discussed, not just the technical requirements. Also, technical courses that involve truly interdisciplinary projects could be developed, with project solutions involving multiple decision criteria that are both technically and socially oriented. These projects should be designed so that social and political constraints play an important part in the decision process. General education courses should be selected to help students develop a sense of creativity, leadership skills, value decision-making skills, and communication abilities—all of which are important when dealing with people and social issues.

### Examples of Involvement

*Smoking in public areas.*    An example of a public policy issue that is receiving some attention in many communities is the problem of smoking in public areas. Some citizens are concerned that smoke from tobacco products used by others presents a health hazard to them; they wish to have smoking banned in public places. Smokers argue that the medical evidence concerning residual smoke is not conclusive and that a ban represents infringement of their freedom. Owners of public services such as restaurants feel that smoking bans will hinder sales, which infringes on their economic freedom. From a simplistic standpoint, the conflict involves the values of public health and freedom. The conflict is magnified because of the uncertainties involved. The risk of health problems is not known, and there is uncertainty about the level of isolation of smokers that would be necessary to eliminate the possibility of smoke presenting a health hazard.

These are problems for which scientists and engineers could provide valuable help, yet they rarely get involved. This is an example of a point made earlier: engineers and scientists ought to be involved in the discussion before the policy is formulated, rather than waiting until the policy has been developed. They should be leaders, rather than servants. How could engineers and scientists be leaders in formulating a policy regarding smoking in public? Certainly, there are a number of medical issues involved, and medical scientists, chemists, and bioengineers could participate together in the evaluation of the medical questions; for example, they could make the risk evaluations that are necessary for establishing policies on the issue. Mechanical engineers could evaluate the ventilation requirements for eliminating the transport of smoke from a smoking area to a nonsmoking area. A materials engineer might examine filter materials that would ensure adequate removal of smoke. Engineering planners might evaluate layouts that would minimize contact between smokers and nonsmokers. If engineers and scientists would attempt to solve such problems prior to the adoption of policies that are founded not on fact but on emotion, they would truly be serving society in that they would be recognizing public health as an important social value.

*Seat belts for school buses.*    Should public policies be developed that require seat belts in school buses? Each day in the United States, 390,000 school buses travel about 3 million miles transporting 21.5 million children. Unfortunately, accidents happen, some resulting in fatalities. Some parents and physicians argue that public policies that require lap belts should be developed. The proponents believe that the belts would reduce fatalities and injuries and would also encourage children to use seat belts when they are riding in the family car. Thus, the proponents cite values of public health and safety, life, and knowledge. Those opposing public policies that require seat belts in school buses argue that they will cause a violent whipping effect, thus causing more severe injuries in frontal crashes. The lap belt opponents also argue that children will use the belts as weapons against other riders. Furthermore, they argue that there are very few fatalities in school bus accidents (one driver and twelve passengers in 1983) and that the requirement of belts represents poor use of public resources. Finally, they argue that redesign of the buses could be just as effective in reducing fatalities and injuries. The opponents thus cite the values of public health and safety and values associated with other uses of the funds that would be required for the seat belts.

This problem in public policy formulation is an example in which the values in conflict are primarily the same—public health and safety. The problem, then, is the lack of accurate estimates of the risks involved. There is an obvious need for engineers and scientists to develop an information base that can be used to improve the public's knowledge of the risks associated with the alternatives. Engineers and scientists would serve the public by investigating the issue and providing a technical basis for solving the value conflict. Transportation engineers could develop traffic policies that would reduce traffic accidents involving school buses, and mathematicians and statisticians could do more rigorous analyses of existing data to improve risk estimates. Computer scientists, in conjunction with transportation and biomedical engineers, could develop computer simulations of alternative accident scenarios to obtain more accurate estimates of the hazards associated with different types of accidents. It might be possible for material engineers to develop improved materials that would reduce injuries due to impact. Industrial engineers, who perform time/space/motion studies, might be able to redesign bus interiors to reduce risks of fatalities and injuries.

Very few communities have promulgated policies on lap belts in school buses, partly because so little is known about the risks. Besides the role for engineers and scientists in solving some of the technical problems associated with the issue, there is also a potential for engineers and scientists to help solve a value conflict and properly formulate a public policy that maximizes public health and safety.

*Use of the oceans.* The oceans are the last unchartered areas of the world. At present, fishing and drilling for oil and gas are the two major uses of the oceans. There are no forward-looking public policies on ocean use; instead public policies reflect stopgap measures for dealing with current problems, such as drilling rights. If we are to make optimum use of ocean resources while minimizing the degradation of the ocean environments, more comprehensive public policies need to be developed. Such policies must reflect uses of the oceans that are expected in the future, such as aquaculture (farming on the ocean floors), mining of the oceans,

recreational use of ocean resources, and the potential of the oceans for energy (geo-
thermal power and energy from harnessing the waves). Engineers could play a role
in evaluating the movement of ocean bottom sediments to determine if it will be
as significant a problem as land surface erosion is for farming on land. Mining engineers and chemists could determine whether acid mine drainage would be a problem in an ocean environment. Besides assessing the possible impacts of various
uses of the oceans, engineers and scientists need to consider how to assess quality-
degrading effects and translate such assessments into policy statements that can
form a basis for public policy formulation. Individual engineers and scientists as
well as professional societies need to look forward, recognizing that these problems
will have to be addressed in the future. Society also has a responsibility to create
an environment in which engineers and scientists have the resources to make both
risk assessments and public policy recommendations.

### Public Participation in Science Policy

To this point in our discussion on public policy, the emphasis has been on
the need for engineers and scientists to participate in its development, especially
for policies dealing with science and technology. The other side of the coin is also
important. There is also a need for other citizens to participate in the formulation
of public policy that is concerned with highly technical concepts. After all, it is
all citizens, not just engineers and scientists, who bear the risks associated with the
deployment of technology. The pluralism of a democratic society should encourage
citizen participation, including in policymaking.

The growth of citizen participation has paralleled the growth of technology.
In particular, citizens are more aware of the ill effects of technology, an awareness
that results in part from the growth of one form of technology—the mass media.
Although some citizen participation has been mandated by law, most is the result
of grassroots action. The most common form of citizen participation has been the
public hearing, but its track record for effectiveness has been limited for a number
of reasons, including the unavailability of expertise, the constrained format of most
public hearings, and the poor timing of the hearings. Other forms of citizen participation include citizen advisory boards, referenda, nonviolent public protest, and,
unfortunately, violent protest. Even where mandated by law, public participation
has had limited success. But this should not mean that public participation should
be taken lightly or that it does not have the potential to be effective. Society can
benefit from citizen involvement

One example of citizen participation in science policy that received a fair
amount of media attention was the attempt by citizens of Cambridge, Massachu-
setts, to be involved in establishing safety guidelines for research in genetic engineering. The citizens were concerned with public health and safety, while the
involved scientists emphasized their freedom to perform their research. This is the
type of situation in which engineers and scientists should encourage some form of

citizen involvement. Both sides had legitimate claims, and the need for public participation in such cases should be evident.

Other cases that have been brought to public attention by the media include:

- The debate over nuclear power facilities, such as the Three Mile Island case.
- The public's demand that saccharin not be banned, despite studies showing that it caused cancer in laboratory animals.
- The public's demand that Laetrile not be banned, even though studies showed that it was of no value in cancer therapy.
- The siting of hazardous and nuclear waste dumps.
- The work-stop order on a dam in Tennessee because of the threat to a tiny fish, the snail darter.

Each of these cases involved value issues as well as technical issues, and the value conflicts inspired public debate. The intensity of such debates is compounded because of our inability to make accurate estimates of the risks involved.

Although technical factors are an important part of science policies, citizen participation is usually demanded only when public values are in conflict. The process of handling value conflicts was discussed briefly in Chapter 2. For our purposes here, it should be sufficient to outline some of the more common value conflicts in science policy formulation. Two types of value questions are involved: the value conflicts associated with public participation versus nonparticipation and the value conflicts associated with the technical alternatives. The second type, as discussed earlier in this chapter and in Chapter 2, involves conflicts between values of public health and safety and values of freedom, either scientific freedom or economic freedom. But for the first type of value conflict, there are both value advantages and value disadvantages to citizen participation. As noted earlier, democratic participation is a value. The citizens who are at risk should have a right to participate in decisions about that risk. On the other hand, if the technical issues are beyond the technical competence of the citizens, would public efficiency, also a value, be optimized by allowing uninformed or ill-informed individuals to have an equal voice in making the decision or the policy? Wouldn't the ill-informed citizens be acting more responsibly by allowing those who have the technical competence to establish the policy or make the decision? The answer is probably yes. But technical competency is not a dichotomous variable; there are all shades of competency. Therefore, the level at which citizens should participate is not so clear, especially when the citizens believe that they have a greater level of technical competence than they really have. The point is that citizens have a right to participate and that engineers and scientists should recognize and encourage that participation. The only question is the most effective means of participation.

In summary, engineers and scientists need to be more involved in public policy formulation, they need to be more involved in the education of citizens about technical issues, and they need to recognize the right of citizens to participate in science and social policy formulation. These efforts are necessary if engineers and scientists are to meet the intent of the stated goals of their codes of ethics—namely, to hold paramount the welfare of the public.

## COURSE SELECTION

Courses in political science are almost always offered by departments of political science or government and politics. However, related courses can usually be found in the sociology and philosophy departments of most universities. You should start with an introductory survey course, which will develop the perspectives mentioned in the first part of this chapter. You may then want to take a course in American government, which will usually be a more sophisticated and more analytical version of your high school civics course, examining the structure and function of local, state, and national institutions. A course in political ideology would certainly be stimulating; such courses explore the concepts of anarchism, communism, socialism, capitalism, and democracy. Most of us are not very clear about the ideological assumptions that govern our opinions; a course of this kind can help correct this lack. For those who anticipate traveling or working abroad, courses in the politics of other countries or geopolitical regions can be both interesting and useful. Courses in political philosophy or theory would expose you to some of the world's great social critics, from Socrates to Ghandi. Finally, for those whose social concern leads them into work in the Third World, a course covering the politics of those diverse areas would be invaluable.

Courses in public policy are numerous, even on campuses that do not have specific programs in public policy. Individual courses might be found in programs in such areas as public affairs, public administration, government and politics, business management, sociology, natural resources, urban studies, industrial management, or law.

The specific content of a course and the context of the discussion on public policy will depend, of course, on the department in which the course is offered. For example, a policy-directed course offered by a business management program might present the material within the framework of the association between business and society or between business and government. A course offered by a department of government and politics might emphasize the role of political processes in establishing policies that reflect voters' interests. A program in natural resources might discuss the use of public policy in the allocation and use of scarce natural resources. Programs in urban studies might discuss policy issues that relate to urban cultures. It should be evident that public policy is not of interest only to engineers and scientists. It is important to other professions and disciplines and in shaping the direction of a society as a whole. When students of engineering and science take courses in public policy, they should attempt to put the policy issues into the context of engineering or science as well as their personal life. Questions such as the following should be asked: (1) What value issues are reflected in the public policy? (2) How would such policies affect the growth of technology? (3) Would such public policy issues affect the practice of engineering or science? (4) How might such policies affect me as a citizen and taxpayer? Finding answers to such questions will enable the student of engineering or science to put public policy in a realistic perspective.

## EXERCISES

16.1. Describe a group of which you have been a member in terms of how power was exercised in the group and who exercised it. Was this exercise of power according to agreed-upon rules or bylaws?

16.2. Give examples from the daily newspaper of each of the four types of political analysis orientations mentioned in this chapter.

16.3. Several examples of the usefulness of studying political science have been mentioned. Give an additional example for each of the principal uses cited in this chapter.

16.4. Give an additional example of each of the political science perspectives described in this chapter.

16.5. What is your principal source of political information? What ideological basis do you think this source has?

16.6. What kind of political involvement do you plan after graduation? What would prevent you from working for a political candidate or party?

16.7. Do you think that science and engineering are unrelated to politics? Why or why not?

16.8. Parents may develop a family policy that teenagers must meet a specific curfew. Describe the value conflict that can result from such a policy.

16.9. Discuss the value issues involved in a public policy that requires dog owners to keep their dogs on a leash.

16.10. During periods of drought, communities often enforce public policies that disallow such uses of water as washing cars and watering lawns. Discuss the value issues involved.

16.11. Federal and state governments have both economic development policies and environmental policies. From a value standpoint, discuss the conflicts that are inherent in these two public policies. Identify ways that engineers and scientists can help reduce the value conflicts.

16.12. Historic sites provide citizens of a community with a view of the culture of past generations. To what extent could engineers and scientists get involved in developing public policies for conserving, preserving, and protecting historic sites? What are the values involved?

16.13. Should public policies be developed to preserve the environmental rights of future generations? To what extent should engineers and scientists be involved in drafting such policies?

16.14. Formulate an environmental code of ethics that engineers and scientists should adhere to as they develop new technologies that might cause damage to the environment.

**16.15.** Because of their involvement in technology, engineers and scientists are often blamed for the ills associated with technology. Discuss why it is important for engineers and scientists to give adequate consideration to the detrimental side effects of new technologies. In your discussion, consider the value issues involved and the possibility that public policies and laws will be developed by others if engineers and scientists fail to consider the ills of new technologies.

**17**

# Development of an Individualized General Education Program

*Richard H. McCuen*

## INTRODUCTION

Each of the chapters in this book has included a discussion of the types of courses that could be useful for students of engineering or science. Obviously, it would not be feasible for students to take courses in all of the topics discussed in this book, nor is it necessary to take courses in all arts and humanities specialties to meet the objectives of ABET (see Chapter 1):

> It cannot be overemphasized that efforts to present coursework in the humanities and social sciences as an integral part of the engineering educational program are encouraged in the interests of making young engineers fully aware of their social responsibilities and better able to consider related factors in the decision-making process.

Students can learn of the social responsibilities of engineers and scientists through judicious selection of only a few courses in the arts, humanities, and social sciences. Of course, the broader the course selection, the greater the reinforcement of the concept of social responsibilities. As has been shown in previous chapters, students can improve their understanding of creativity from courses as diverse as the fine arts, literature, and psychology. Similarly, courses in history, psychology, and management can enhance students' understanding of leadership. The importance of human welfare can be illustrated in philosophy, sociology, and business courses. Thus, although a broad-based exposure to the arts, humanities, and social sciences would be desirable, the ABET objectives can be met through just a few courses—but only if the student is aware of the importance of a general education program and knows that important knowledge can be gained from these courses.

This chapter is intended to tie together the concepts developed in the preceding chapters to help each student develop a program that will meet the general education requirements and fulfill the intent of the GERs, as indicated by ABET. Because every university or college has a different set of requirements and different resources, only a general outline will be presented here. For example, some universities allow for three electives, while the remaining general education credits are in required courses such as literature, history, American or state government, and technical writing. Other universities have fewer required courses and as many as eight electives. The strength and size of programs are also factors. Obviously, if a university does not offer a course in sculpture, it would not be possible for a student to experience the benefits of such a course that were discussed in Chapter 13. Thus, the resources of each student's university will be an important factor in developing a specific program.

## OBJECTIVES OF GENERAL EDUCATION COURSES

Although this entire book has dealt with the objectives of general education courses, it may be useful to summarize these objectives here. First, and probably foremost, the GERs are intended to make students better citizens. Individuals have obligations to themselves, their families and friends, their communities, and society. Understanding the importance of value goals and knowing how to make value decisions are necessary conditions for being a good citizen. Individuals who act only in their own self-interest will fail to meet the moral obligations of citizenship.

In addition to the responsibilities of their personal lives, all engineers and scientists must recognize the social responsibilities of professionals. The ability to make proper ethical decisions in a professional setting is an essential requirement for being a responsible professional. The first step in understanding social responsibility is to be aware of fundamental human values. Problem solving in engineering and science often involves human values in conflict, very often because of the uncertainty in risk assessments. To solve these value conflicts, a professional must understand the basics of value decision making, which has many characteristics similar to those of technical decision making but is considerably more complex. Therefore, one objective of the GERs is to introduce both values and value decision making, which are necessary for understanding the social responsibilities of engineers and scientists.

In addition to these two objectives, the GERs can develop important skills, such as communication ability, self-confidence, and creativity. These are fundamental characteristics of leadership. The vicarious experiences afforded by the GERs enhance each of these skills, especially when students recognize their importance. Such skills should be given serious consideration when selecting courses to fulfill the GERs.

## CRITERIA FOR COURSE SELECTION

Why do students select the general education courses they do? In an informal survey (McCuen, 1983b), a number of reasons were identified: personal interest (84 percent); easy work load (56 percent); high grade (41 percent); ease in scheduling (39 percent); improvement of general knowledge (5 percent); and because it's what friends take (5 percent). Are these legitimate reasons for selecting GERs, given the importance of the underlying objectives of the GERs? Although personal interest is a valid reason, one would hope that courses would be selected for reasons other than the grade, the work load, and the ease of scheduling. Such reasons are not legitimate given the importance of the courses in developing a socially responsible engineer or scientist.

What criteria should engineering and science students use in selecting courses to fulfill the GERs? Before discussing specific criteria, we must assume that the students recognize and believe in the intent of the GERs; only then can criteria be established. In the aforementioned informal survey, general interest was the number one criterion, and it certainly is a legitimate criterion. However, education implies an expansion of interests, not just a reinforcement of existing interests. Someone who had two years of Spanish in high school should not necessarily take a first course in college Spanish to fulfill the GERs; it would be better to select an advanced-level Spanish course. Or if the individual is interested in languages, a course in a different language might be more interesting in the long term, more educational, and more beneficial. Thus, although personal interest is a legitimate criterion, developing new and varied interests is probably a better one.

A second criterion for course selection is whether or not a course will help fulfill the ABET objectives. Some courses will do so directly; however, when such courses have prerequisites, it may be necessary to use one of the courses allocated to general education to obtain a necessary prerequisite. It is hoped that all courses selected will enhance students' capacity to be useful citizens—useful to themselves as well as society. Course descriptions should be reviewed and evaluated to determine whether or not the material has some relation to the social responsibilities of engineers and scientists. In addition, the content of each course should be evaluated by reviewing the texts in the campus library or bookstore and by discussions with faculty who teach the course. Evaluating a course before registering for it can help place the course in perspective with respect to both the social responsibility of a professional and the overall general education program that is being selected.

Education does not end with a baccalaureate degree; it continues for life and contributes significantly to personal pleasure. Since personal pleasure is a dominant human value, one that is a behavior determinant, an objective of one's formal education should be the development of self-confidence in one's ability to tackle new learning experiences. Taking courses that are different from one's background can develop self-confidence as well as contributing to educational variety. Thus, a third criterion to use in selecting general education courses is to choose one or more courses in unfamiliar areas. The development of new interests adds variety to life.

Some students have multiple career goals. For example, a student may intend to pursue an MBA after completing a baccalaureate degree in engineering or science. Another may intend to obtain a medical degree after the baccalaureate degree and pursue a career as a biomedical engineer. Although career plans change even after completing the baccalaureate degree, it would be valuable for students to take one or more courses that would expose them to material in the area of their intended second degree. Thus, a fourth criterion to use in selecting general education courses is to select courses that relate to other educational plans. This can help the student determine the desirability of continuing to work toward these other educational objectives.

## LIMITATIONS ON COURSE SELECTION

General education requirements vary from one university to another, and the limitations on course selection also vary. The number of courses required varies from program to program, and other limitations are usually imposed within each program. For example, a program may require at least one course each in areas such as literature, psychology, philosophy, and history. Another program may require a certain number of upper-level (junior and senior) courses. Although such constraints limit the depth to which a student can pursue a specific area of interest, they also add variety to every student's program.

Resources also vary from one university to another. Obviously, students cannot learn about sculpturing at a university that does not offer such a course, but they can still develop an appreciation for the arts from other courses. The lack of specific program resources is a constraint only with respect to specific material; it should not prevent a student from meeting all of the broad objectives of general education requirements.

When a program allows for only a few general education electives and it is difficult to find basic courses that discuss material involving social values, it may be difficult to develop a sequence of courses that provides sufficient depth to develop an appreciation for the social responsibilities of a professional. As noted earlier, upper-level courses that provide in-depth discussions of social value issues may have one or more prerequisites, which can be a severe limitation. When a student wishes to take such an upper-level course but cannot do so within the framework of the university requirements, the student may request a waiver of the prerequisites or a waiver of other required credits so that they can be used to take the prerequisites. Waivers may also be required when some general education courses are limited to students who are majoring in the area. For example, a business course may be closed to nonbusiness majors because of overcrowding in the business degree program. However, engineering or science majors may be allowed to take the course if they explain to the business school that they intend to pursue an MBA after finishing the baccalaureate program.

In summary, although there are a few limitations, the available general education courses can meet all of the objectives so long as students give considerable thought to selecting the courses they use to fulfill the GERs.

## PROGRAM DEVELOPMENT

A primary goal of this book is to guide the reader in developing a general education program. This can best be done using a slight modification of the systems process. According to McCuen (1985), the systems process involves seven elements: goals and objectives, resources and constraints, alternatives, decision criteria, model, decision, and feedback. This process can be used to develop a personalized general education program.

### Goals and Objectives

A personalized general education program should be designed to meet personal goals. Therefore, these goals must be identified. This requires self-evaluation, which involves an assessment of existing knowledge and expected future interests. It also requires an assessment of one's abilities. Self-evaluation can be a long but interesting and educational process. For our purposes here, we will reduce the self-evaluation to an assessment of three items: interests, present knowledge, and abilities. Since the self-evaluation is for the purpose of selecting general education courses, the student should evaluate his or her interests and present knowledge of each of the general education topics discussed in this book, which are summarized in Table 17.1. An interest/knowledge table (Table 17.2) can be used to facilitate the analysis. The interest/knowledge table is a two-way table relating level of interest (personal and professional) and level of present knowledge of the general education discipline. The student should review the items in Table 17.1, add other areas or disciplines of interest, and place them in the appropriate lines/columns of Table 17.2. Both the column and the row variables are separated into three classes: low, medium, and high. (Note that topics other than those listed in Table 17.1 can be included in Table 17.2.)

### TABLE 17.1  General Education Disciplines

| Code | Discipline |
| --- | --- |
| HI | History |
| CC | Contemporary culture and sociology |
| FA | Fine arts |
| PA | Performing arts |
| LI | Literature |
| LA | Language |
| PH | Philosophy |
| PB | Psychology and human behavior |
| BE | Business and economics |
| HF | Health, fitness, and nutrition |
| PP | Politics and public policy |

**TABLE 17.2   Interest/Knowledge Table**

| Level of Present Knowledge | Level of Interest[a] | | |
|---|---|---|---|
| | High | Medium | Low |
| Low | | | |
| Medium | | | |
| High | | | |

[a]Insert discipline code from Table 17.1 in the appropriate line/column here.

In filling in the interest/knowledge table, the reader should try not to associate the two variables, interest and knowledge, too highly. A lack of knowledge in a particular general education discipline does not necessarily indicate a lack of interest. As suggested earlier, variety is an important human value; taking courses in disciplines with which you are unfamiliar can provide much pleasure, develop self-confidence, and increase motivation for learning. It may be helpful to review the earlier chapters when trying to assess your interest level.

An assessment of your abilities is also important in making a self-assessment. The ability assessment table in Table 17.3 can be used to evaluate important abilities. This table should not be filled in quickly. Consider each ability seriously and think of examples of situations in which the abilities were used. For example, if you have been an officer in several youth groups or captain of an athletic team, you might give yourself a high rating in leadership; otherwise, a medium or low rating may be more realistic. If you have made speeches to groups without being nervous or have written reports that were praised for their quality, you have reason to believe that you have good communication skills. Remember that being truthful to yourself is a requisite of self-assessment, and self-assessment is necessary for improving your abilities. The completed ability assessment table should accurately reflect your abilities. The list of abilities can be expanded to reflect other personal characteristics that you believe are important.

Having completed the interest/knowledge and ability assessment tables, you can now establish goals to be achieved through general education. The goals should not be a list of specific courses to be taken. Instead, they should be statements of

**TABLE 17.3   Ability Assessment Table**

| Ability | Level of Ability | | |
|---|---|---|---|
| | High | Medium | Low |
| Communication skills | | | |
| Creative ability | | | |
| Leadership | | | |
| Self-confidence | | | |
| Social awareness | | | |
| Value decision-making ability | | | |

the results you hope the general education courses will help you achieve. The following are some examples:

- Develop better communication skills
- Develop self-confidence in social situations
- Develop creative talents
- Develop leadership skills

A set of operational objectives can then be developed for each goal. Based on the four goals provided as examples, the following operational objectives might be selected:

- Develop better communication skills
  - Learn TV/radio broadcasting
  - Study speech therapy methods
  - Study writing techniques in journalism
- Develop self-confidence in social situations
  - Study personality theories
  - Perform independent research in a social science discipline
- Develop creative talents
  - Learn to interpret creative literature
  - Study creative advertising
  - Participate in creative dance performances
  - Study creative art
- Develop leadership skills
  - Learn motivation methods in management
    Participate in a performing art or a group sport
  - Study biographies of leaders

Although the operational objectives provide some direction for selecting courses to be taken, specific courses should not be listed as operational objectives.

### Resources and Constraints

In addition to goals and objectives, it is necessary to have a clear picture of the framework within which the general education courses are taken. As discussed in the earlier section on limitations, several items are of special interest: how many credit hours are required; whether courses that are primarily skill courses are allowed for fulfilling the GERs; whether course sequences are required; how many credit hours must be in upper-level courses; whether prerequisites restrict registration for some courses. Each of these constraints, and others, must be considered in selecting specific courses. However, they should not be allowed to prevent you from fulfilling your goals and operational objectives.

## Decision Criteria

The criteria to be used in selecting general education courses were discussed in an earlier section. The interest/knowledge table can be used in selecting both general types of courses and specific courses. If you wish to develop new interests, the general disciplines you rated "low level of present knowledge" can be given special consideration. If you wish to challenge youself to learn a topic for which your initial interest is low, those general disciplines you rated "low level of interest" can be given special consideration. Then, for the disciplines you identify, you can select specific courses. When you are selecting specific courses, you can use the ability assessment table, as well as the specified operational objectives, in your attempt to select courses that meet all of the operational objectives.

It is important to recognize that the decision process for selecting specific courses involves multiple decision criteria. First, the operational objectives need to be met. Second, the ABET objective of making students aware of the social responsibilities of engineers and scientists should be considered. Because general education courses do not deal specifically with engineering and science but do deal with human values, you can use the values listed in Table 17.4 as a guide in selecting specific courses. You should assess and consider the likelihood that such values will be discussed in a course before making a final selection. Finally, you should consider the constraints along with the goals and operational objectives.

## Model and Decision

The model and decision steps of the systems process are operated on jointly. The model consists of a proposed plan for fulfilling the GERs, and the decision will be to use a plan that best fulfills the decision criteria. If there are only a few general education electives, it may be difficult to meet all of the operational objectives as well as develop a social awareness. In such a case, a plan that most nearly meets the decision criteria should be used.

TABLE 17.4  Human Values

| | | |
|---|---|---|
| Beauty/aesthetics | Honor | Preservation (natural resources) |
| Brotherhood | Justice | Prudence |
| Cleanliness | Kindness | Public health/safety |
| Courage | Knowledge | Respect |
| Diligence | Life | Responsibility |
| Efficiency | Love | Reverence |
| Equality | Loyalty | Security |
| Equity | Mercy | Truth |
| Freedom/liberty | Orderliness | Variety |
| Gratitude | Performance | Wisdom |
| Honesty | Pleasure/happiness | |

### Feedback

Over the course of a four-year program, your interests will change. Also, courses will be dropped from the course catalog, new courses will appear, and other courses will change in content. And as time goes by, your level of knowledge will increase. All of these factors require periodic reassessment of your general education plan. For example, if operational objectives change, the general education plan should also change. This periodic reassessment corresponds to the feedback loop of the systems process. Through continued reassessment of the plan, you will glean maximum knowledge from your general education program.

## EXERCISES

17.1. For your current or planned major (e.g., electrical engineering, computer science) identify how a course in each of the following might be of value: government and politics, psychology and human behavior, philosophy, dance.

17.2. (a) Using the interest/knowledge and ability assessment tables, perform a self-evaluation and identify the goals and objectives of your personalized general education program. Discuss your reasons behind the self-evaluation and the specified goals and objectives.

   (b) Identify the existing constraints you are subject to in setting up your personalized general education program.

   (c) Establish the decision criteria you will use in selecting a program. Specify the relative importance of each of the criteria.

   (d) Based on your self-evaluation, select four of the areas from the table of general education disciplines (Table 17.1) and identify three courses from each area that discuss values, society, technology, or culture and that might discuss material that would meet the ABET objective of developing a social awareness. Also consider course prerequisite requirements.

   (e) Select courses that can be used to fulfill the GERs and fill out a course program that shows the term (semester, quarter, etc.) in which the courses would be taken. Identify alternative courses that could be used as replacements.

   (f) Evaluate the extent to which the proposed program meets (1) the ABET objective of developing social awareness and (2) the goals and objectives identified in part (a) of this exercise.

**18**

# The Importance of a Social Sensitivity to Engineers and Scientists of the Future

*George E. Dieter*

## INTRODUCTION

You hardly could have reached this concluding chapter without becoming convinced from your reading that serious study of humanities and social science courses is important to the career success of an engineer or scientist. But, you might ask: "What are the future prospects that a successful engineering career will require more or less knowledge of humanities and social science?" "How will future jobs in engineering differ from those of today?" or the sixty-four-dollar question, "What will the world be like in 2010 when I am at the peak of my professional career?"

In this brief concluding chapter, we will try to peer into the future, realizing all the while that such predictions are fraught with a high degree of uncertainty. For example, which of you would have predicted in 1980 that world oil prices would be undergoing a steep and apparently steady decline in 1986? The crystal ball of the future is always murky and never approaches the precision of 20/20 hindsight. But since the future is the place where we will be spending the rest of our lives, there is a natural human curiosity about what it will be like.

## A LOOK AT THE FUTURE

In this section we present a brief summary of some of the most plausible predictions about what the world will be like in the next thirty years. We will follow with more specific ideas of technological trends and of which technologies are likely to be important to society in the twenty-first century.

These forecasts are not the products of clairvoyants or seers. They are generally obtained from the collective wisdom of broad-based experts in a field (the Delphi technique) or by extrapolating the present to the future (technological forecasting) using sophisticated statistical techniques (Martino, 1983). Such forecasting tends to be correct over the long term, but it cannot be expected to predict short-term perturbations.

The general public seems to sense that we are entering an era of accelerated social change that is driven by an unprecedented era of technological change. This has spawned a number of futuristic studies aimed at the general public (Tofler, 1970, 1980; Naisbitt, 1982). John Naisbitt, the author of *Megatrends* and a futurist with a large corporate clientele, sees ten significant trends that are affecting the United States:

1. *Decentralization:* Through most of this century, social, economic, and political forces have been directed at creating centralization of power, authority, and responsibility in private- and public-sector organizations. Now society is creating decentralized alternatives for almost every centralized type of organization. The breakup of the national telephone system and the growing trend toward sources of energy other than the central power plant are but two examples of this pervasive trend.

2. *Deinstitutionalization:* There is a steady trend toward dismantling and reshaping many of the institutions that were created to provide the delivery of private and public goods and services. We see this in the changes taking place in the banking system, the postal service, and the mergers within the airlines and the petroleum-producing companies.

3. *North-south shift:* The population center of the nation is moving southwest. Much new investment in manufacturing is taking place in the Sun Belt states, where land and labor supply are more plentiful and less costly.

4. *Information economy:* The shift from an agricultural to an industrial economy that took place in the early part of the twentieth century is giving way to a shift from an industrial base to an information base. Capital is being replaced by knowledge as the critical strategic resource. The implications of this evolution are profound in terms of the skills, attitudes, expectations, and motivations of the work force.

5. *High-tech/high-touch:* As high-technology products pervade our lives, there is a rapid change by society to adjust in ways that maintain human contact and relationships (high-touch). This is identified as one of the chief pacing elements in technological change. As technology alters or replaces our social relationships, either we tend to reject the technology or, if we accept it, we find intensified human contact elsewhere.

6. *Biology as the dominant science:* Innovations in the biological sciences, led by DNA technology, will generate new technologies in the future, just as physics and electronics fueled the current predominant technologies.

7. *Computer as liberator:* Old fears about the computer are rapidly breaking down as the computer pervades the business world and provides cheaper ways of gathering and processing information.

8. *"Organization man" to entrepreneur:* The traditional "organization man" stereotype of management is giving way in many places to a more entrepreneurial approach. Corporate hierarchies are being restructured to enhance innovation.

9. *Multiple options:* Individuals are being given greater opportunity to express their individual tastes and choices. This is true not only in consumer goods but also in other aspects of society, such as entertainment and religion.

10. *Truly global economy:* The world has become a truly interconnected global economy. The number of nations capable of producing industrial goods has increased dramatically. Fueled by major shifts in costs of fuel and materials, entirely new producing nations have evolved and will evolve for many commodity products.

We can see that these changes in the world will alter the value base of the society in which engineers and scientists work. The trend toward greater decentralization and deinstitutionalization should bring engineers closer to the public in their working life; thus, the individual engineer will have greater opportunity for exercising social responsibility. The trend of the north-south shift is having a strong impact on social institutions—for example, underenrollment of schools in the North and overenrollment in the South. It is interesting that a major limitation to the continuation of this trend could be the limited water resources of the southwestern United States. A major political controversy over obtaining the federal funds and water rights for engineers to extend the water resources is likely. Engineers should be major contributors to the concomitant controversy over the environmental and ecological consequences of such a major engineering undertaking.

The development of the information economy that is being propagated by the ubiquitous computer will have a major impact on the value structure of society. It could be that society will value the services of the possessors of certain knowledge to the same degree that certain skills are currently valued in athletics and entertainment. If knowledge becomes a commodity of high monetary value, will we be so willing to exchange and share knowledge as we currently do within the universities and professional societies?

We can also project how greater individual understanding of the arts, humanities, and social sciences can help us cope with these changes of the future. A stronger grounding in human behavior and philosophy should help engineers adapt their developments to satisfy the "high-touch" needs of the population. Also, with more emphasis on innovation and entrepreneurship, there is a need for greater understanding of the personal behavior that results in enhanced creativity. A better understanding of psychology would be beneficial in this area. In a world that will be increasingly concerned with multiple options, the broadest possible background in literature and the arts will be of value in making wise decisions among cultural and consumer options. Finally, the one-world economy into which we are moving so rapidly requires a far greater emphasis for engineers and scientists on language skills and knowledge of the culture of foreign countries. In the future, an increasingly greater percentage of American engineers and scientists will find that a major part of their practice will be outside the United States.

## FUTURE TECHNOLOGY

Many of the important technologies that engineers and scientists will deal with in the twenty-first century can be predicted with considerable certainty because their antecedents are with us now. What we cannot do is predict the scientific breakthroughs that will occur in the next twenty years and that will lead to even more dramatic technologies. More important, we cannot predict how those scientific breakthroughs will change the social and institutional framework in which engineers and scientists have to work.

It seems clear that the current respite from the energy crisis will not last very long. Certainly, by the twenty-first century the growing population and spreading industrialization in what we now call Third World countries will put even greater pressure on the world's energy resources. The massive engineering problems required to harness fusion energy will most likely be solved in the first quarter of the twenty-first century, but before that, nuclear reactors of a new and safer design probably will have revived that moribund industry. Economical ways of producing auto fuel from hydrocarbon-bearing plants will have been developed, but new developments in electric storage batteries and fuel cells finally will make the electric car a strong competitor to the automobile with an internal combustion engine.

The full flower and impact of the biotechnology revolution will be upon us by the twenty-first century. Starting first in specialized areas of animal nutrition and agricultural modification, it will bring mass production of now rare and expensive pharmaceuticals, cures for fatal hereditary diseases by gene therapy, and innovations in extracting minerals from ores and in converting biomass to useful fuels.

The first quarter of the twenty-first century will see the full impact of the computer revolution, which is driven by the marvels of microelectronics. Integrated circuit (IC) chips with 100 million elements are predicted, and eventually biotechnology may produce microcomputers with a circuit density one billion times that of current IC chips. These advances in microelectronics will continue to reduce the cost of computer power and make possible the potential of artificial intelligence. This will have far-reaching consequences on information processing and on the engineering functions of design and manufacturing. In manufacturing, there will be an increasing trend toward decentralization and away from mass production, providing greater flexibility in product and process.

The materials with which we build will also undergo major changes. Ceramics will be employed successfully in autos and aircraft. New forms of polymers will be developed, and composite materials combining metals, polymers, and ceramics will be developed to a high level of design sophistication.

## THE ENGINEERING PROFESSION OF THE FUTURE

As we have just seen, the future will be strongly influenced by technological change. There is no question that technology will have even a greater impact on society in the twenty-first century than it does today. Since engineers and scientists are the creators and implementers of technology, we can predict a strong future employment market in these fields. However, part of the technology engineers have created will play a major role in significantly modifying the future of the profession.

At present, the engineering profession is beginning a major transformation of the way engineering is practiced, a transformation brought about by the computer revolution. The first glimpse of this change was in the area of computer-aided drafting, where computer graphics has replaced a great deal of the manual drafting function. Powerful individual computer workstations are coming into the marketplace and are being adapted into the engineering design function. Currently, these are being used to move complex design calculations from mainframe computers to the more convenient personal workstations or to enhance the ability to design for problems with a higher degree of complexity. However, the next phase, already under way in the research labs, will be to greatly enhance the design process through application of the methods of artificial intelligence. These methods will substitute for much of the experience factor in design, and as the research progresses, the engineering design process will be elevated intellectually and will increase productivity significantly. Many of the lower-level jobs in the design process will disappear, just as many drafting jobs were eliminated by computer-aided drafting. The long-term result will be a considerable elevation in the professional status and compensation of the engineer and a clearer distinction between the engineer and the engineering technologist and the technician. The engineer will be concerned with designing the systems for design and manufacturing, while the technologist will carry out the design and manufacturing using the greatly enhanced tools of computer-aided engineering. The total employment opportunities for the spectrum of technological occupations will increase significantly in the future, but it is not clear whether the number of engineers who are really practicing professionals will increase very much. What is clear is that the professional status of and rewards for these engineers will be much greater as society recognizes their true value.

As engineering is thrust into a more central role in society, its responsibilities toward society will increase dramatically. The U.S. economy will be increasingly dependent on innovation and discovery and less dependent on exploitation of natural resources and high-volume manufacturing. One of the problems that lies ahead is the danger of an increasing stratification of our work force, with more highly trained individuals becoming more essential to our productive welfare while relatively unskilled persons become economically more expendable. Engineers have contributed to this problem through such developments as automation and microelectronics, and they should devote some of their talents to addressing the problem. A greater involvement of the engineering profession in the "nuts and bolts" of educating our population is one positive way for engineers to help provide a solution.

## ENGINEERING EDUCATION FOR THE FUTURE

Engineering is the only profession that attempts to provide adequate preparation in a four-year undergraduate program. With the inexorable growth of knowledge, however, this has become harder and harder to do.

In the 1960s, engineering education underwent a major transformation in which traditional practice-oriented subjects were removed from the curriculum and emphasis was given to newly developed engineering science courses. These courses gave the curriculum a much stronger analytical orientation, and by using a more basic approach, they provided a broader background for the professional engineering courses. The importance of a strong engineering science core is well established in engineering education, and it is not likely to be eroded in the future. Moreover, since engineering specialty areas have a way of disappearing or transforming dramatically over a period of twenty years or less, it is important for every engineering graduate to have a firm foundation in basic mathematics, science, and engineering science. Such knowledge will make retraining easier and less stressful.

At present and into the future, the impact of the computer is likely to provide the greatest pressure on the engineering curriculum. Currently, it is clear that engineers need more background in computer science than simply learning a computer language and being introduced to computer-based numerical methods. They need to understand how to manipulate data bases, they need to know the fundamentals of computer graphics, and they need to be conversant with many of the techniques of artificial intelligence. This requires additional space in the curriculum, which is hard to find. In a few years, when the impact of the computer on design and manufacturing comes into fruition, there will be great pressure from that direction.

Of course, the theme of this book is the importance of humanities and social science courses to the education of the engineer, and we hope that we have made a good case for the importance of these subjects in your education and your future career. Unfortunately, however, there usually is no natural constituency on the engineering faculty for enhancing or expanding this segment of the curriculum. Engineering faculty usually are caught up in the excitement of their research and rarely step back far enough to see the importance of the nontechnical areas. Therefore, students have traditionally been left on their own to give the proper emphasis to this part of their education. If you have read this far in the book, you should have the knowledge and motivation to do an adequate job.

Will the aforementioned curriculum pressures force engineering and science educators to abandon the four-year program in favor of a five-year program? We think not, at least in a formal sense. Most B.S. graduates in engineering and science take employment in industry or government immediately after receiving their degree. They find jobs mostly with large corporations or agencies that view these graduates as a valuable manpower resource, since they are the brightest and best-trained group of students graduating in large numbers from the colleges and universities of the nation. Many of these graduates are hired for corporate careers in engineering, but a growing number are hired for broader corporate careers. So as long as industry values this manpower resource, and pays a premium starting salary to attract it, it is unlikely that engineering and science schools will be willing or able to deviate from the four-year B.S. curriculum. At the same time, there is recognition today in many fields that the M.S. degree is necessary for competent practice in the design and development areas of engineering. This recognition is likely to be widely acknowledged in the future, so that the true professional will be expected to be educated to at least the M.S. level.

There are many paths by which an individual can achieve an engineering education:

1. Four years of undergraduate study at an engineering school leads to the B.S. degree.

2. Two years of pre-engineering plus two years at an engineering school leads to the B.S. degree.

3. Three years at a liberal arts college plus two years at an engineering school leads to a B.A. degree and a B.S. degree.

4. Five years of cooperative study at an engineering school leads to the B.S. degree.

5. A B.S. degree plus one year full-time in an engineering school leads to the M.S. degree.

6. A B.S. degree plus three years of part-time study in an engineering school leads to the M.S. degree.

7. An integrated five-year B.S./M.S. program leads to the B.S. and M.S. degrees.

Path 1 is the traditional method, in which a student enrolls as a freshman in an engineering school. Although the curriculum is normally four years long, many students require more time to complete the requirements. One good reason for this is that some students take more than the minimum requirement of humanities and social science courses.

Many students follow Path 2, in which they first enroll in a community college or liberal arts college for the basic math and science courses and then transfer to an engineering school for the last two years.

An attractive variant of this is Path 3, the "3-2" program. The student completes three years at a liberal arts college and then transfers to an engineering school for the last two years. This program allows greater depth in liberal studies than Path 1 or 2 and generally results in a B.A. from the liberal arts college and a B.S. from the engineering school. This is an attractive program for producing broadly educated engineers.

About 20 percent of the engineering graduates in this country follow a five-year cooperative program, in which periods of industrial experience are interspersed with academic work on campus. Although cooperative programs are especially designed to give undergraduate students real-world experience, they also give students the opportunity to expand their nontechnical education by taking evening courses or programs of directed reading during work periods.

None of the paths that lead to an M.S. degree in engineering offer opportunities to expand the students' nontechnical education in a formal way, since study at the master's level is highly specialized in professional subjects. Therefore, it is important that you gain as broad an education as you can in your undergraduate program.

## A PLAN FOR YOUR FUTURE

Your educational program for a B.S. degree will shape your future ideas and actions. Therefore, it is worth spending a few minutes to consider what you might do *now* to enhance your *future*. The following is a short list:

1. *Keep an open mind.* Try to view your education as a true learning experience, not as a series of hurdles to be gotten over (or around) as easily as possible. It may be hard to appreciate now, but later you will look back on your undergraduate days as the most carefree time of your life. In choosing your liberal arts courses, select them for breadth of interest and intellectual content. Try to build for yourself a course of study that, within the rigid requirements of the engineering curriculum, allows you to feel that you are a truly educated person.

2. *Challenge yourself.* Failure can be frightening, but failure that follows a serious attempt is better than no attempt at all. Very often, students elect general education courses that will offer little resistance in their quest for good grades. You should be aware, however, that the grades you receive in general education courses will have little impact on your career. Therefore, use these credits to challenge yourself. Prove to yourself that you can confront a new and very different topic and not only master it but enjoy it. Meeting these challenges will develop your self-confidence, which will surely help you face the challenges with which your future career will continually confront you.

3. *Talk with older people.* Seek out people older than you—your parents, employers, instructors, or counselors—and ask them what courses they found most helpful or, conversely, what they believe were the major deficiences of their own education. Then try to plug these gaps. Although you may think older people are somewhat narrowminded, their experience as adults has given them a broader perspective on life.

4. *Enhance your creativity.* Creative thinkers are distinguished by their ability to synthesize new combinations of ideas and concepts into meaningful and useful forms. We are all born with an inherent measure of creativity, but the process of maturation takes its toll on our native capacity. Moreover, a technical education, with its emphasis on precision of thought and correct solutions to mathematical problems, is especially deadly to creativity. What, then, can you as an engineering or science student do about this?

First, you should be aware that the world of work values creativity more than your present environment does. You should also know that creativity can be rekindled and stimulated by formal courses of study and by practice (Osborne, 1965). Moreover, in your nontechnical courses you will find tidbits of knowledge that will be helpful in developing this important characteristic. Grab them as they come along and put them where they can be retrieved when you need them. Do not assume that the material in the arts and humanities courses cannot enhance your creativity and be of value in your future. Art, music, and literature are creative efforts just as much of the work that you will do in the future will be creative.

5. *Prepare for a lifetime of learning.* You should already be aware that the four-year undergraduate programs in engineering and science are inadequate for a lifetime of professional practice. They are intended to provide you with the fundamentals that you will need as you add to your formal education in response to the changes that developing technology will bring. Industry clearly recognizes the need to reeducate the work force. A recent study revealed that U.S. corporations are training about eight million people per year—close to the total enrollment in colleges and universities—and they spend as much in doing this as more traditional educational institutions do (Eurich, 1985).

Part of your future educational needs will be provided by corporate sources or by educational institutions, but part will have to be provided by you—in the form of self-study. It is hoped that you are now developing the discipline and techniques for successful self-study. Refine them and keep them intact; you will need them in the future. You should not believe that you can learn everything necessary for a successful career in just four years.

The need for a lifetime of learning is not restricted to the technical sphere. You also have a lifetime to grow culturally. It is hoped that your courses in history, literature, philosophy, art, and music will have instilled in you an interest in the subject and a thirst for more knowledge. Take the opportunity to prepare lists for future reading—after graduation, when you are freed from the tyranny of required classes, tests, and reading assignments. An excellent guide to the liberal arts has been prepared by the distinguished engineer Samuel C. Florman (1968). This book presents a brief discussion of the development of thought in history, literature, philosophy, fine arts, and music and provides selected reading lists in each discipline that are particularly tailored to the needs and interests of the engineer. The young engineer who is aware of the need to grow culturally as well as technically could hardly do better than to devote some time each week to Florman's lists of suggested reading.

## SUMMARY

In this final chapter, we have indicated that the world is becoming more dependent on technology and on the works of engineers and scientists. Therefore, almost by definition, there will be a greater need for engineers and scientists who have the greater social sensitivity that comes from an appreciation of the liberal arts and social studies that comprise our culture. The accelerating rate of technology will have a major impact on the way the engineering and science professions will be practiced. At the creative, upper level of the profession, this will greatly enhance the value and prestige of the professional, but many engineers and scientists who work at the bottom, near the level of technologist, may have their jobs eliminated or downgraded by technological change. The future will call for a broadly educated professional who is well steeped in technical fundamentals and in nontechnical subjects. The successful engineer or scientist will have learned to be an independent self-starter who is able to pursue a lifetime of learning.

## EXERCISES

**18.1.** List and briefly discuss reasons why courses in the arts, humanities, and social sciences will be important to the engineers and scientists of the future.

**18.2.** Provide arguments why courses in the arts, humanities, and social sciences do *not* have a place in the engineering and science curricula. Also provide counterarguments for each point made.

**18.3.** Many executives of engineering corporations have educational backgrounds in the liberal arts, rather than engineering. Discuss how such backgrounds have enabled them to succeed in the engineering profession.

**18.4.** The U.S. economy has moved from an agricultural base to a manufacturing base to a service base to an information base. Discuss the possible roles of engineers and scientists in each type of economy and discuss how the need for engineers and scientists to understand social issues has increased.

**18.5.** Identify the human value issues in the following Fundamental Principles of the ABET Code of Ethics for Engineers:

> Engineers uphold and advance the integrity, honor and dignity of the engineering profession by:
>
> I. using their knowledge and skill for the enhancement of human welfare;
>
> II. being honest and impartial, and serving with fidelity the public, their employers and clients;
>
> III. striving to increase the competence and prestige of the engineering profession; and
>
> IV. supporting the professional and technical societies of their disciplines.

**18.6.** For the engineers and scientists of the future who are applying artificial intelligence, provide an interpretation of how Fundamental Principle I in Exercise 18.5 would apply.

**18.7.** Discuss why someone employed in the field of genetic engineering should have a humanistic perspective.

18.8. As a practicing engineer or scientist, you will have to continue your technical education beyond the B.S. program, either with an advanced degree in engineering or science or short courses and workshops on specific topics. Discuss why continued education in the arts, humanities, and social sciences should also be part of your long-term program of self-development. Discuss ways in which this can be done.

# Bibliography

"A Call to [Linguistic] Arms: Improving America's Foreign Language Competence." *Today's Education,* vol. 69, p. 73GE, September-October 1980.

Accreditation Board for Engineering and Technology (ABET), *49th Annual Report.* ABET, New York, 1981.

*American Heritage Dictionary of the English Language,* William Morris (ed.). Houghton Mifflin, Boston, 1969.

Anderson, F.II. *The Philosophy of Francis Bacon.* Octagon Books, New York, 1971.

Arnold, J.E. "The Creative Engineer," in *Creative Engineering* (pamphlet). American Society of Mechanical Engineers, New York, c.1956.

Bailey, R.L. *Disciplined Creativity for Engineers.* Ann Arbor Science Publishers, Ann Arbor, Mich., 1978.

Bernal, J.D. *Science in History, Volume 2: The Scientific and Industrial Revolutions.* MIT Press, Cambridge, Mass., 1971.

Bremer, O.A. "Is Business the Source of New Social Values?" *Harvard Business Review,* pp. 121-126, November-December 1971.

Brown, R.W., et al. *Language, Thought, and Culture,* Paule Henle (ed.). University of Michigan Press, Ann Arbor, 1966.

Burke, J.G. "Bursting Boilers and the Federal Power." *Technology and Culture,* vol. 7, no. 1, pp. 1-23, 1966.

Cassidy, H.G. *The Sciences and the Arts.* Harper and Brothers, New York, 1962.

Cravens, H. "The Impact of Evolutionary Thought on American Culture in the 20th Century." *Intellect,* pp. 83-86, August 1977.

Cummings, E.E. "Since Feeling Is First," in *Complete Poems, 1913-1962.* Harcourt Brace Jovanovich, New York, 1972.

Dahl, R.A. *Modern Political Analysis* (3rd ed.). Prentice-Hall, Englewood Cliffs, N.J., 1976.

Dickinson, E. "Success Is Counted Sweetest," in *The Poems of Emily Dickinson,* Thomas H. Jackson (ed.). The Belknap Press of Harvard University Press, Cambridge, 1955.

Dougherty, N.W. "Methods of Accomplishing Professional Development." *Transactions, ASCE,* vol. 126, part V (Paper No. 3184), pp. 1-6, 1961.

Eastman, M. *The Literary Mind.* Octagon Books, New York, 1969.

Eulau, H., and March, J.G. *Political Science.* Prentice-Hall, Englewood Cliffs, N.J., 1969.

Eurich, N.P. *Corporate Classrooms: The Learning Business.* Princeton University Press, Princeton, N.J., 1985.

"Few on Layoffs Will Be Rehired; U.S. Push in World Market Urged." *New York Times,* May 14, 1983.

Fishman, J.A. *The Sociology of Language: An Interdisciplinary Social Science Approach to Language in Society.* Newbury House Publishers, Rowley, Mass., 1972.

Florman, S.C. *Engineering and the Liberal Arts: A Technologist's Guide to History, Literature, Philosophy, Art, and Music.* McGraw-Hill, New York, 1968.

Florman, S.C. *The Existential Pleasures of Engineering.* St. Martin's Press, New York, 1976.

Fodor, J.A., and Katz, J.J. *The Structure of Language: Readings in the Philosophy of Language.* Prentice-Hall, Englewood Cliffs, N.J., 1964.

Fowler, C.B.; Guffen, J.I.; et al. *Economic Handbook: A Visual Survey.* Thomas Y. Crowell, New York, 1955.

Fyle, C. "National Languages and Cultural Identity." *UNESCO Courier,* vol. 36, p. 6, July 1983.

Garfoot, R.F., and Simon, J.R. "The Professional Engineer and His Values." *Journal of Professional Practice, ASCE,* vol. 89, pp. 15-21, 1963.

Goldman, S.L., and Cutcliffe, S.H. "Responsibility and the Technological Process." *Technology in Society,* vol. 1, pp. 275-286, 1979.

Harris, D.G. "Multilingualism in a Global Economy: Internationalism and Concern with Cultural Issues." *Vital Speeches of the Day,* vol. 49, p. 332, March 15, 1983.

The Harvard Committee. *General Education in a Free Society.* Harvard University Press, Cambridge, 1948.

Heilbroner, R., and Thurow, L. *Economics Explained.* Prentice-Hall, Englewood Cliffs, N.J., 1982.

Herzberg, F. "One More Time: How Do You Motivate Employees?" *Harvard Business Review,* vol. 46, pp. 53-62, January-February 1968.

Janson, H.W. *The History of Art.* Prentice-Hall, Englewood Cliffs, N.J., 1976.

Kestin, J. "Creativity in Teaching and Learning." *American Scientist,* vol. 58, pp. 250-257, May-June 1970.

Kimel, W.R. "Engineering Graduates: How Good Are They?" *Engineering Education,* pp. 210-222, November 1979.

Koestler, A. *The Act of Creation.* Hutchinson Publishers, London, 1964.

Kohlberg, L. "The Child as a Moral Philosopher," in *Readings in Values Clarification,* S.B. Simon and H. Kirschenbaum (eds.). Winston Press, Minneapolis, 1973.

Kohlberg, L. "Moral Stages and Moralization: The Cognitive-Development Approach," in *Man, Morality, and Society,* T. Lickona (ed.). Holt, Rinehart and Winston, New York, 1976.

Korman, A.K. *Organizational Behavior.* Prentice-Hall, Englewood Cliffs, N.J., 1977.

Levine, S. "Stimulation in Infancy." *Scientific American,* pp. 80–86, May 1960.

Machail, J.W. *Classical Studies.* Books for Libraries Press, Freeport, N.Y., 1968.

Martin, G.B. "Industrial Robots Join the Workforce." *Occupational Outlook Quarterly,* pp. 2–11, Fall 1982.

Martino, J.P. *Technological Forecasting for Decision-Making* (2nd ed.). American Elsevier, New York, 1983.

Mason, R.O., and Mitroff, I.I. *Challenging Strategic Planning Assumptions.* John Wiley & Sons, New York, 1981.

McCuen, J., and Winkler, A. *Readings for Writers.* Harcourt Brace Jovanovich, New York, 1974.

McCuen, R.H. "The Ethical Dimension of Professionalism." *Engineering Issues—Journal of Professional Practice, ASCE,* vol. 105, no. E11, pp. 89–105, 1979.

McCuen, R.H. "Solving Ill-Structured Sociotechnical Problems." *Journal of Professional Issues in Engineering, ASCE,* vol. 109, no. 2, pp. 113–126, 1983a.

McCuen, R.H. "Engineering Students' Perception of General Educational Requirements." *Journal of Professional Issues in Engineering, ASCE,* vol. 109, no. 4, pp. 256–264, 1983b.

McCuen, R.H. *Statistical Methods for Engineers.* Prentice-Hall, Englewood Cliffs, N.J., 1985.

Melville, H. "The Paradise of Bachelors and the Tartarus of Maids." *Harper's New Monthly Magazine,* vol. 10, pp. 670–678, April 1855.

Munro, T. *The Arts and Their Interrelations.* The Press of Western Reserve University, Cleveland, 1967.

Murray, P., and Murray, L. *The Penguin Dictionary of Art and Artists.* Penguin Books, Hammondsworth, Middlesex, England, 1983.

Naisbitt, J. *Megatrends.* Warner Books, New York, 1982.

National Society of Professional Engineers (NSPE). *A Guide for Developing Courses in Engineering Professionalism.* NSPE Publication No. 2010. NSPE, Washington, D.C., November 1976.

Noble, D.F. *American by Design: Science Technology and the Rise of Corporate Capitalism.* Alfred A. Knopf, New York, 1977.

Osborne, A.F. *Applied Imagination* (3rd ed.). Charles Scribner's Sons, New York, 1955.

Peters, T.J., and Waterman, R.H., Jr. *In Search of Excellence.* Warner Books, New York, 1982.

Piaget, J. *The Moral Judgment of the Child.* Free Press, Glencoe, Ill., 1948.

Pollock, T. *The Nature of Literature: Its Relation to Science, Language and Human Experience.* Gordian Press, New York, 1965.

Poulson, B.W. *Economic History of the United States.* Macmillan, New York, 1981.

Pound, E. "In a Station of the METRO," in *The Imagist Poem,* W. Pratt (ed.). E.P. Dutton, New York, 1963.

Rabbitt, M.C. "John Wesley Powell: Pioneer Statesman of Federal Science," in *The Colorado River Region and John Wesley Powell.* USGS Professional Paper No. 669. USGPO, Washington, D.C., 1969.

Redfield, R. "Research in the Social Sciences: Its Significance for General Education." *Social Education,* pp. 568–574, December 1941.

"Robots in the Labor Force." *Business Week,* June 9, 1980.

Rosenberg, N. "Technology, Economy, and Values," in *The History and Philosophy of Technology,* G. Bugliarello and D.B. Doner (eds.). University of Illinois Press, Urbana, 1979.

Rubinstein, E.A. "Television and the Young Viewer." *American Scientist,* vol. 66, pp. 685–693, November-December 1978.

Rutherford, C.S. "Liberal Arts in Business/Business in Liberal Arts." *Arts and Humanities Magazine,* vol. 1, no. 1, pp. 12–13, Spring 1985.

Sabo, S.R. "Remembering History's Kings, Conquerors, and Crusaders." *Leadership,* pp. A14–A19, December 1984.

Schaeffer, K.H., and Scalar, E. *Access for All: Transportation and Urban Growth.* Penguin Books, New York, 1975.

Senger, J. "Managers' Perceptions of Subordinates' Competence as a Function of Personal Value Orientations." *Academy of Management Journal,* pp. 415–424, December 1971.

Shoolman, R., and Slatkin, C. *The Story of Art: The Lives and Times of the Great Masters.* Halcyon House, New York.

Slusser, G., and Guffey, G. "Literature and Science," in *Interrelations of Literature.* Modern Language Association of America, New York, 1982.

Steger, J.A. "Engineers as Managers." *Journal of Management in Engineering,* ASCE vol. 1, no. 2, pp. 105–111, April 1985.

Styron, W. *Sophie's Choice.* Bantam Books, New York, 1979.

Sypher, W. *Literature and Technology.* Random House, New York, 1968.

Taebel, D.A., and Cornehls, J.V. *The Political Economy of Urban Transportation.* National University Publications, Kennikat Press, Port Washington, N.Y., 1977.

Thompson, S.M. *The Nature of Philosophy: An Introduction.* Holt, Rinehart and Winston, New York, 1961.

Thornburg, H.D. "Behavior and Values: Consistency and Inconsistency." *Adolescence,* vol. 8, no. 32, pp. 513–520, 1973.

Totler, A. *Future Shock.* Random House, New York, 1970.

Tofler, A. *The Third Wave.* William Morrow, New York, 1980.

Toulmin, S.; Rieke, R.; and Janik, A. *An Introduction to Reasoning.* Macmillan, New York, 1979.

Transportation Research Board. *55: A Decade of Experience.* National Academy Press, Washington, D.C., 1984.

Tribus, M. "The Engineer and Public Policy-Making." *IEEE Spectrum*, pp. 48–51, April 1978.

Vonnegut, K. *Player Piano*. Dell, New York, 1952.

*Webster's New World Dictionary of the American Language*. World Publishing, Cleveland and New York, 1958.

Weiss, L.W. *Economics and Society*. John Wiley & Sons, New York, 1981.

Wengert, N. *Natural Resources and the Political Struggle*. Random House, New York, 1955.

White, L., Jr. "The Historical Roots of Our Ecological Crisis." *Science*, vol. 155, no. 3767, pp. 1203–1207, March 10, 1967.

Winner, L. *Autonomous Technology: Technics-out-of-Control as a Theme in Political Thought*. MIT Press, Cambridge, Mass., 1977.

Woodberry, G. *The Appreciation of Literature*. Kennikat Press, Port Washington, N.Y., 1967.